Ed Finn

A Journalist's Life on the Left

BOULDER
PUBLICATIONS

CCPA
CANADIAN CENTRE
for POLICY ALTERNATIVES
CENTRE CANADIEN
de POLITIQUES ALTERNATIVES

Published by

Boulder Publications
Portugal Cove-St. Philip's, Newfoundland and Labrador
www.boulderpublications.ca

Canadian Centre for Policy Alternatives
500-251 Bank St., Ottawa, ON K2P 1X3
TEL 613 563-1341 FAX 613 233-1453
ccpa@policyalternatives.ca
http://www.policyalternatives.ca

© 2013 Ed Finn

Cover illustration by Dirk Van Stralen
Layout by Susan Purtell

Printed and bound in Canada

Boulder Publications acknowledges the financial support of the Government of Newfoundland and Labrador through the Department of Tourism, Culture and Recreation.

Boulder Publications acknowledges the financial support for our publishing program by the Government of Canada and the Department of Canadian Heritage through the Canada Book Fund.

Library and Archives Canada Cataloguing in Publication

Finn, Ed, 1926-, author

    Ed Finn : a journalist's life on the left / Ed Finn.

Issued in print and electronic formats.

ISBN 978-1-927099-31-5 (pbk.).—ISBN 978-1-927099-39-1 (epub).—

ISBN 978-1-927099-40-7 (mobi).—ISBN 978-1-927099-41-4 (pdf)

1. Finn, Ed, 1926-. 2. Journalists—Canada—Biography. 3. Labour leaders—Canada—Biography. 4. Newfoundland and Labrador New Democratic Party—Biography. 5. Newfoundland and Labrador—Biography. I. Title.

PN4913.F55A3 2013   070.92   C2013-906755-8   C2013-906756-6

Dedication

To Dena, Kevin, Kerri-Anne,

Gwynneth, Arun,

Garrett and Heather

iv   Ed Finn

Table of Contents

Essays

Ed Finn

Preface

*"The urge to write one's autobiography,
so I have been told, overtakes everyone
sooner or later."*
—Agatha Christie.

MANY OF MY FRIENDS, relatives, and co-workers had been urging me to write my memoirs ever since I reached my late 60s and early 70s. I put it off until I became an octogenarian — for several reasons.

First, I thought that writing a book about my personal experiences would be the supreme act of egotism. Not being inclined to narcissism or self-indulgence, that was not a project I felt I could undertake with much enthusiasm.

Second, I have never kept personal records, a diary, or copies of my correspondence, so would have to rely mainly on a far-from-perfect memory for many of my reminiscences.

Third, I still had a full-time job as editor of the *CCPA Monitor*, the monthly journal of the Canadian Centre for Policy Alternatives (CCPA), and was reluctant to spend my weekends working on my memoirs instead of spending time with my family and reading the books I'd accumulated.

As now seems clear, I was able to overcome these three impediments. I realized first that, although the story of my life would have little appeal for the general public, it might prove interesting and informative for my family and other relatives, friends, and co-workers, and perhaps for many Newfoundlanders, union members, and members of the CCPA.

I never aspired to celebrity status, but my 70-year working career has been unusually diversified. I was a printer's apprentice; a linotype operator;

columnist, sports writer, and editor of the Corner Brook *Western Star*; a journalist with the *Montreal Gazette* and columnist for the *Toronto Star*; first provincial leader of the NDP in Newfoundland and an NDP candidate in four elections there; a public relations officer for the Canadian Labour Congress, the Canadian Brotherhood of Railway, Transport and General Workers, and the Canadian Union of Public Employees; a member of the board of directors of the Bank of Canada; and currently editor of the *CCPA Monitor*.

I also had the privilege of working closely with Tommy Douglas for several years and helped promote and defend his pioneering Medicare legislation in Saskatchewan during the 1962 doctors' strike.

To some extent, my account of all these experiences may prove readable.

I was able to find enough written material from my Newfoundland years to supplement my memories of that often turbulent period. Also helpful were copies of some of my speeches, and my *Toronto Star* and *Labour Gazette* articles, eight cartons of which I had packed away under the stairs in our basement. My columns and editorials written for the *CCPA Monitor* were all easily available, most of them later published in three CCPA anthologies, the last one in 2007 titled *The Right is Wrong and the Left is Right*. You'll find some samples as appendices at the end of this book.

As for the time I needed to write these memoirs, I reduced my work schedule with the CCPA in 2011 from five days a week to three, which still left me time for reading books as well as writing one.

I should confess that I've taken some liberties to fill gaps in this chronicle for which I was unable to find precise dates and names. All the events I describe did happen, but some not necessarily at the time or place that my faulty memory recalls. This may have resulted in some embarrassing and even egregious mistakes, for which I welcome corrections, but I'm pretty sure that 99% of what I've written is fairly accurate.

Most of the questionable statements probably are contained in the Prologue that follows, a narrative of events that occurred before I was born. My mother told me about them when I was in my late teens, but unfortunately I've forgotten some of the details and have been compelled for the sake of the narrative to invent a few names, dates, and places. The events my mother told me about, however, *did* happen, and I think their narration (even with some improvisation) leads nicely into the memoirs.

Prologue

AT 7 A.M. ON THE morning of April 3, 1910, Raymond Mifflin's new windup alarm clock rang. He reached over from his bed to look at the time, and groaned. He thought he had set it to go off at 8.

It was a Sunday morning, and normally he could sleep in even longer, but he was a school teacher with a few dozen student essays to read and grade before school reopened after the weekend. That would take him most of the day, and he had left the essays at the school across the bight.

Ray decided that, since he was awake, he would leave earlier than planned. A widower who lived alone in his bungalow in Caplin Cove, a small outport in an inlet in Newfoundland's Bonavista Bay, he quickly washed and dressed, then prepared and ate a breakfast of hot oatmeal and kippers. After a cup of tea, he donned his winter jacket, scarf, breeks and logans, and stepped out into the snow-cleared path leading to the village's main road.

Since the bight was still safely frozen, he decided to leave the road and take a short cut across the ice. The sun was just rising, providing a clear view of Critchville on the opposite shore a mile away. The spire of the Anglican church was visible, as was St. Andrew's School where Ray taught students the basics of reading, writing, and arithmetic.

He thought at first he was alone on the ice, but then he saw that a young woman was walking briskly about 200 yards ahead and to the right of him. He could recognize her from the distinctive red woollen winter coat she wore. She was 18-year-old Sarah Prince, who was obviously on her way to the early church service.

Ray was concerned to see her leave the usual pathway across the ice to strike out on a more direct route toward the church. He thought the ice near the shore at that point might not be as thick. He opened his mouth to shout at her to be careful, but it was too late. He was horrified to see the ice crack beneath her, plunging her into the frigid water.

He heard her frantic cries for help as he sprinted over to her rescue. He had to be careful not to fall in himself, so he stretched out on his stomach and wriggled as close as he dared. Then he pulled his long woollen scarf off and tossed it to the edge of the hole.

"Grab onto the scarf," he gasped, "and I'll pull you out."

Sarah was thrashing about desperately, but she managed to close her numbed hands around the scarf.

Pulling her to safety was not easy, but slowly and carefully Ray was able to draw her back out onto the ice. He was aware, however, that if he didn't get her somewhere warm in a hurry, she could still die from hypothermia.

Sarah was soaked to the bone and shivering violently as Ray picked her up and carried her as fast as he could to the shore. Fortunately, a house near the beach had its kitchen light on and smoke was rising from the chimney.

Ray ran to the unlocked front door and burst in without knocking. "I've got a girl who just fell through the ice!" he shouted. The residents, Fred Dunphy and his wife Betty, immediately saw the urgency of getting Sarah out of her wet clothes. Betty soon had her stripped and dried and into a warm housecoat, then bundled into a chair in front of the kitchen stove.

Sarah was young and healthy, and soon had completely recovered. But she knew that, without Ray's help, she would have drowned. She never forgot him.

Like most pretty girls, she attracted several suitors. Her favourite was Joseph Ingram Quinton, a fish merchant, and they dated for a year before becoming engaged when she was in her late teens. She looked forward to marrying him.

But Ingram was not so committed. During a visit to St. John's, he met another girl, Alice Payne, and fell in love with her. When he broke off the engagement with Sarah, she was heartbroken.

By time time she had been working for several years as a telegraph operator, and one of her co-workers at the telegraph office in Clarenville was a young man named Edward Finn. They had been close friends, but no romantic attachment had developed. After the breakup with her fiancé, however, their relationship warmed up and they later married in 1923.

Sarah Prince, as you may have surmised, was my mother. I started these memoirs by recounting a few of her pre-marital experiences for two reasons. First, because she was so remarkably gifted and intelligent — the most intellectually brilliant woman I have ever known — and had such a strong influence on my upbringing and later life. The fact that she became one of the very few female telegraph operators — at a time when women who wished to work outside the home were usually confined to nursing, teaching, or clerical work — speaks for itself.

The second reason for prefacing my memoirs with these life-changing incidents in my mother's life before she married my father is to reflect on how everyone's life is shaped by either choice or chance. The experiences that befall us through circumstances beyond our control are often life-changing. And so are the decisions we make on our own — for good or ill — at crucial turning points in our lives.

These turning points can be imperceptible at the time they occur. If Ray Mifflin had not set his alarm clock incorrectly; if he had decided to sleep another hour anyway, he would not have been on the ice to save my mother when she fell in. If Ingram Quinton had not made that trip to St. John's, he would not have met the woman who displaced my mother in his affections and would presumably have gone ahead with the planned marriage to Sarah. If Sarah, following the termination of her engagement to Quinton, had not then decided to marry her fellow telegrapher (who probably got her "on the rebound"), I would obviously never have been born, nor my brothers and sisters, nor our children and grandchildren.

When Ray Mifflin saved Sarah Prince's life, he also saved ours. So did an alarm clock that went off an hour sooner than its owner intended. So did the woman in St. John's who captured the heart of Sarah's fiancé.

Chance and choice. Our lives all turn and change as those two powerful forces come to bear on us. The rest of these memoirs relate how chance and choice played decisive roles in how the narrative of my life unfolded.

Chapter 1

Mom and Dad (and Grandpa)

MY MOTHER, SO FAR as I know, never took an IQ test. If she had, she would probably have registered well up into the genius level and qualified to join the select ranks of Mensa.

She taught me to read and write before I was five, mostly using the Burgess Bedtime Stories in the local weekly paper, the *Western Star*, as her "primer." The enthralling adventures of Peter Rabbit, Reddy Fox, Old Man Coyote, and the other denizens of the Burgess forest stirred my imagination. They fuelled my desire to become proficient in the written word as soon as I could — much more than would any dry First Grade Reader.

I was not Mom's first-born. A girl, Mary Florence, preceded me, but died from a "blue-baby" birth defect shortly after her christening. That was a year before I came into the world on June 4, 1926, in Spaniard's Bay, a small outport about a hundred miles from the Newfoundland capital of St. John's. We lived there till 1931, when Dad applied for and was offered an accounting job at the new paper mill that had just been built at Corner Brook on the west coast. By that time, the family had grown to include my sister Mary, a year-and-a-half younger than I, and baby brother Bill. We were later joined by brother Thomas Michael (called Mike for most of his life) and finally Patricia to complete the family.

Unlike my short-lived first sister, I've remained alive for 87 years and counting as I tap out these words on my Apple computer keyboard in Ottawa. Such is the stark disparity in the span of individual human survival. We are all placed on "death row," as it were, at the moment we emerge from the womb (or, some would say, at the moment we are conceived). The only difference for each of us is when and how the "execution" is to be carried out. Will it be even before we become self-aware, before our mother can teach us to read and write? In childhood or youth, from a fatal accident or infectious disease? In early middle age, from the kind of brain tumour that took my younger sister Pat in her mid-40s? Or from a stomach cancer like the one that doomed my mother to an agonizingly slow and painful death before she reached her 70th birthday?

Only her surviving children and a few relatives and friends now in their eighties and nineties still remember Sarah Finn, née Prince. She lived at a time and place when a woman with her keen intellect and aptitudes was denied the opportunity to develop them. Had she been able to pursue a career in the arts, in academia, in politics, in almost any profession, she would surely have won fame and acclaim. She would be remembered by millions, not just the few people still alive who had the great good fortune to have known and loved her, and to have benefited from her affection, her guidance, her wisdom.

Her early years as a telegraph operator helped broaden her knowledge and hone her sharp intellect. She was one of the first telegraph operators to receive and relay the S.O.S. signal from the *Titanic* after it struck an iceberg off the Newfoundland coast in April of 1912. She later filled two scrapbooks with newspaper accounts, photos, and other memorabilia from the doomed passenger liner.

As one of her sons, I am not of course an objective judge of her character or potential. But for many years I saw at close quarters the evidence of her percipience and creativity; her skill in raising and nurturing five children on a paltry budget in the midst of the Great Depression; her ability to manage the household affairs despite the difficulties of living with a husband who fell far short of matching her in ability or dedication.

She was 31 when she wed my father, nearly a decade past the usual marrying age for a woman in those days. She was no doubt widely considered by then to be an unmarriageable spinster, perhaps even by herself. I can only speculate that her prolonged single status was a legacy of the breakup of her engagement to Ingram Quinton, and perhaps her subsequent distrust of the fidelity of men in general. It is quite likely that, instead of being "dumped" by him, it was she who broke off the engagement after learning about his dalliance with another woman.

She may well have resigned herself to lifelong spinsterhood, only to have the deep instinctual desire to bear children finally come to the fore. She may not have "fallen in love" with Ed Finn while working beside him as a railroad telegrapher, but she was no doubt fond of him. The fondness bloomed into love, I think, over the next 12 years, as they were blessed with the children she yearned for.

It was customary in those days to have large families. Mom, despite being late to wedlock, gave birth to three boys and three girls between 1924 and 1936, all but one of whom lived into adulthood.

My memories of my mother would fill a book on their own, but here I'll relate only a few that especially stand out.

She was a convert to Catholicism. Dad was forbidden by the Church to marry her unless she converted, so she took lessons in catechism from a priest for several months before being admitted to the Catholic congregation. Like many converts, she became more devout in practising her new faith than those born into it. And her children were expected to live up to the high religious standards she herself set. Confession and communion every two weeks. Abstinence from sweets during Lent. No meat on Fridays. Absolutely no profanity, of course, and a "hell" or a "damn" — even an "oh heck!" — drew stern glances. She never spanked us (all physical punishment being left to Dad), but a reproving look from her was all it took to move us to tears.

My faith in the Catholic Church was so deeply instilled — by the priests and nuns as well as my mother — that it wasn't till my mid-20s that I completely discarded it. But I never had the nerve to break the news of my apostasy to my mother. She died believing she would be reunited with Dad and her children in the Christian afterlife, and it was a consolation I would never have forgiven myself for undermining in her during her long final illness.

Until the stomach cancer afflicted her, she was vigorous and robust, rarely ill with anything more serious than a cough or cold. She provided most of the "doctoring" that was needed, for us as well as herself. Nostrums like castor oil, Castoria, milk of magnesia, Brick's (Not So) Tasteless, and other potions were freely dispensed when needed for upset stomachs, as were bread poultices, liniment, and other skin lotions for cuts and bruises.

Apart from reading books and listening to radio programs like the Lone Ranger, Little Orphan Annie, Jack Benny, and Fibber McGee and Molly on the radio, we had to provide our own entertainment. One of Mom's and our favourites was Anagrams, a precursor of Scrabble. It consisted of several hundred letters on hard cardboard squares kept in a tin can. Up to six people could play, each in turn blindly drawing a letter from the tin and placing it face up in front of him or her. When eventually a short word could be formed, other players could "capture" it by using another letter to form a different word. Words would thus be formed, reformed, taken, and retaken until one of the players became the first to safely form and hold on to ten words.

Mom would invariably win nine out of ten of these word games — not just when playing against us as children, but even when we were in our 20s and 30s. She easily bested me despite the proficiency I acquired as a writer and editor. I suspected she let us win an occasional game to keep us from getting completely discouraged. Her mastery of English often deepened my regret that she had no outlet for her gift with language, other than the splendidly written letters she wrote to us after we'd left home and to her sisters and cousins who lived elsewhere in Newfoundland. Whether she herself was dispirited by her confinement to parenthood and housework, I never knew. She certainly never betrayed to us any sign of deprivation or embitterment. But of course she was also an expert in self-abnegation.

The worst years of the Depression took a toll on Mom. Luckily Dad kept his job at the paper mill in Corner Brook, being laid off only a few times and then for only a few weeks. His pay, however, was barely enough to keep the seven of us adequately fed and clothed, and often Mom's ability to keep us out of debt was sorely tested. One incident in particular seared the distress and anxiety of the mid-1930s into my memory.

My grandfather, who had been living with us, died in 1937. His bed then went unused for several months before Mom decided to strip off the mattress and blankets and sell the bedstead. She thought it was worth at least a couple of dollars. I was 12 years old at the time, and my brother Bill was eight. We managed to get the bedstead out in the front yard. It had wheels, and Mom asked us to push it down to Broadway, the West Side's main street, and over to Sammy White's emporium. She told us to ask him for $2 for the bedstead, and settle for $1 at the very least.

But Sammy White couldn't be persuaded to offer us any more than 50 cents. So we sadly trundled the bedstead back home and broke the bad news to Mom. It was one of the few times I saw tears in her eyes. She wiped them away with her apron and told us to wheel the bedstead back to Sammy White's store and accept the 50 cents.

At High Mass the next Sunday, the choir as usual sang a hymn that extolled the angels: the cherubim and seraphim. It was the first time I'd really listened to the Latin words. After Mass, I asked Father Doyle, who was saying farewell to the parishioners, why the hymn was praising Sarah Finn. He didn't notice I was mispronouncing the word. "Seraphim is the name God has given some of his angels," he told me.

As I walked home holding my mother's hand, I said to her, "Mom, I'm the luckiest guy in the world to have an angel as my mother."

She looked down at me, smiled, and squeezed my hand.

"I'm the luckiest Mom in the world," she said, "to have a son who thinks I belong in heaven."

After she died, my deepest regret was that I hadn't told her nearly as often as I should how much I loved her. She knew that, of course, even if I only put it into words on Mother's Day and her birthdays. But I think the unintended compliment I paid her after mistaking seraphim for Sarah Finn was the one she treasured most.

Dad

My father was born with a crippled lower left arm, a disability that frustrated and embarrassed him. He could make limited use of it, mainly to grasp things and supplement his good right arm, but most of the time he kept that misshapen hand tucked into his pocket. It was a handicap he was never able to accept and cope with, and I think it also crippled his outlook on life.

While not the best of fathers, he was far from the worst. He was a hard worker, a good provider for his family. He never mistreated Mom or any of his children. But he was often morose and withdrawn. He rarely displayed his affection for us. I can't remember ever hearing him laugh aloud.

He didn't quite know what to make of me. I spent too much time reading, he thought, and my first attempts to write short stories and draw my own comics drew his disdain rather than encouragement. He left that kind of "coddling" to Mom. My concern for animals baffled him. He set wire-traps for rabbits, went moose hunting every fall, occasionally decapitated one of the chickens he kept in a henhouse in the back yard, and had no qualms about taking a new-born litter of kittens from our cat, tying them in a burlap bag, and throwing them in the brook.

Of course, hypocritically, I ate my share of the chicken and rabbits and moose that I could never kill myself. Had I been the family food supplier, we would all have had diets seriously lacking in protein. Growing up in Newfoundland, where people tended to look at other animals mainly as prey and dinner fare, I was considered rather weird — and not just by Dad.

He gave up trying to change my hypersensitivity to other creatures after taking me trout-fishing with him when I was about 12. Not only did I refuse to do anything to harm a fish, but I even balked at first impaling a helpless worm on the hook. That was my first and last fishing trip with Dad.

A few years later, I came home from school sporting a big purple bruise on my forehead. Dad was hopeful that I'd finally gotten into a fight in the schoolyard. But I told him and Mom that I had walked into a light-pole.

"Weren't you watching where you were going?" Dad asked.

"No, I had to keep my head down," I explained. "There were lots of ants on the sidewalk and I had to be careful not to step on any of them."

Dad rolled his eyes and went back to reading the paper. Mom, of course, simply advised me to look up occasionally.

My relations with Dad while in my teens and 20s were cordial, but could never be called close. We had very little in common and he rarely joined in our card or Anagram games or other family activities. Always a moderate drinker while we kids were growing up, he began to imbibe more in his later years; but I never saw him so inebriated that he couldn't walk or talk.

It wasn't until after Mom's tragic death that he became an alcoholic. He devoutly loved my mother, and he depended on her. She was the brightest light in his otherwise drab existence, and her death plunged him into a downward spiral of drunkenness, despair, and maudlin self-pity.

He retired from his job at the paper mill, sold our house on Howley Road, then squandered the money from the sale — along with most of his pension income — on liquor. All of his children — my brothers Bill and Mike, and my sisters Mary and Pat — joined me in trying our best to sober him up, but our efforts were futile. He would sometimes stop drinking for a few days, even weeks, but always fell off the wagon.

Mary and I shared an apartment in Ottawa in the late 1960s, and he came to visit us, promising he wouldn't "take a drop" while he was there. But he soon found a compliant taxi driver who would bring him bottles of whiskey during the day while Mary and I were at work. He hid the empty bottles under his bed, but the smell betrayed him. Reluctantly, we had to put him on a plane back to Corner Brook.

To his credit, he later succeeded in controlling his alcoholism, perhaps with the help of some old friends who had kicked the habit themselves, possibly on his own. (And perhaps it would not be unkind to surmise that he had by then also depleted his bank account.)

In the fall of 1972, Dad drove up to Ottawa to visit my wife Dena and me, and to see our son Kevin, who had been born on January 3 of that year. He never touched a drink in the few weeks he was with us. A highlight of his visit was that, a few days before he left, Kevin at nine months began to walk, and he toddled first across the living-room floor into Dad's waiting arms. Dad was overjoyed, and this image of him hugging Kevin is one that mitigates the not so pleasant memories of my father that preceded it.

Dad died at a rest-home in Corner Brook a few years later. From the reports Dena and I heard from the staff when we went down for his funeral, he was well-behaved, socialized well with other residents, and enjoyed his time there. He even seemed to have become a favourite with some of the nurses and attendants.

Dad went to bed one night at the home and never woke up. I like to think that in the final stage of his life, he made peace with his inner demons, that he finally shook off the inferiority complex that his disability had afflicted him with.

He lies buried beside Mom in the Catholic cemetery in Corner Brook. If he had kept his faith, he may have died believing he would be reunited with her in heaven. If so, it was a comfort that Mom would certainly not have begrudged him. Nor do I.

Grandpa

My paternal grandfather was a maintenance-of-way foreman on the Clarenville-Bonavista branch line of the Newfoundland Railway. After retiring in 1930, he came to Corner Brook and helped defray the cost of building our two-storey, four-bedroom home on Howley Road. He lived with us until his death in 1937. He merits a mention here, if only because I've never forgotten his quirky character and sage philosophy.

He was as robust and astute in old age as he must have been in his prime working on the railroad.

"I stopped getting sick," he used to say, "when I found out it was bad for my health."

This was his sardonic reply to people who marveled at his seeming immunity to disease — even the common cold — well into his 80s.

His genes could no doubt take most of the credit, but Grandpa also had a healthy lifestyle. He kept physically fit and supplemented a nourishing diet with two cloves of garlic and a mug of cider vinegar every day. His death, at 86, resulted from a fall off the roof, where he had been fixing some loose shingles. Up to then, his vigor had been undiminished.

I found myself thinking of my grandfather more often as I neared the age when his life ended. I think mostly about his philosophy — his answers to the great questions of life and death.

Most vivid in my mind is an afternoon I spent with him on one of the few sandy beaches to be found near Corner Brook. I had just passed my 11th birthday. It was shortly after one of my school chums had died of a ruptured appendix before he could get medical help. I was upset, and told Grandpa that I'd thought death was something that happened only to old people.

He picked up a stick and drew a line in the sand from the grassy fringe down to the water, a distance of about thirty feet.

"Think of this line as the progression of time," he said, "from the birth of the universe to infinity." He took out his pocket-knife and cut a thin slice across the time-line.

"That's my life-span," he said.

"And where's mine?" I asked him.

He carefully drew the blade down the same cross-slash, widening it less than a millimetre. "Your life-span overlaps mine, but in the vastness of time it's barely perceptible."

"Jimmy's was even shorter," I said glumly.

Grandpa was silent for a while. Then he told me that each human being gets an allotment of time to exist.

"For some it's longer than for others, but what you should try to understand, Eddy, is that each of us is immortal, regardless of how long or short our individual lives."

Grandpa was an agnostic — another of his eccentricities — so I knew he wasn't referring to a religious after-life.

"Basically," he explained, "what happens is that, when each person is born, the universe is simultaneously created for that person; and when he or she dies, the universe also ends."

That concept was far too metaphysical for me to grasp at the time. Later, when I dabbled a bit in philosophy myself, I thought at first that Grandpa must have been a solipsist. But later I came to understand what he was getting at.

His argument was that the universe exists for each of us only through our senses. If we couldn't see it, hear it, feel it, or smell it, then for all practical purposes it would not exist. So life and time are both subjective, and Grandpa was right: the universe is indeed created and destroyed with the birth and death of every sentient creature.

"It's pointless to worry about dying," he told me that afternoon. "Like everyone else, you are going to live from the beginning to the end of time and the universe — as time and the universe exist for you. In that very real sense, you are immortal. So am I. So is or was everyone else — including your friend Jimmy, as hard as that may be for you to believe."

Seeing that I remained unconvinced, he pointed to the line in the sand that led down to where he had bisected it. "Were you sad or worried because you weren't alive before you were born?"

I laughed. "Of course not, Grandpa. I wasn't alive, so I couldn't feel anything."

He nodded, then pointed to the remainder of the line that led down from the cross-slash to the water. "The same is true of all the time that will follow you. You won't feel anything then, either."

He gripped me by both arms and looked into my eyes. "Always remember this, Eddy: You can never be sorry you're not alive."

I used to think that was a flippant remark, but as I grew into adulthood I came to believe it was rather profound.

Grandpa didn't try to deny the objective reality of time and matter, but he insisted that their interaction with each individual was purely subjective. He would argue, for example, that human feelings, whether of pain or pleasure, could not be quantified, since these and other emotions could only be experienced by the person in whose mind they existed. For him, a plane crash that killed a hundred people was no more tragic and inflicted no more pain or grief than a car crash that killed one person. Each person's mental reaction to anything that happens outside him or her, he maintained, is felt only by that person in his or her unique universe.

Still, he thought it was important for each of us to be aware of the entire life-cycle of the species to which we belong. He thought we should reach out with our minds and imagination and try to comprehend what went before and what will come after us. His view was that even a vicarious encompassing of the past and future of humankind would enrich our own short lifetimes.

So he read hundreds of history books and historical novels and biographies, and so had a keen sense of what had preceded his universe. The future was more of a challenge. Science-fiction was still in its infancy, but he read the futuristic novels of Jules Verne, H.G. Wells, and other science-fiction pioneers. He would have loved the later tales of space and time travel spun by Ray Bradbury, Isaac Asimov, A.E. Van Vogt, and other early sci-fi masters. And he would have delighted in the *Star Wars*, *Star Trek*, *Babylon-5*, and *Battlestar Galactica* movies and TV series.

He wasn't sure that any of the speculative stories he read accurately portrayed the future, but he appreciated the authors' attempts to extrapolate from contemporary social, economic, and political trends into the centuries ahead. They gave him the sense of completion that he sought.

I sometimes wonder what passed through his mind in the last few seconds of his life. He would not have been human if he felt no fear or regret, but I like to think that, at some intellectual level, he simply thought as he was falling that here was the answer to the one question that had hitherto eluded him: At last he knew how and when the universe would end.

He had few possessions to leave his family. His watch and other personal belongings he bequeathed to my father, and his property in Spaniard's Bay he divided among Dad and his other two sons.

A hastily-written note was found pinned to his will: "To Eddy, I leave the universe."

That cryptic note puzzled everyone else, including my parents, and I could never explain it to their satisfaction. But, although not an official part of Grandpa's will, it's a legacy I've never forgotten.

Chapter 2

Growing up in Corner Brook

MY BROTHERS, SISTERS, and I grew up during the Great Depression. Those years for most Newfoundlanders were lean and grim, as they were for most people everywhere. Poverty was rife, unemployment high, and food sometimes scarce; but in Newfoundland nobody starved. Newfoundlanders have always looked after one another, and there were always fish to catch; moose, caribou and rabbits to provide meat; and wild berries of all kinds that grew in profusion, as did hazel-nuts in some parts of the island. Many people, like our family, were able to grow potatoes, carrots, turnips, and other vegetables in their back yards — and we also had a dozen hens that kept us supplied with eggs for breakfast.

So poverty was not abject. Many Newfoundlanders still found work in the fisheries, forests, and mines, and lived moderately well. In Corner Brook, the paper mill remained in production almost all through the Depression, shutting down only a few times and for only a few weeks, so unemployment in the town never reached the levels that devastated other communities.

We children enjoyed our early years. With other kids in the neighbourhood, we played "cowboys and Indians" and went berry-picking in the woods during the summer, built snowmen and snow forts and had snowball fights during the winter. Our parents never worried about our excursions in the forest. They knew we'd be safe. Even if we did get lost, the mill whistle would emit piercing blasts audible for miles to guide us home.

In the evenings, when we weren't doing our homework, we would get our entertainment from the radio. Those were the hey-days of the vaudeville comedy shows, like Jack Benny, Edgar Bergen (Charlie McCarthy),

Fibber McGee and Molly, Fred Allen, Amos and Andy, and many others. For thrills and chills, we were enthralled by radio shows such as Little Orphan Annie, Terry and the Pirates, Red Ryder, the Lone Ranger, Suspense, and The Shadow. *(Who knows what evil lurks in the hearts of men? The Shadow knows!)*

We didn't lack for reading material, either. Since Newfoundland at the time was a virtual British colony, all the kids' magazines came from Britain. The three we boys read from cover to cover were *The Wizard*, *The Skipper*, and *The Rover*. They were packed with adventure stories, such as those featuring *The Wolf of Kabul*, a secret agent battling sinister villains in Afghanistan and India. I got my first dose of science-fiction in those magazines, and can still recall the title of one series: *Full Speed Ahead to the Worlds of Fear!* The space ships were powered by gravitational pull. Just open the outside panels facing the nearest planet or moon, and gravity would take you there. (I don't know why NASA keeps ignoring this form of propulsion!)

These weekly magazines cost 7 cents, which ate up nearly all of a boy's weekly allowance of 10 cents. So several of us would each buy one and swap them so we could eventually read them all — plus two British comic books, *The Dandy* and *The Beano*.

My love for science-fiction and fantasy became a lifelong addiction. Like my grandfather, I devoured the novels of Jules Verne and H.G. Wells that I found at the local library, but stories by contemporary writers of the genre were published only in American pulp magazines that weren't readily available in Newfoundland at the time. Later, after I went to work and had enough money, I was able to order copies of the pulp sci-fi mags from the United States. Those were the only publications that carried the early works of the best writers of imaginative fiction, such as John W. Campbell, Robert Heinlein, Ray Bradbury, Theodore Sturgeon, A.E. Van Vogt, Arthur C. Clarke, and Isaac Asimov.

These magazines, however, as imports from the U.S., had to clear the Newfoundland Customs, so I had to pick them up at the government building near the railway station. This would normally have been a routine visit, but in pre-Confederation times, the Customs Office also served as the censor of imported reading material. To my dismay, the covers of the early sci-fi and fantasy magazines invariably displayed scantily-clad heroines, usually firing ray-guns at BEMs (bug-eyed monsters). The Customs official who unwrapped the parcel containing a dozen of these garishly illustrated pulps was one of our neighbours, Mr. Howell. He stared at the covers, visibly shocked, and shot me an accusing glance.

"Now, Eddy Finn," he tut-tutted, "what do we have here?" He obviously thought he had caught me trying to slip pornography past him, and the magazines' names — *Amazing Stories, Thrilling Wonder Stories, Weird Tales* — did little to allay his suspicion.

"But they're just science-fiction stories," I assured him. "There's nothing dirty or indecent about them." This was certainly true. Most of the stories didn't even have female characters in them, and those that did were as devoid of sexual content as the local church bulletins. The half-naked cover girls were solely intended to boost sales at the magazine shops.

Mr. Howell, however, was not convinced. He kept me waiting nearly two hours while he painstakingly scanned page after page, trying to find some passages in the text that matched the bawdy cover art. He finally gave up and grudgingly allowed me to take the magazines home, even resisting the impulse to first rip off the offending covers.

A few years later, most of the pulps were allowed to be imported and displayed and sold in the local newsstands. So I was free to pick up the sci-fi mags, the Wild West pulps, and the other "men's" periodicals like *The Shadow, The Spider, Doc Savage, Blue Book*, and *Argosy*. It was in the latter two that I first came across the early *Tarzan* stories by Edgar Rice Burroughs, and the Zorro yarns of Johnston McCulley.

If it seems that I devoted more of my time to reading fiction than fact, that was probably true till I reached my early 20s, but it was important, I think, to stimulate my sense of wonder and open my mind to alternative ways and worlds. In later years, when I read more non-fiction, this openness to alternatives helped me, I think, to better evaluate the merit of ideas and policies proposed by academics and politicians.

Chapter 3

My Education

MY FORMAL EDUCATION ended when I was half way through Grade Eleven. That a high-school dropout could later succeed as a writer and editor is a testament to the times. Today, a university degree in communications is the least an aspiring professional writer must have on his or her resumé — and that just to get a toehold on the bottom rung of the journalism ladder. Sixty years ago, however, you could be hired by a daily newspaper on the basis of your demonstrable writing ability alone, or perhaps on the experience of writing for a weekly tabloid or newsletter for a few years.

My mother gave me a good head start. When I was old enough for kindergarten, the good Presentation Sisters, who taught all the elementary and middle grades at Our Lady of Perpetual Help School, soon found out that I could read and write at a Grade Three level. Unencumbered by any rules of student advancement in those days, the Mother Superior promptly "promoted" me past the first two grades. So I was only 16 — four months short of graduation — when I left school to enter the work force.

I was a better-than-average student in all but the eighth grade, when I slipped a few notches. That was the year I fell while running down a hill near St. Henry's School during recess, gashing open my left knee. The doctor who sewed it up (his last name really was "Hack") didn't clean all the dirt out, so the knee became badly infected, swelling up to nearly twice its normal size. This was shortly after the Christmas break. Without antibiotics to speed up the healing process, it took nearly two months for me to recover and get back to school. My sister Mary helped make up for the gap in my schooling by bringing me home three or four books a day from the library while I was bedridden.

Some of the other pupils accused me of what today would be calling "sucking up" to the nuns or being "teacher's pet." The Sisters probably did consider me a model student, since I hardly ever failed to do my homework or be late for a class. But I got my reputation as a toady mainly from my careful avoidance of the most dreaded instrument of a Sister's wrath: her cane or strap.

Corporal punishment in the schools was not only tolerated, but also strongly encouraged and ardently practised. All the teaching nuns had their favourite strap or cane in the top drawer of their desks, and wielded it to punish the slightest deviation from their strict rules of behaviour. Some of them would today probably be considered sadists, so evidently did they enjoy the cries of pain from the boys (seldom girls) whose palms they whacked. (Occasionally, a boy who dared defy or talk back to a nun was forced to bend over and have the strap applied vigorously to his backside. It was a spectacle that horrified the other boys, while drawing grins and giggles from the girls.)

I was adept at judging how far I could depart from impeccable conduct with each of the nuns without incurring her displeasure. Only once did I have my own posterior flayed, and it was by a nun I had always thought to be the kindest: Sister Mary Aloysius Claver. She taught the catechism class in Grade Seven — the subject I had the most trouble comprehending. I preferred to have a logical basis for what I was taught, and found most of the stories in the Bible — especially the Old Testament — so illogical as to border on the incredible.

I was especially baffled by being told that God was all-knowing as well as all-powerful, and that he could foresee the consequences of everything he did. Why, then, I wondered, when he was creating Adam and Eve, didn't he give them the wisdom to obey his command not to eat the forbidden fruit? Why did he put that tempting apple tree in the Garden of Eden in the first place? Why, when Adam and Eve ate the apple (as he knew they would), did their sudden knowledge of good and evil justify their expulsion from Eden? And what possible justification could there be for extending the punishment to all their descendents who were innocent of the Original Sin?

I didn't dare pose these questions about Adam and Eve to Sister Mary Claver, but when she turned to the subject of the Devil and Hell, I ventured to put my hand up. She smiled at me and asked if I had any questions. The following exchange then took place:

Me: "Sister, the catechism says that Satan was originally an angel, so he must have been created by God."

Sister M.C.: "Yes, Eddy, of course. God created all the angels. The one who led the rebellion against him was called Lucifer, and we know him now as Satan, or the Devil."

Me: "But God, being omniscient, must have known *before* he created Lucifer that he would become evil, that he would rebel. If God didn't want that to happen, he could have decided not to create Lucifer in the first place, couldn't he? Or he could have made Lucifer as pure as all the other angels he created."

Sister M.C. (testily): "It is not for any of us, certainly not a young boy, to question the will of God."

Me (recklessly): "But I'm just trying to understand, Sister. Okay, maybe God did have a good reason to create Lucifer and the other bad angels. But did he really then have to create Hell to send them to? Couldn't he have just made them repent, heard their confessions, and converted them back into good angels instead? And why doesn't he *keep* Satan and the other bad angels in Hell instead of letting them leave whenever they want so they can tempt human beings into sinning and also get sent to Hell? It really doesn't seem to make sense..."

Sister M.C. (now enraged): "That's quite enough! I never thought I would hear such blasphemy from a boy I thought would never question the Word of God! You have committed a mortal sin, young man, and you must confess it as soon as you can, or the gates of Hell will be opening for you, too! In the meantime, let me give you a small taste of the punishment you deserve for such sacrilegious heresy!"

As I saw her reach into the drawer of her desk and pull out her strap, I knew my tongue — usually so discreet — had gotten me into serious trouble. I looked around at my classmates, all of whom were beaming with anticipation. Seeing their usually most timid and well-behaved (and thus most disliked) fellow student finally incur a strapping was to be a highlight of their school year.

And indeed it was a painful lesson I learned about the folly of applying logic to the tenets of religion. Sister Mary Claver was incensed by my impiety, so she had me bend over my desk so she could administer the dozen strokes directly on my buttocks. They were as vicious and painful as she could make them. I was so sore from the flagellation that I couldn't sit comfortably again for another three days.

This, however, was my only fall from grace with the good sisters. I thenceforth dutifully suppressed my heretical doubts about the Old Testament and left their tutelage after Grade Eight to enter high school, where the teachers — and students — were all male. The church didn't trust boys and girls to occupy the same classrooms after they reached puberty, so thereafter we were educated in separate schools.

The most prominent teacher (and *de facto* principal) of St. Henry's High was Fred Scott, who had a strong influence on my mental development, both as educator and mentor. Fred (or Mr. Scott, as I always called him), was the most erudite person I had so far encountered. He was probably no more intellectually gifted than my mother, but far more formally educated. He had mastered four languages, including Greek, and had a wall full of framed degrees in history, philosophy, mathematics, and several other esoteric disciplines.

I wondered why such a brilliant scholar was teaching in the relative backwater of a Newfoundland paper mill town. He confided in me later that he, like many other young people with an inquiring mind, became obsessed with the deep mysteries of human existence. What was the meaning of life? Was there life after death? Were there answers to be found in the writings of the great philosophers? In any of the major religions?

He pondered many ideological and speculative theories, but what he was searching for was both credence and certitude. None of the great thinkers satisfied him, nor did any of the ancient creeds or cultures. It wasn't until he immersed himself in the teachings of the Roman Catholic Church that he found the authoritativeness he yearned for. The Church set down the precepts for the "good life" with the assurance that they came from God himself, and those commandments had withstood the trials and tests of two millennia.

When I expressed my own doubts about the Catholic doctrines that struck me as irrational, Fred told me I had to learn to distinguish between faith and reason. "When it comes to material things," he said, "you can rely on logic for understanding. But when it comes to your immortal soul and its purpose and ultimate destination, faith must be your one and only guide."

He somehow managed to reconcile those two conflicting perspectives, and it gave him a serenity that I always envied. I could never suspend my own reasoning faculty to embrace any faith-based system, but Fred managed that intellectual duality for the rest of his life. (As did my mother.) He went on to become a bureaucrat in the provincial government's Department of

Education, and later a deputy minister. We didn't see much of each other after I left school, except during the 1959-60 loggers' strike when we were on opposite sides of a province-wide controversy; but his influence on my early formative years was profound, and I remember him with fondness and respect.

Chapter 4

Mary and the Confessional

IN A TOWN WHERE Catholic children were not so much taught religion as indoctrinated with it, I always found it difficult to equate the catechism and the commandments with my sense of logic. So did many other kids. When we dared question some of the more incredible tales from the Bible, however, the priests and nuns would sternly tell us we had to accept them as "the Word of God." Faith should always prevail over reason, we were repeatedly told.

This was an intellectual constraint that I had a lot of trouble with as I grew up. One of my greatest difficulties was with the Catholic ritual of confession. We had to confess our sins to a priest every two weeks, promise each time to "go and sin no more," then return a fortnight later to relate how many times we'd broken that promise.

One day in the late fall of 1940, when I was 14, I complained to my sister Mary, then nearly 13, about having to go back to Father Doyle's confessional again on Saturday.

"What's the problem?" she asked.

"I hardly ever have any sins to confess," I told her, "so I usually make them up."

"And of course these sins you invent are always venial ones, I suppose?" Mary said. Though still only 12, she had already mastered sarcasm.

"I guess they're venial," I admitted. "I tell Father Doyle I was a few minutes late for school one day, or that I forgot to make the sign of the cross before saying my prayers, or that when I made the stations of the cross I skipped a few stations, that sort of thing."

"They're not even good venial sins," Mary said scornfully. "Does he even give you any penance for them?"

"Three Our Fathers and three Hail Marys, usually," I told her. "The only time he gave me five Our Fathers and five Hail Marys was when I confessed I'd fallen asleep during one of his sermons. And that happened to be a sin I really *did* commit. But I was running out of sins to invent, so I decided the last time I went to confession to tell him that I had nothing to confess."

Mary was appalled. "What the hell were you thinking of? Did you really expect Father Doyle to believe you could remain entirely sin-free for a whole two weeks?"

"Well, he always tells me after giving me absolution to go and sin no more," I reminded her, "so I thought he'd be pleased that I obeyed him this time. But after I said, 'Bless me, Father, for I have not sinned since my last confession,' he snapped back at me, 'Well you've just committed one sin, young man, by lying to a priest.' "But I'm telling you the truth, Father," I said. He got mad at me. 'Now there's another sin, contradicting a priest!' I was aghast. "I'm sorry, Father—" I started to say I was sorry he didn't believe I had no sins to confess, but he interrupted me after I said the first three words. 'So you're sorry,' he said. 'Good. I'll accept that as your act of contrition. Your sins are forgiven, and your penance is to say ten Our Fathers and ten Hail Marys. Now go and sin no more.'"

Mary sighed when I told her about this pseudo-confession. "And now you're worried about what to confess to Father Doyle this Saturday," she said. "I suppose you plan to invent and confess more fictitious sins?"

"What else can I do?" I asked her.

She sighed again. "Look, Eddy," she said, "your problem is that you don't understand what the Church is all about. The Church is all about forgiveness. That's its job — to forgive Catholics for the many sins they commit, and are *expected* to commit. If every Catholic was like you instead of me, the Church would go out of business. Why do you think I swear so damn much? It's to make sure I have lots to confess and don't get into the kind of pickle with Father Doyle that you've got yourself into."

I had never realized before that my failure to commit sins was threatening the future of a religion that had endured for nearly two thousand years.

I was worried. "So what do I do?" I asked Mary.

"You have to convince Father Doyle," she said, "that you've become a loyal and dependable Catholic sinner. That means you have to start confessing real sins — mortal ones."

I was horrified. "But mortal sins are going to be a lot harder to invent," I protested.

Mary threw up her hands in disgust. "You can't just make them up. You actually have to commit them!"

"No way," I said. "I could never take the name of the Lord in vain like you do. And I'm not going to risk committing a mortal sin and then dying and being sent to hell before I can confess it and be forgiven."

Mary heaved another sigh. "No, I suppose not. You're too much of a goody-two-shoes to even say 'damn' or 'shit,' let alone a really good swear-word. But it's important that you have at least one good mortal sin to confess to Father Doyle on Saturday."

She thought for a few minutes, then her face brightened. "Eddy, I have just the right mortal sin for you!"

I was skeptical. "What one?"

"Well," Mary said, "this is Thursday, and you know Mom always serves sausages or blood puddings for supper on Thursdays. All you have to do at the table tonight, when Mom and Dad aren't looking, is pinch off a little bit of meat and put it in your pocket. Then you eat it tomorrow."

My jaw dropped. Eating meat on a Friday was indeed one of the worst things a Catholic could do in those days. Definitely a mortal sin, but it would be easier for me to do than curse or swear.

"I'll do it," I promised Mary. And I did. It took as much courage as I could muster, but I pulled off a bit of sausage at supper, then put it under my pillow before I went to sleep. As soon as I woke up next morning, before I could lose my nerve, I popped the forbidden morsel in my mouth and swallowed it.

As I felt it slide down my esophagus, I also felt my soul slowly turning from snow-white to pitch-black. I was now a *bona fide* mortal sinner. I really had mixed emotions about that. Would God strike me down before Saturday afternoon and cast me into the flames of hell?

Mary assured me I would live long enough to escape from my state of iniquity back to a state of grace. She accompanied me to the Church of Our Holy Redeemer Saturday afternoon, and was waiting for me when I left the confessional.

"Did it work?" she asked eagerly. "Was Father Doyle impressed? Is he confident that from now on he can rely on you to be as sinful as a good Catholic is supposed to be?"

"Well, not as confident as he is in you, I suppose," I said, "but let me put it this way: he increased my penance to a complete rosary!"

"Congratulations, Eddy!" she enthused. "I knew you could do it!"

I was on a roll. "But you know what, Mary? I'm not going to recite all five decades of the rosary, only four. That way I'll have another sin to confess to Father Doyle next time because I really will be disobeying him."

Mary was ecstatic. She beamed at me. "Good for you, Eddy! Now you're getting the hang of it!"

She turned to go, but I grabbed her arm.

"Mary, I really appreciate your help with my confessions," I told her. "I couldn't have done it without you. But now that you know all *my* sins, it would only be fair, wouldn't it, for you to tell me all yours?"

She gave me that withering look she had perfected by the time she was six or seven, and turned away disgustedly.

"In your dreams, Buster," she said over her shoulder as she walked away.

I never did learn what sins Mary used to confess, other than her occasional profanity, but of one thing I'm absolutely certain — that she never had to invent any of them.

* * *

Mary had a long and active life that was terminated by a stroke in her 84th year. I had started writing my memoirs before she died, and showed her what I'd written about her help with my confessional problem. She thought I'd embellished the story somewhat, especially about her salty language, but laughed with delight as she read it.

"It'll be good to have this bit of humour in your memoirs," she said. "It will help balance all the stuffy political, labour, and journalism chapters."

Chapter 5

From schooling to printing to writing

OUR DESTINIES ARE shaped by the decisions we make — or are made for us — at crucial turning points in our lives. During my sixteenth year, a major event decisively changed the course of my life: my formal education was terminated before I could finish Grade 11 and graduate from high school. Knowing my parents' financial limitations, I knew they couldn't afford to put me through university where I could prepare myself for the career in journalism to which I aspired; but I'd hoped at least to finish high school. (Later, my brother Bill and sisters Mary and Patricia won scholarships that helped fund their higher education for careers in engineering and nursing, but that avenue was closed to me.)

My high school education ended when our school had a visit from Albert Bergeron, manager of the printing department in the Bowater paper mill. He was looking for an apprentice — or, as it was called in the printing business, a "printer's devil." The boy who took this job would spend four years learning the trade before becoming a full-fledged "journeyman."

Fred Scott, principal of St. Henry's boys' school, recommended me. I said I would have to consult my parents. I didn't want to leave school before graduating, and I hoped Mom and Dad would agree. To my dismay, they both advised me to accept Mr. Bergeron's offer. They shared Mr. Scott's opinion that a high school diploma would add nothing to my future prospects, since I wouldn't be going to university, and would have to enter the work force soon, anyway.

My starting salary as a printing apprentice would be $25 a month, a welcome boost to the family's meagre income. It was 1942, and my Dad's job as an accountant at the mill was secure, but his pay barely covered the basic necessities for a family with five children.

The first few months of my apprenticeship were onerous and depressing. I was taught how to operate the huge press which printed the big Labrador-dog labels that were pasted at each end of the huge rolls of newsprint the mill produced. I hated this job because of its monotony and the frequent lacerations of my hands. The press had to be hand-fed the knife-edged labels and, if you didn't pull your hand back in time, you got a nasty cut when a sheet was yanked away by the cylinder-grips. Some days I ran through a dozen or more Band-Aids.

I was so unhappy during that time that I cried myself to sleep most nights. I had a bedroom to myself and I muffled my sobs so the rest of the family wouldn't hear them. If Mom knew how dejected I was, she never showed it, and I took solace from that because the last thing I wanted was to make her and Dad feel guilty.

I had no way of knowing then that my training as a printer would be the first step on a path that led me, if circuitously, into the career in journalism that I had always wanted. This switch from the printing to the editorial side of publishing didn't happen for another few years; but the stage was set in 1943, when the weekly newspaper the *Western Star,* then based in the nearby town of Curling, was sold to Bowater's by the Barrett family and moved to the Bowater mill.

The print-shop was enlarged and equipped with a bigger press, as well as five linotypes to provide the galleys of metal type needed to format the newspaper pages. These typesetting machines can be found today only in science and technology museums, having been made obsolete by offset lithography printing and computer typesetting. They produced lines (or "slugs") of type by injecting molten lead into matrices that dropped from slanted "magazines" when the operator pressed the appropriate letters, numbers, or punctuation marks on the big 90-character keyboard. The assembled lines of matrices were then cast as slugs in a process known as "hot metal" typesetting, and the matrices then returned to the magazines for further use.

I was overjoyed to be made the operator of one of these machines, and first learned to type on the linotype keyboard, which was completely different from the standard typewriter's "QWERTYUIOP" board. It had six rows of keys instead of four. There were separate keys for lower-case and capital letters, for numbers and punctuation marks, and for other characters such as the dollar and percent signs, brackets, ampersand, etc. The alphabet was also more conveniently arranged, so that the most-often-used letters were the easiest to reach. I can still rattle off the alphabet in the order it appeared on the linotype keyboard: ETAOIN-SHRDLU-CMFWYP-VBGKQJ-XZ.

I was told that it would take four years for me to advance from an apprentice to a journeyman — an operator who could produce a galley of type in an hour. Within seven months I was producing one-and-a-half galleys an hour, and the shop foreman, Cyril Barrett, told me to slow down. "You're making the other operators look like they're slacking," he explained.

Embarrassed, I quickly lowered my galley production, using my spare time to do some original composition instead of typesetting the editorial staff's copy. I remember writing for the St. Henry's alumni paper, *The Vinculum*, and doing a story on the *Western Star's* annual picnic at George's Lake. (I was one of the very few linotype operators — perhaps the only one — who composed and set his own stories directly into press-ready type instead of using a pen or typewriter.)

I got along well with my fellow linotype operators (after learning to pace my productivity), and with the other printers, too. I still recall some of their names: Jack Robbins, Charlie White, Ernie LeMoine, Bert Butler, Phonse Bouzanne, and the Pinsent brothers.

Working as a printer in my teens also brought me into contact with organized labour for the first time. I was still being paid only $55 a month in 1944 when the International Printing Pressmen's Union signed up the printing staff and negotiated our first collective agreement. Imagine my delight when my monthly pay was more than doubled to $120 a month!

Needless to say, I've been a strong supporter of unions ever since.

During the last years of World War II, the *Star* was full of war news, and I have vivid memories of typesetting the report of the D-Day landings in Normandy, and the later stories of the Allied troops' advance through France, the Netherlands, and then into Germany.

Among the local news were articles about the local Ladies' Auxiliary, whose members sent monthly care packages of hand-knit clothing to the Corner Brook boys in the Armed Forces. These notes from the secretary of the group were usually typeset and printed exactly as written, but on one memorable occasion we let an embarrassing "typo" get through that caused quite a commotion. Even the best linotype operator could slip up if one of the channels holding the matrices got sticky, usually from inadequate graphite. When that happened, the letter in that channel didn't always drop when the key was tapped. In this case, which occurred a few months after D-Day, one of my "g's" got stuck. So a sentence that should have read, "The evening was spent in glove-making, which was enjoyed by all" came out instead as "The evening was spent in love-making, which was enjoyed by all."

When the proofreader (intentionally or not) also failed to catch the missing "g," the shocking behaviour of the ladies was revealed for all to see in print. There was much speculation about whom they could possibly have made love with that evening, since almost all the eligible men were off to war.

I can still summon a vision of the furious group of women who came marching into the Printing Department that afternoon. They barged into Mr. Bergeron's office and, although the door was shut, we could see them through the office window, gathered around his desk and shaking their fists at him. The poor man did his best to convince them it was an unfortunate typographical error, but they left still clearly incensed, shooting venomous glares at all of us as they stamped out.

Mr. Bergeron made a half-hearted effort to reprimand me and the proofreader, but soon all three of us started laughing and couldn't stop.

"Too bad it wasn't the Ladies' Auxiliary that stormed the beaches of Normandy," Mr. Bergeron chuckled. "The Germans wouldn't have stood a chance."

From linotype to typewriter

My transition from the printing to the editorial department came soon after the *Western Star* was expanded from a weekly to a daily paper in 1946. I had to take a $25-a-month cut in pay, since the editorial staff were not unionized, but it was a sacrifice I was only too glad to make, so eager was I to become a full-time journalist.

I was first asked to pinch-hit for our sports writer, Jimmy Murphy, when he fell sick and couldn't cover a baseball game at Jubilee Field. Not knowing much about baseball, I spent a few hours before the game reading the rulebook and talking with a few of the players. One of them, the shortstop, was my brother Bill. When I wrote the story that night, I braced myself for a torrent of criticism from the players and knowledgeable fans, but instead got compliments. As a beginner, I wasn't nearly as proficient a baseball writer as Jimmy, of course, but I managed to turn in a passable account of the game.

My permanent shift to the editorial digs also included a change of work-place when the *Star* was moved out of the mill to its own new building on Brook Street. The editorial department was understaffed, so I had to take on a much heavier workload than when I was a printer. But I was so thrilled to become a full-time writer/editor that I never complained about the longer hours. I did general reporting, sports reporting, edited copy, and wrote headlines.

Soon I also started writing a daily column called *Back Talk,* as well as some of the editorials. And, because of my experience as a typesetter, I was able to work with the printers in laying out the page-forms and cutting stories to fit. A typical work-day was from 7 a.m. to 7 p.m., but if there was a baseball or hockey game or a town council meeting, I was often banging away at the typewriter until well past midnight.

(The typewriter, incidentally, was my worst handicap when I first "went editorial." Having learned to type on the linotype keyboard, I was frustrated by the standard typewriter when I knew a much more efficient keyboard existed. For some time I fantasized about rearranging the typewriter keys to match those on the linotype, but eventually, reluctantly, had to surrender to what I considered the inferior and haphazard "QWERTYIOP" disarray. I still can only type with two fingers.)

Confederation

The years passed. In 1948 and '49, the big news was the battle over Newfoundland's future. Should it be restored to the self-rule it enjoyed before the Great Depression and near-bankruptcy forced Britain to install a colonial "Commission of Government?" Should the colonial status be retained? Or should Newfoundland become a province of Canada? The debate raged in the pages of the *Western Star* as it did in other papers, on the radio, at political meetings, in the Bingo and church halls, and in people's homes.

Most people were aware that the standard of living in Newfoundland lagged behind that of the majority of Canadians, Americans, and Europeans, and needed to be improved. The person who was most effective in raising this awareness, particularly in the immediate post-war years, was Joey Smallwood. As a journalist and on his radio show "The Barrelman," he constantly argued that the best way for Newfoundlanders to improve their lives was through Confederation — by becoming a province of Canada.

But that was not a popular view. Newfoundlanders were proud of their independence and self-reliance. Granted, they had to give up self-government in the early 1930s because of the economically crippling effects of the Depression, but by the late '40s, with the war over and the island's economy again thriving from the war's stimulus, a return to self-rule was a tempting prospect. Certainly, Britain intended to cut Newfoundland loose again, along with most of the rest of its overseas empire. So the two obvious choices for the future in a referendum were to return to self-rule or join Canada.

The champions of an independent Newfoundland (and Labrador) were numerous and vocal. They included most of the business and church leaders, educators, and the media — a powerful coalition. The pro-Confederation side also had some able and dedicated proponents, but most lacked the eloquence and influence of the anti-Canadians. Fortunately for the pro-Confederates, however, they had Joey Smallwood with them, and not just as a supporter, but as their leader. And what a fluent, fervent, spellbinding leader he was.

Joey was gifted with an oratorical ability that in Canadian politics I would rate second only to that of Tommy Douglas — and I've listened to speeches by both of them. Just as Tommy is deservedly known as the Father of Medicare, Joey deserves his acclaim as the last Father of Confederation. He also had the advantage of being widely known as a journalist and radio commentator. In the national convention called in 1948 to discuss and debate the island's future, Joey's distinctive voice over the airwaves was the most clear and compelling. The vision of prosperity as part of Canada that he outlined so lucidly swayed many who might otherwise have shunned Confederation.

Even with Joey's silver tongue, the referendum vote in favour of Confederation in 1949 passed by a margin of less than 2%. I was 23 at the time, and one of the pro-Canada votes was mine. I suppose you could also call it a pro-Joey vote. Smallwood undoubtedly merited most of the credit for Newfoundland's becoming a province on April 1, 1949. It was his crowning achievement, and the adulation heaped on him at the time was richly deserved.

After the Confederates emerged victorious, the debate turned into what kind of provincial government would follow. Everyone knew that whatever party Smallwood decided to lead would easily win the first election, and there was speculation that, as a former labour organizer and still an avowed socialist, he would set up and lead a provincial branch of the Co-operative Commonwealth Federation (CCF), then the principal left-wing party in Canada and the governing party in Saskatchewan under Tommy Douglas. Indeed, a delegation of union leaders went to St. John's to urge Smallwood to follow that course. One of them, Baxter Fudge, then president of the big Pulp, Sulphite and Paper Mill Workers' local at the Corner Brook mill, told me later about that meeting.

Joey listened to the union leaders, and said he agreed with their support of the CCF. But, he reminded them, the CCF outside of Saskatchewan was weak and, in the Atlantic region, almost non-existent.

"We have to be realistic," Joey argued. "The Liberals are in power federally and will likely remain in power for a long time. And we are going to need federal support if we want to get this new province on a sound footing. So let's form a provincial branch of the Liberal party in Newfoundland. What's the difference what label we put on it? We'll call it Liberal, but I promise you that, when it comes to policies, they'll be exactly what the CCF would adopt. We'll have a socialist government here under a Liberal name."

The union leaders were persuaded by this rationale, and Joey didn't let them down in his first few years as Premier. He had always been an outspoken foe of "the Water Street Gang," as he called the dominant business leaders, and seemed sincere in wanting to break their stranglehold on the island's economy and workforce. His popularity with the labour movement lasted until he broke the loggers' strike in 1959. (More about this historic strike later, if only because it became a decisive turning point in my life, as well as the lives of many other Newfoundlanders.)

The night Joey announced on the radio that he was decertifying the International Woodworkers of America (IWA), and expelling it from the province, Bax Fudge took his framed and autographed photograph of Smallwood off his living-room mantelpiece and threw it in the garbage can. Although Bax was close friends with the Premier up till then, he never spoke to Joey again.

A Disappointing Premier

I, too, was an early admirer of the feisty Smallwood, but I soured on him long before the loggers' strike. He had been superb as the leader of the pro-Canada crusade, and, on a scale of 1 to 10, I'd give him an 8 or even 9 for that performance. As a premier, however, as the leader of a provincial government, I'd rate him no higher than a 3. He was a terribly disappointing Premier, and his failure to govern well was not the result of inexperience or ineptitude, which might be an excuse, but by a conscious decision to form and administer a government patterned on a model of autocracy and corruption. He did bring several of his most capable followers into his cabinet, but demanded unquestioning loyalty from them, as he did from the many bumblers and sycophants he gathered around him.

Smallwood's failure as a premier was made evident by the type of men he picked to run key government operations and develop the province's resources. They were either greedy, high-rolling promoters like John C. Doyle and John Shaheen, or outright crooks like Al Vardy and Alfred Valdmanis. Joey later claimed to be unaware of their misdeeds, but really he was too intelligent *not* to know of the malfeasance with which they riddled his administration.

Perhaps the most obvious evidence of Joey's dereliction as premier is that, without exception, all the competent, principled individuals who worked closely with him during the campaign for Confederation became so disgusted with his behaviour that they broke with him. One by one, the erstwhile friends and allies he put in his cabinet — Greg Power, Harold Horwood, Ed Roberts, Bill Rowe — resigned in protest against his political and economic folly. Joey promptly denounced them all as "traitors" and vilified them with slurs so odious that they would have been considered libelous if uttered outside the legislature.

I was also among the former admirers of Smallwood who became disenchanted by the incompetence and corruption that tainted his government. Since the *Western Star* had by then been sold by Bowater's to the Herder family in St. John's, some of my columns in the *Star* castigating Joey were also run in the Herders' flagship paper the *Evening Telegram*. I soon received a letter from Joey, handwritten on the Office of the Premier stationery, and dated November 23, 1951. For some reason I've held onto it. The ink has faded badly, but it's still legible. It reads:

> Dear Mr. Finn:
> This is the first time I have ever written to the author of anything written about me. Your piece in *The Western Star* of Nov. 9, however, is so clever that I write to congratulate you. I do this, not as the subject of the article, but as an old-time journalist.
> Sincerely, J.R. Smallwood.

Perhaps Joey hoped his flattering letter would win me over, or at least induce me to tone down my sniping at his administration. It didn't. If anything, as evidence of his government's corruption and venality continued to leak out, my rebukes became sharper. The nadir for me was reached during "the Valdmanis Affair."

The Valdmanis Affair

Alfred Valdmanis, a Latvian, was a federal Department of Industry bureaucrat in Ottawa when then federal Industry Minister C.D. Howe recommended him to Joey to run his economic development projects. Valdmanis was supposedly a brilliant planner and administrator with three doctorates and with a record of having escaped both the Nazis and Russians during World War II.

Joey immediately made him his Minister of Finance, Economics and Trade, and soon afterward his Director-General of Economic Development. Today, someone like Valdmanis would not be considered qualified to run a corner store, let alone the economy of an entire province. He was incompetent both as economist and manager, but quite cunning in the dubious arts of kickbacks, fraud, and padding his expense accounts. It was his idea to set up factories for making rubber boots, shoes, gloves, and chocolate bars, all foredoomed market flops, but, incredibly, Joey kept him in charge of the provincial economy for four years.

Altogether, the Valdamis economic follies ate up more than $50 million and drained the province's treasury. It was only when his scandalous past as a former Nazi collaborater came to light that Joey called in the RCMP and had him arrested.

Like many Newfoundlanders, I was shocked when it was announced that the inquiry into Valdmanis's misdeeds and his subsequent trial were to be conducted *in camera*, first by a Grand Jury, and then, also in secret, by the province's Supreme Court.

I wrote an editorial for the *Star* criticizing the secrecy of the justice system in dealing with Valdmanis. He was, after all, a public servant accused of stealing millions from the taxpayers of Newfoundland, and therefore accountable to them. How much, I asked, did he steal, how was it done, and were any of the elected politicians involved? (We never did find out.)

The morning after my editorial was published, I was visited by the local Sheriff and served with a contempt of court summons. I was taken to St. John's to appear before the province's Supreme Court. I told the honourable Justices that I was not impugning their integrity, but simply contending that the people of Newfoundland deserved to have all the pertinent information about this public servant's alleged misconduct made public.

My argument fell on deaf judicial ears. I was found guilty of contempt of court and fined $400 — a not inconsiderable sum in those days, more than my monthly salary. Fortunately, and to their credit, the Herders paid the fine for me, since the offending editorial had been published in one of their newspapers.

After the secret trial, the Court issued a statement that Valdmanis had pleaded guilty to "a lesser charge of fraud," for which he was sentenced to a four-year term in the minimum-security first-offenders' prison farm near Deer Lake. He was allowed to go fishing or hunting on weekends and then released after "serving" one-and-a-half years of his sentence.

As for how much he misappropriated, estimates ranged as high as a million, but insiders suggested it was a great deal more. How much of these ill-gotten gains he gave back, if any, is also unknown. He moved to Montreal, bought a mansion in Westmount, and, a few years later, while I was working as a reporter for the *Montreal Gazette*, I saw him being driven around in a chauffeured limousine. I think it's safe to assume he didn't leave Newfoundland empty-handed.

Harold Horwood, who shortly afterward quit the Smallwood cabinet in disgust to resume his journalistic career with the *Evening Telegram*, told me he had reason to believe that Valdmanis was given a secret trial and a token sentence because "he knew where the bodies were buried." An open trial, with the prosecutor and defence attorney asking Valdmanis and witnesses pointed questions, might have inculpated other senior government officials and probably more than a few politicians. An *in camera* trial, a wrist-slap sentence, and permission to keep most of his stolen loot were almost certainly the terms exacted by Valdmanis for keeping his mouth shut.

(An interesting sidelight of the Valdmanis affair is that, as soon as he was arrested, he phoned Ottawa to ask John Diefenbaker — then still practising law — to be his defence attorney. Dief accepted and immediately hopped on a plane, but the deal to keep Valdmanis quiet was evidently made while Diefenbaker was in the air, because he was met at the St. John's airport by representatives for Valdmanis who told him his services would not be needed.)

Chapter 6

At The Montreal Gazette

AS MUCH AS I enjoyed working for the *Western Star*, I was conscious of its limitations as a small-town paper. I began to think that my writing ability could be honed and my experience broadened by getting a job with a big-city daily — at least for a few years. Being a long-time fan of the *Montreal Canadiens* (one of just three people in Corner Brook at the time who were not *Maple Leaf* supporters), I applied for a position as reporter with the *Montreal Gazette*. This was in 1955, several years before the eruption of the not-so-"Quiet Revolution" by Quebec nationalists, and I was promptly hired on the basis of samples of my writing that I enclosed with my application.

The ability to speak French — or even a willingness to *learn* to speak it — was not one of the qualifications required to work for the *Gazette*. In fact, there were three English dailies in Montreal at the time — the *Montreal Star* and the tabloid *Montreal Herald* were the other two.

Moving from a tranquil unilingual English community of 30,000 to a bustling city of more than a million francophones was a stressful transition, made all the more challenging by the jarring culture shock. Granted, I had no trouble communicating with francophone Montrealers, since almost all those I met were fluently bilingual. But I was always conscious that their first language was French and that they were fiercely proud of it — and of the distinctive culture in which it was rooted.

Shortly after I took a desk among the dozens of reporters in the *Gazette's* editorial offices on St. Antoine Street, I wrote what I thought was an amusing piece for the editorial page. I said I was puzzled about not hearing French spoken that often, and wondered if Quebec really was a French-speaking province. It was quite insensitive of me, and the editorial page editor warned me it might even be considered insulting.

"I'm going to publish it," he said, "but you should brace yourself for a backlash."

It wasn't long coming, starting the next morning with a scathing editorial in the leading French daily *Le Devoir* by its renowned editor, Gerard Pelletier. I'll always remember the heading: "Oui, M. Finn, on parle français ici!" He didn't appreciate my feeble attempt at humour. I was properly chastised, and tried during the rest of my time in Montreal to be more respectful of the French language and culture.

This wasn't always easy, since the volatile Gallic temperament was often on display in public demonstrations. A few months before my arrival in Montreal, a riot over the NHL's suspension of *Canadiens* star Maurice Richard from the playoffs had left St. Catharine's Street littered with broken glass. One of my first assignments as a reporter that fall was to cover another riot that broke out to protest an increase in the streetcar fare from a dime to 12 cents. Angry commuters pulled stanchions across the streetcar tracks to stall them so they could hurl rocks and bricks to shatter coach windows. Some protesters stormed onto the stalled streetcars and slashed the leather seats. A few attempts were made to set the immobilized cars on fire, but, apart from a few side-panels, they were inflammable.

What shocked me most was that these protesters were clearly not hoodlums. Some were young students, but most were well-dressed shirt-and-tie adults, and several appeared to be clerks emerging from nearby office buildings and gleefully joining the melee.

A large new hotel was being built downtown at the time. It was a project of Canadian National Railways and, when finished, would surmount the Sun Life building as the tallest edifice in Montreal. The CNR planned to call it the Queen Elizabeth Hotel, a choice of names that infuriated Quebec nationalists. They argued that the tallest building in the city (and the province) should be named Hotel Maisonneuve after one of Quebec's historic founders, not after the Queen of England.

Donald Gordon, who was then president of the CNR, was impervious to this argument, and apparently puzzled by it. At one of his press conferences that I attended, he asked querulously, "What are they so upset about? She's the Queen of Canada, isn't she? And Quebec is a part of Canada, isn't it?"

This insensitivity to the aspirations of Quebec nationalists was typical of the anglophone business élite that — together with the Roman Catholic Church — dominated the province prior to the 1960s. The Queen Elizabeth Hotel incident undoubtedly provided one of the sparks that fuelled the franchophone revolution.

As I was walking to work a few days after Donald Gordon's disdainful comments, I saw several students climbing the girders of the Queen Elizabeth Hotel's still unfinished structure. They were carrying what appeared to be a rolled-up banner. I ran to the *Gazette* building and asked one of the paper's photographers to come back with me. We got there just in time to get a good panoramic shot of the banner that was unfurled between the girders: *HOTEL MAISONNEUVE!* it proudly and defiantly proclaimed. Of course, it was soon torn down, and never did grace the portals of the Queen Elizabeth, even though I thought that would be one of the first acts of the first PQ government headed by Réné Levesque.

During my two years with the *Gazette,* I gained the deeper and more diverse experience in the newspaper field that I had hoped for. I covered a wide range of assignments as a reporter, ranging from train wrecks to sunken treasure finds in the St. Lawrence, from civic elections to interviews with distinguished guest speakers at various events.

One of my interviews was with labour leader Claude Jodoin, after he was elected first national president of the Canadian Labour Congress (CLC) at its founding convention in Montreal in 1956. Had I known that three years later he would hire me to work as a public relations officer for the CLC, I might have been more interested in him and the labour movement than I was while interviewing him.

Another of my interviews was with Arthur Scammell, composer of *The Squid-Jiggin' Ground*, one of the most well-known Newfoundland sea chanteys. He was then living in a Montreal suburb. The main thing I remember from that interview was his being peeved that all the other songs he had composed (some of which he felt were superior to *The Squid-Jiggin' Ground*) were all but forgotten and hardly ever performed. I asked him to sing a few, which he did, and they were pretty good, but I left privately agreeing with most Newfoundlanders that they were not nearly as singable as his pre-eminent composition. Well, that one rousing ditty is more than enough to assure Art Scammell a certain degree of immortality.

Although my first feeble attempt at writing a humourous article incurred the wrath of Gerard Pelletier and other nationalists, the editors accepted and ran dozens of other jocular pieces I submitted. Here are some excerpts from one published on April 1, 1956.

The anniversary of a significant date in Canadian history occurred today, although it will probably pass unnoticed here. April 1, 1949, was the date of Canada's confederation with Newfoundland.

Newfoundlanders are apt to say it was rather the day on which they "annexed" the Canadian mainland. Actually, of course, our takeover of Canada became a *fait accompli* nearly half a century earlier. April 1, 1949, was merely the day we got around to proclaiming the coup.

It was a bloodless conquest, effected so gradually and unobtrusively that it is doubtful a single native Canadian is yet aware it has happened. So insidiously, in fact, was the entire operation conducted that its details may be divulged without fear that they will be given any serious credence.

Newfoundlanders multiply rapidly, yet its population has remained virtually static at 400-500,000 for the past 200 years. This ethnic equilibrium was maintained by systematically exporting the surplus progeny across the gulf to Canada and the United States. Since 1600, it is estimated that approximately 3,000,000 Newfoundlanders have migrated to the mainland, most to the various Canadian provinces (or what were destined eventually to become provinces).

Assuming these expatriates retained their levels of procreation, it is safe to assume that by now their descendants comprise at least one-third of Canada's English-speaking population. A sufficient number of them now hold enough influential positions in politics, business, and the arts to exert a controlling force in the nation's internal affairs.

Fantastic? Of course it is. That's the beauty of it. Who would ever believe that a country as large as Canada could be occupied and vanquished by a process of systematic infiltration from an obscure island off its eastern coast? That's why I can so freely reveal so much. Even if some of you did believe it, what could you do? It's far too late now to stop us. We are too solidly entrenched at this stage to be displaced; and we can't be deported back to Newfoundland now that we have all been given Canadian citizenship papers.

The discerning reader may enquire as to the ultimate goal of our long-range conquest through infiltration. This information, unfortunately, I am unable to divulge with any authority. I can tell you, however, that our infiltration of the United States is proceeding satisfactorily and according to plan.

When the *Gazette* editors found out I also had experience editing, writing heads, and covering hockey and baseball games, I became the all-purpose staffer, serving on the editing desk, covering the police and education beats for a while, and even spending several months in the sports department.

I had the pleasure of seeing some of my hockey heroes perform at their finest at the fabled Montreal Forum, including "The Rocket" and his illustrious linemates Toe Blake and Elmer Lach, and later the equally stellar trio of Jean Beliveau, Dicky Moore, and Bernie "Boom Boom" Geoffrion.

I also got to cover some home games of the Montreal Royals, a farm team of the Brooklyn Dodgers. This was several years after the Dodgers signed up the first black player in the major leagues, Jackie Robinson, and had him play his first season with the Royals.

As much as I enjoyed working with *The Gazette* in Montreal, I never planned to stay there long. I had kept in touch with the Herders and with Wallace McKay, the *Western Star's* business manager, and they kept urging me to return to Newfoundland and the *Western Star*. As an inducement, they offered me the editor's position, as well as a munificent salary increase to $500 a month. Wow! How could I refuse? After bidding farewell to my colleagues at the *Gazette*, I hopped a plane in the fall of 1956 to resume my newspaper career in Corner Brook.

Down to Earth

The name of our planet is often erroneously written with a lower-case e instead of the capital E to which it is entitled. Why is it that the names of all the other planets — Mars, Venus, Jupiter, etc. — are always capitalized and the name of our own planet so often lower-cased?

Some confusion arises because we also refer to the soil we walk on as "earth," which *shouldn't* be capitalized. But when clearly referring in print to the planet and not the dirt beneath our feet, it should always be spelt with a capital E.

Another mistake in writing the name of our planet, even when properly capitalizing it, is to precede it with the definite article: "the Earth." There is no need for the "the," and in fact it's grammatically incorrect to use it. We don't say or write "the Mars" or "the Venus," or "the Saturn," so why say or write "the Earth"?

Maybe it's partly because we have a large satellite that has been left with no official name, so we just call it "the moon." Accustomed to referring to "the moon," we've fallen into the bad habit of also saying and writing "the earth."

The widespread misuse of our planet's name could quickly be remedied if we changed it to "Terra." That's the Latin word for "earth" and one that many science-fiction writers have adopted and capitalized — just as they've also given our moon the Latin name Luna. It's unlikely that people would spell Terra with a lower-case t or refer to it as "the Terra," or to the moon as "the Luna" — but, alas, equally unlikely that Terra will ever replace Earth or Luna replace the moon as widely used names for our planet and satellite. (A ray of hope, however, is that the word "terrestrial" — a derivative of Terra — is commonly used to describe our planet's qualities and resources.)

In any case, I'll try to keep setting an example by capitalizing Earth in my own writings, and doing my best always to omit the "the."

Chapter 7

Back to The Western Star

WHEN I RETURNED to Corner Brook in the fall of 1956, after my two-year sojourn in Montreal, I took over as editor, but that promotion didn't appreciably lighten my workload. I quickly slipped back into a 12-hour daily routine. I covered city council meetings, shared the sports beat with reporters Alex Powell and Mark King, wrote most of the lead editorials, and resumed my daily column (but changing the name from *Back Talk* to *Minority Report*).

I had an outstanding team of journalists working with me. Tom Buck served as city editor. He had graduated from McGill University with a degree in engineering, but had done so much writing for *The McGill Daily* that he decided to embark on a career in journalism instead. Tom Cahill doubled as our wire copy editor and editorial cartoonist, and Alex Powell did yeoman duty as our all-purpose reporter. Several other talented writers joined our staff for various stretches, including Bill Callahan, who went on to a stellar career in journalism and politics in St. John's, and Ron Pumphrey, who later became a Newfoundland icon as a politician and radio talk-show host.

One of the best-known journalists in the province at the time was a young chap named Max Keeping, who covered sports for the St. John's *Evening Telegram*. He wrote a sports column which was called — what else? — *Keeping Score*. (Max later moved to Ottawa, where he gained fame as a broadcaster with the city's CTV station and as a prominent personality in that community.) When our sports writer, Mark King, was given his own column in *The Star*, we naturally called it *MarKing Score*.)

One of my first initiatives on returning to *The Star* was to resume my interrupted running feud with Bowater's. Corner Brook was — still is — a paper mill town, and the huge Bowater's mill at the time was the world's largest, employing nearly 3,000 workers in the mill and as many as 2,000 loggers in the woods.

I was appalled to learn that this huge international paper company paid no provincial taxes, no royalty or stumpage fees for deforesting large tracts of Crown land, and not even a cent in municipal property taxes even though it was by far the largest property owner in the city. After Confederation in 1949, the company even had the gall to refuse to pay any federal taxes, either, since its charter granted by the former Representative government gave it complete exemption from taxes of any kind. It argued its case for federal tax exemption through the Canadian courts and all the way to the Privy Council in Britain. Only when the Privy Council ruled that Bowater's, like every other business firm in Canada, was obliged to pay federal taxes did the company reluctantly start sending payments to Ottawa. But it was still allowed to remain tax-exempt at the provincial and municipal levels.

In effect, Bowater's had been given freedom to exploit the province's forest resources with no reciprocal obligation other than to provide jobs for paper mill workers and loggers. And the number of those jobs was steadily declining as the company proceeded to mechanize and automate its operations, both in the mill and in the woods.

Bowater's eventually (and reluctantly) agreed to pay city council an annual sum "in lieu" of a property tax, but it amounted to far less than the rate assessed on individual home owners. So I kept hammering away at Bowater's refusal to act like a good corporate citizen and pay its fair share of the cost of provincial and municipal services. In one editorial, citing the continued elimination of mill and forestry jobs by labour-saving technologies, I asked sarcastically how long Bowater's would be allowed, in effect, to set its own "mill" rate. Would it still enjoy a free tax ride if eventually it employed just one person in the mill to push a start-up button every morning?

I kept churning out my indignant editorials, but to absolutely no effect. I was the proverbial voice crying in the wilderness of political indifference — or more likely it was the deep-rooted fear of offending the city's largest industry and employer. Whatever the reason for the lack of support for my lonely crusade, I was permitted to keep publishing my jeremiads without any effort by the company to muzzle me.

At a City Hall ceremony, when I bumped into the mill manager, Monty Lewin, he told me that some of his fellow executives wanted the company to put pressure on the publishers (the Herder family in St. John's) to fire me.

"We could easily have you sacked, all right," he told me, "but I told them that would only make a martyr of you, and as a martyr you might well give us a lot more trouble than you can as an editor. I reminded them that nobody was paying any attention to your rants, anyway, so why should we worry?"

A few years later, Bowater's power and arrogance *was* effectively challenged by a labour union, the International Woodworkers of America (IWA), when it began organizing the company's underpaid and mistreated loggers, and those of the other big paper firm in the province, the Anglo-Newfoundland Development Company based in Grand Falls. The two companies refused to negotiate in good faith with the union, which was eventually forced to take the loggers employed by the AND company out on strike after that company rejected a conciliator's proposed modest first contract.

I'll write more about that strike in the next chapter, because it turned out to be a pivotal turning point in my life, and indeed in the lives of many other Newfoundlanders. Had the strike not happened, I would probably have continued as editor of the *Star* for many more years, and might even have stayed there for the rest of my working life.

In any event, my editorial clash with Bowater's was my first eye-opening encounter with the exercise of unbridled corporate power. It planted the seed of a life-long aversion to Big Business bullies that I later cultivated while working as a communicator for several labour organizations and for 14 years as a labour columnist for *The Toronto Star*.

Bowater's, of course, with the help of the Smallwood government and the provincial media, emerged unscathed from the loggers' strike. Twenty years later, after harvesting the most accessible timber on the island, and putting its huge (mostly tax-free) profits into building new mills in the Scandinavian countries and the southern U.S., Bowater's simply shut down its Corner Brook mill. It was left to the provincial government to find another company to take over papermaking operations that Bowater's felt were no longer as lucrative as it could find elsewhere.

If only the angels had a union...

All of the woes that now plague humankind could have been avoided if the angels had been unionized.

Our progenitors, Adam and Eve, lived in the Garden of Eden, or Paradise, until Eve was tempted by the "Serpent" — Satan — to eat the forbidden apple. That original sin doomed them and their descendants (us) to the evils of neoliberalism and corporate rule.

But why did evil exist at all when God created Adam and Eve? It certainly didn't exist when he created Heaven, the original Paradise.

The answer, of course, is that evil originated with Lucifer, the angel who led the foredoomed rebellion against God. After Lucifer (aka Satan) and his fellow insurgents were defeated, God (their employer) relieved them of their celestial duties and cast them down into Hell, which presumably he had created earlier in anticipation of Lucifer's insurrection. (The rebel angels thus became the first workers ever to get "fired.")

God, however, for His own inscrutable reasons, chose to allow Lucifer and the other "fallen" angels to leave Hell whenever they wished and roam around the planet tempting and corrupting Adam and Eve's descendants — with appalling success.

We now have a global economic system that is the embodiment of evil. The Ten Commandments have been supplanted by the Seven Deadly Sins (especially greed) as the tenets of the new corporate religion. If this is not Hell on Earth, it's a close facsimile.

Now, imagine what could have happened if the angels had been represented by a trade union at the time Lucifer and his followers first thought of rebelling. Instead of resorting to violence, they could have gone on strike, which conceivably could have led eventually to a settlement with the Almighty that preserved celestial harmony.

Or Lucifer could simply have filed a grievance. And, who knows, maybe his grievance could have been settled to both his and the Boss's satisfaction, and the rebellion thus averted.

Of course, a lot would have depended on the nature of Lucifer's complaint. It's hard to think of angels having anything to gripe about, living as they do in what we're told by all the major religions is a place of perfect happiness. Still, Lucifer apparently wasn't happy enough. Maybe he was passed over for a promotion to Archangel. Maybe he disliked working long shifts at the Pearly Gates.

The point is that, with a union, a collective agreement, and a grievance procedure, he would have had the means to resolve his complaint, whatever it was, peacefully. Without a union and a grievance procedure, he had no outlet for his resentment, so it festered, eventually erupting in a vain "hostile takeover" attempt.

We all know the catastrophic consequences: Hell, damnation, disease, hunger, poverty, unemployment, global warming, capitalism, privatization, deregulation, NAFTA, the WTO, and George W. Bush and Margaret Thatcher.

And all because the angels didn't have a union.

Chapter 8

The loggers' strike

THE TWO PAPER mill towns in Newfoundland — Corner Brook on the west coast and Grand Falls in central Newfoundland — were fierce rivals in both hockey and baseball. Sports writers for the Corner Brook *Western Star* and the Grand Falls *Advertiser* often visited each other's communities when their teams were playing in the "enemy's" baseball field or hockey rink.

Late on a brisk November day in 1957, I was driving my Austin-Mini along the highway to Grand Falls. I planned to attend a game in Grand Falls between the towns' all-star hockey teams. But I never got there.

It began to snow heavily shortly after I passed Deer Lake, and about 40 miles later, taking a sharp curve, the car skidded off the road into a ditch. Both headlights shattered, and the engine conked out. There was no chance of completing the trip. With the snow falling more heavily, not much chance of being seen and rescued by another car, and given the now perilous driving conditions, I faced the prospect of having to spend the night in the car. Foolishly, I hadn't brought any food or blankets, so it would have been a very uncomfortable experience, to say the least.

Twenty minutes later, I was spared that ordeal by a logger, one of eight in a nearby logging camp who had heard the screeching of the brakes. I first saw his lantern flickering through the snow as he approached.

"I've never been happier to see anyone before in my life," I told him as he helped me out of the wreck. His name was Jeff Pritchard.

"You were lucky you went off the road so near our camp," Jeff said. "You might have survived without heat and grub, but it would've been a shockin' fierce night." He made sure I was unhurt except for a few bruises, then led me a few hundred yards down the road and off on a narrow path to what passed as a logging camp in those days.

It was little more than a clapboard-and-canvas hovel, infested with rats and other vermin. The loggers had to sleep on green birch boughs. The only heat was from an oil drum converted into a makeshift stove. I was appalled to learn that it was typical of the living quarters provided to the loggers by the two big paper companies.

I have to confess that, prior to this forced visit, I had no idea that the loggers' working conditions were so appallingly bad. Their food consisted mainly of boiled navy beans, baloney, and occasionally salt fish or salt beef, supplemented by hard-tack, rice, and black tea. There were no bathrooms, toilets, or kitchen facilities. They could only wash if there was a stream nearby or snow to melt.

They were paid at the prevailing rate for unskilled labourers: then $1.05 an hour. They were not supplied with appropriate safety equipment or training, so frequent accidents occurred, many resulting in the loss of hands or feet, or lifelong disability. A dozen or more loggers were killed on the job every year.

"What you guys need is a strong union," I told the loggers who were my hosts that memorable night.

Jeff grinned. "We joined one a few months ago," he told me.

It was the International Woodworkers of America (the IWA), which already represented loggers in most other provinces as well as in the United States. This union had been asked by the Newfoundland Federation of Labour and the Canadian Labour Congress to take on the arduous task of organizing the loggers in Newfoundland, and had begun signing them up the previous spring.

(At the time, the loggers were "represented" by the Newfoundland Lumbermen's Association, a compliant "company union" that had maintained a cosy relationship with the paper mill companies since it was founded by Joe Thompson in 1936. By the mid-1950s, it had managed to raise the loggers' pay to just $10 a day, and had done nothing to improve the atrocious conditions in the logging camps.)

The next morning, after my first and last night sleeping on tree boughs, Jeff helped me flag down a logging truck that took me back to Deer Lake, where I rented a car to return to Corner Brook.

I became a lot more interested in the loggers' plight after that, and avidly followed the IWA's efforts to organize and represent them. The union's organizers, led by Harvey Landon Ladd, Eastern Canadian director of the IWA, spent more than two years trying to overcome all the obstacles the two paper companies mounted against them. Simply getting to the isolated camps and gaining access to the loggers was made as difficult as possible. Organizing the loggers who supplied the Bowater's mill was especially hard because the company signed contracts with individual private logging outfits, forcing the IWA to seek certification separately for each of their work-groups.

This was such a labourious undertaking that the union decided to concentrate on the Anglo-Newfoundland Development (AND) company in Grand Falls, whose loggers were all direct company employees. The IWA could therefore apply to the province's Labour Relations Board for one certification to cover them all.

Even so, it wasn't until a year later that the IWA was able to sign up a majority of the AND loggers and submit its first bargaining proposals to the company. They were quite modest: a wage increase to $1.30 an hour, a work week reduced from 60 hours to 54, and some improvements in the camps' abominable working conditions.

Not unexpectedly, however, the company refused to make a single concession, so the IWA applied for a conciliation board to adjudicate the dispute. The board, in its report, recommended that the modest reduction in working hours sought by the union be granted, along with minimal upgrading of camp conditions, and a wage increase to $1.22 an hour. It was less than the modest IWA demand, but the union leaders were desperate to get a first contract, so they agreed to accept the board's report.

But the company was determined not to bargain with the union on any basis, so it flatly rejected the conciliation board's recommendations and refused to make a counter-offer. The mill manager claimed that acceding to the board report would cripple the company's entire operations. What he was referring to, of course, was not the few additional cents an hour in wages, but the cost of building decent, liveable camps for the loggers. Central heating, hot and cold running water, flush toilets, showers, kitchen stoves, dishes and cutlery would certainly have run into several million dollars. But these were all workplace facilities that other paper companies in Canada willingly provided without significantly reducing their operating profits.

The IWA was backed into a corner. Faced with an intransigent employer and with a labour relations board that refused to exercise its authority to compel the company to bargain in good faith, the union had no alternative but to take a strike vote. Its members responded with an overwhelming 98% majority favouring a walkout.

Many reports, newspaper articles, and books have been written about the ensuing strike. It dominated all other events in the province for the next several months, and became front page news across the country. It polarized communities, split families and friendships, and generated anger, frustration, and controversy on a massive scale. The province's radio stations and newspapers — with the sole exception of the *Western Star* — sided with the two paper companies against the union and the loggers. So did the business leaders and most of the clergy. Many priests and ministers preached anti-union sermons from their pulpits. They all accepted the AND company's absurd claim that acceding to the IWA's moderate demands would cripple the mill's operations and could even force it to shut down.

The day the strike started, I called a meeting of the *Western Star's* editorial staff.

"I don't have to tell you," I said, "that this strike is obviously going to be the biggest news-maker in Newfoundland for a long time. With anti-union sentiment running so high, it will be a challenge for this paper to maintain its objectivity, but I know you will support me as editor in reporting on this dispute in a manner that's fair to both the company and the union."

Tom Buck, Tom Cahill, and Alex Powell quickly gave me that assurance. So did the other reporters, though not with quite so much fervour.

We had one major geographical problem covering the strike. Since it was directed mainly at the AND company, almost all the developments would be in or around Grand Falls, while Bowater's mill in Corner Brook remained free to continue its operations.

As the *Star* was now owned by the Herder family, I phoned Steve Herder, editor of the Herders' flagship paper in St. John's, the *Evening Telegram*, to ask if he was sending a reporter to Grand Falls to cover developments there.

"No, why would I do that?" he responded. "We can get all the information we need from the company, or from the police if there's any violence or law-breaking by the loggers."

"But what about the union?" I asked. "Surely we'll want to give their side of the story as the strike goes on."

"Oh, that won't be necessary," Steve said airily. "They'll make their side of the story quite obvious from their actions."

I was shocked, but kept my composure. "I was going to suggest that we share the cost of sending at least one reporter to Grand Falls who would cover the strike for both our papers, but I see I'll just have to send one there from here and cover the cost out of The *Star's* budget."

He was silent for a minute. "Well, you're the editor and I suppose that's your decision to make," he said. "But I think you're mistaken that we actually need a reporter on the scene."

After I hung up, I told Alex and the two Toms that we were evidently on our own. "The Herders' sympathies seem to be solely with the paper companies," I said. "They won't try to dictate how we cover the strike, at least not yet, but if our coverage diverges significantly from theirs, we may well find our editorial freedom curbed from St. John's."

"If that happens," Tom Cahill said, "we may each have a hard decision to make, sooner or later."

We all nodded. We knew that what might well be at stake was the fundamental principle of objective journalism that we revered so highly.

Our fears, unfortunately, turned out to be well founded — but not for another eight months.

Alex volunteered to be our "foreign" correspondent in Grand Falls. His dispatches were informative and insightful, and he scrupulously quoted both company and union representatives when an "incident" generated opposing views. Such incidents mostly occurred in or near the adjacent logging camps, sparked by the company's attempts to continue logging with strikebreakers and to transport logs through the picket lines.

Two other factors seriously complicated the dispute. One was a deep and dangerous split in the labour movement. Most unions and their locals in the province were firmly in support of the IWA and the loggers, but — to the consternation of union leaders — members of the paper mill union locals in Grand Falls took the company's side in the dispute. They lived in company-subsidized housing that the company warned could be in jeopardy if it were burdened with the "heavy" costs of a settlement with the IWA. And many of the mill workers had also been turned against the loggers by the vicious anti-IWA propaganda that had been vented by most of the media in the province.

The other complicating factor was the arrival in Newfoundland of reporters dispatched there from several mainland newspapers and The Canadian Press. Unlike the anti-union coverage spewed out by the media in Newfoundland (other than The *Western Star*), the reports on the strike sent back to their papers by these mainland journalists often portrayed the loggers in a sympathetic light — as the victims of heartless and greedy corporations that were exploiting and mistreating them.

When this apparent "pro-union" coverage was made known in Newfoundland, the mainland reporters on the scene became even more unpopular than the leaders of the IWA. At first, the public reaction in Grand Falls was to hurl insults at these reporters, spit at them, and warn them to get back to the mainland. Then, as they continued to send back stories that infuriated the town's mill workers, they were evicted from the local hotels and some of the rooming houses, and a few were chased through the streets by a mob of vigilantes.

We were careful to keep The *Star's* coverage of the dispute fair and balanced; but Alex's reports, too, were resented by the Grand Falls citizenry — perhaps even more so than those by the visiting journalists. The *Western Star*, after all, could not be lumped in with the "biased" press outside Newfoundland, and so was pilloried as treasonous and traitorous — as giving credence to the "distorted" stories about the strike in the mainland media.

Fearing for Alex's well-being, we recalled him home, but continued to have union leaders interviewed by phone, as well as company and police spokespersons, whenever a significant event occurred. When it seemed necessary to maintain objective coverage, we even dared to quote the views of the few courageous mainland journalists who braved the growing public hostility and stayed in small bed-and-breakfast homes near Grand Falls.

One of these plucky reporters was Ray Timson of the *Toronto Star*. We came to rely on his accurate, detailed, well-documented accounts of the ongoing strike. It became clear from his and other mainland reporters' stories that, despite all the anti-union hysteria that was whipped up, the IWA was actually coming close to winning the strike. The stockpile of logs at the AND mill was shrinking and not being replenished. The mill would soon have to close down, and the company seemed on the verge of having to capitulate and start genuine negotiations with the union.

Many of the loggers' leaders continued to be arrested and jailed for simply exercising their right to picket company premises or roads through which strikebreakers were being escorted. But their places were promptly and courageously filled by their wives, girlfriends, or sisters — women who proudly supported the strike and believe it wholly justified.

It was at this crucial point, however, that Premier Joey Smallwood decisively intervened in the dispute, and, shockingly, it was to side with the paper companies against the union.

On the night of February 12, 1959, he took to the radio network to denounce the IWA as a "vicious bunch of thugs from the mainland" bent on seizing control of one of the province's most important industries. He claimed that IWA leader Harvey Landon Ladd and the union's organizers, Jeff Hall and Jack McCool, were spreading class hatred and he accused them of fomenting class warfare.

"It is not a strike they started, but a civil war," Smallwood declared. "How dare these outsiders come into this decent Christian province and try to seize control of our main industry? How dare they spread their black poison of class hatred and bitter bigoted prejudice?"

It was such a fierce anti-union tirade that it stunned the entire labour movement in Newfoundland and across Canada, not just the IWA and the loggers. They had hoped that Joey — a former union organizer himself — would indeed intervene to end the strike, but to force the company back to the bargaining table, or at least have the dispute settled through third-party arbitration. That he would decide instead to become a legislative strikebreaker and keep the loggers in company-controlled serfdom was an act of brutal anti-unionism unparalleled in Canadian history, before or since.

On March 6, Smallwood had the House of Assembly pass what he called an "emergency" bill to decertify both locals of the IWA in Newfoundland. This was the harshest and most blatantly anti-labour legislation ever enacted by a Canadian government. It was (and still is) the only time that a union was simply named and abolished by law, and it was almost certainly a violation of the Canadian Constitution.

The legislation was widely condemned all over the country (except Newfoundland) and indeed around the world. But Smallwood sneered at the volleys of censure directed at him. The IWA was not only to be stripped of its right to represent the loggers, but was also to be driven from the province.

For the loggers, their position now seemed hopeless; but many of them were so infuriated by Smallwood's strikebreaking legislation that they continued to block roads to the camps. This led to an incident near the little town of Badger, about 20 miles west of Grand Falls, that extinguished whatever small ray of hope the union had to survive in the province.

Joey responded to the blockage of camp roads near Badger by sending in every RCMP constable who was available in central Newfoundland and reinforcing them with a few dozen policemen from the Newfoundland Constabulary in St. John's. Altogether, he sent 72 police officers to the little town.

The loggers there, most of them residents of the town, refused to disband their picket lines. The police then marched on them, and the ensuing melee was graphically described by the *Toronto Star's* Ray Timson, the only reporter to witness it.

According to Timson, the police charged the loggers without provocation or warning, using their nightsticks to club two of them unconscious and knock several others to the ground. The loggers' wives and children screamed at the police to stop, but, Timson reported, their attack on the mainly defenceless loggers went on for an hour or more. In the melee, one of the policemen, William Moss, fell after being struck on the head. Immediately the police arrested nine of the loggers they had clubbed and knocked to the ground, including Ronald Laing, whom they later charged with striking Moss.

Moss later died in a Grand Falls hospital, and this gave Smallwood the fuel he needed to further inflame public fury against the IWA. As Harold Horwood later wrote in his biography of Smallwood, the premier turned the death of Moss into a stage production, complete with the parade of a flag-draped coffin and an honour guard at the graveside. The real criminals, Smallwood declared, were not the striking loggers, but the mainland IWA organizers, especially the union's east coast director, Harvey Ladd.

Public outrage against the union had already been whipped up to a fever pitch before the Badger incident, but now it boiled over. The "murder" of a valiant police officer was unforgivable and "proved" that Smallwood's strikebreaking action had been justified.

(A few months later, when the accused logger, Ronald Laing, was brought to trial on a charge of murdering policeman Moss, the Crown had not a shred of evidence to back up the charge. In the darkness, Moss could easily have been struck accidentally by another policeman's club. The verdict was prompt and unanimous: Not guilty. By then, however, Moss's death had served its purpose. It provided the final blow to the IWA's image and credibility.)

The Badger incident also led to the final breakdown of relations between the Herder family and the *Western Star's* senior editorial staff. Up till then, we had been able (with great difficulty) to defy or ignore the publisher's increasingly forceful "suggestions" about how the loggers' strike should be covered (or not covered). The alleged murder of a policeman by a "lawless" mainland union, however, was not something the Herders would tolerate being reported as anything but a crime and an atrocity.

We received a directive, not a suggestion, that forbade any reference to Timson's eyewitness account of the Badger clash. In addition, further stories about the strike or its repercussions were not to include any quotes or comments from union sources.

Faced with direct orders of this kind from the publisher, Alex, Tom Buck, Tom Cahill and I met in my office to discuss our options.

"If we obey the Herders' orders," I said, "you know it would mean a betrayal of the basic principles of journalism. We'll each have to make our own decision, but I can tell you that I will be sending them my resignation before I leave the office today."

Alex and the two Toms quickly agreed to resign as well.

"We have no choice if we want to maintain our self-respect," Alex said.

"We could never work again as respected journalists if we follow the Herders' edicts," said Tom Buck.

"I'd like to keep looking in the mirror every morning without feeling ashamed of myself," said Tom Cahill.

In retrospect, we did have one honourable alternative: we could have continued disobeying the Herders, kept reporting the strike fairly and fully, and dared them to fire us. But in our anger and disgust at the publisher's unacceptable directives, we didn't consider that option. We simply quit.

Rather than leave the Herders without a senior editorial staff at the *Star*, we did offer to defer our resignations for a few weeks to give them time to find replacements for us — provided, of course, we were allowed to cover the strike as we saw fit until then. But of course they were so furious that they ordered us to vacate the paper's premises as fast as we could. They seconded editorial employees from their flagship paper, the *Evening Telegram*, and flew them to Corner Brook that evening to take over from us immediately.

All four of us were unmarried at the time, with no family responsibilities, and with some savings in local bank accounts. So it wasn't as difficult as it otherwise might have been to quit our jobs. We knew, given the unpopularity of our coverage of the strike, that it would not be easy to find alternative employment as journalists in the province. But I have always felt certain that our decision to resign rather than desecrate journalistic ethics would have been the same even if we had all been married with families dependent on our incomes. It would have been much more difficult, and we'd have felt guilty about subjecting our families to stress, dislocation, and possible deprivation (however temporary), but fortunately that was not a price we had to pay.

Instead, being carefree bachelors, no longer having hard editorial work to keep us busy, Tom Buck, Alex and I piled into my little Austin-Mini and drove down to Florida for a month-long vacation. It was early April in 1959, shortly after the revolutionary guerilla force headed by Fidel Castro overthrew the corrupt Batista dictatorship in Cuba. We arrived in Miami to find laudatory pro-Castro posters and banners everywhere. He was quite popular with Americans before he decided to shut down the casinos, drive out the racketeers, and nationalize the sugar cane, banana, and pineapple plantations.

We paid $31 a week for a three-bedroom apartment just across from Miami Beach, spent time swimming, golfing, and just relaxing on the beach. We drove down to Key West, and would have taken a ferry from there to Havana if our finances had been less skimpy.

Tanned and reinvigorated, we returned to Corner Brook to consider our respective future careers. Our prospects didn't appear promising. But Tom Cahill, surprisingly, soon got a job with the CBC in St. John's and went on to distinguish himself there, both as a broadcaster and as a playwright whose stage productions garnered many awards. Alex decided to become a teacher and was an outstanding member of the teaching staff at the local public high school till his retirement in the mid-1990s. Tom Buck, with his degree in engineering and experience in journalism, was a natural to become editor of a *Maclean-Hunter* engineering journal in Toronto. (As for me, I went into politics, an unexpected transition I'll reminisce about in the next chapter.)

Before we went our separate ways, however, we met and talked at some length with local union officials, government and business people, and even the few journalists willing to be seen with us, such as Harold Horwood and Malcolm ("Mac") Maclaren. We wanted to get their views on why Joey Smallwood broke the loggers' strike, because its consequences had changed our lives so dramatically. Had Joey intervened instead to broker a fair settlement or even send the dispute to arbitration, the Badger incident would have been averted, and so would our job-ending clash with the Herder family.

Why did Smallwood break the logger's strike?

This question has often been asked since 1959: why did Premier Joey Smallwood, a former union organizer and self-professed socialist, become an implacable strikebreaker? His ruthless anti-unionism was all the harder to understand when it crushed a union effort to help the most exploited, mistreated, and underpaid workers in the province.

I think Joey had four incentives for becoming a strikebreaker.

First, there was the immense economic and political power of the two big paper companies. They were the largest industrial employers in the province, and they warned Smallwood, whose government was then struggling with a growing deficit and a slumping economy, that a victory by the IWA would have serious economic repercussions. The AND company even talked about shutting down its Grand Falls mill and leaving the island. A bluff, no doubt, but it had the desired effect.

The next three reasons for Joey's attack on the IWA had to do with its leadership by Harvey Landon Ladd. Ladd had one outstanding personal skill in common with Joey -— a gift for oratory that was as spellbinding as the premier's. He made the tactical mistake of putting his impressive rhetoric on display in meeting halls all over the province, thus presenting himself as a potentially dangerous political rival.

Ladd went further to anger and alienate Smallwood by hinting strongly that, once the IWA had built a strong base in Newfoundland, he intended to mould it into a political force. Organizing the loggers, he predicted, would be just the first step in building a broader movement that would establish a new and much improved social and political order in Newfoundland. This was a serious strategic blunder. Ladd was warned by his labour allies not to antagonize Joey in that way, but he wouldn't listen. He badly underestimated Joey's oratorical and political influence.

Perhaps Ladd's worst tactical mistake, however, was to declare publicly that, once his union was established in the province, it would make sure that logging became a full-time job for its members. No more hiring people to work seasonally or from month to month. If achieved, that would certainly have been a boon for the permanent loggers, but it would have dealt Joey's government a hefty financial blow.

Why? Because at that time the province's fishermen didn't qualify for federal unemployment insurance benefits. Once the fishing season was over, many hundreds of them got off-season jobs in the woods, logging for the paper companies. Ladd's plan would have denied them that option, so they would have been forced to turn to the provincial government for financial help in the form of social assistance or welfare benefits. The drain on Smallwood's treasury would have been huge.

I had — and still have — a high respect for Harvey Ladd. His efforts to lift the province's loggers out of a life of exploitation, poverty-level pay, scandalous working conditions, and virtual bondage were admirably motivated and pursued. He held meetings with them in which they voted democratically on their contract demands. He listened to their suggestions. He insisted that local support committees set up during the strike be comprised mainly of women — a decision that generated full family commitment to the campaign and supplied the picket lines with some of their most militant recruits.

Ladd also made sure, once the strike began, that no logger or his family would go hungry, lack food or shelter or medical care as long as the strike lasted. At first, the cost of providing these living costs were borne by the IWA and unions affiliated with the Newfoundland Federation of Labour and the CLC; but soon labour organizations all across Canada began contributing to a national strike fund that eventually raised $865,000 to help the Newfoundland loggers — the largest ad hoc strike fund in Canada's history.

So Harvey Ladd eminently deserves the respect and adulation bestowed on him for the valiant campaign he led on behalf of the Newfoundland loggers. It's unfortunate that he inadvertently undermined his own endeavours. His long-range plans for the loggers were laudable, but there was no need to make them public prematurely. I'm not implying that, had he refrained from flaunting his eloquence and long-term plans, his union's strike would not have been crushed by the provincial government. Joey probably still would have intervened to terminate the strike, but might have stopped short of outlawing the IWA. He might even have sent the dispute to arbitration. But if he ever had any reservations about enacting some kind of strike-ending legislation, Ladd himself helped to dispel them.

Whether he might have averted Smallwood's vicious strikebreaking legislation by moderating his verbosity is something we can only speculate about. What is certain is that Smallwood himself, no matter what his motivation or provocation, indelibly tarred his own image when he became the worst political strikebreaker and destroyer of basic union rights in Canadian history.

Harold Horwood, in *Joey*, his book about Smallwood, called Joey's betrayal of the loggers his one unforgivable act, one in which he abandoned everything he had once stood for. As Horwood noted, Joey fuelled the violence and hysteria that gripped the province as the strike progressed, and gave the people inflammatory rhetoric instead of statesmanship.

It was the beginning of Joey's decline and fall. He had exposed himself as an egotistical, power-mad demagogue, intolerant of the slightest dissent, and opposed to fundamental democratic processes. He managed to cling to power for another 10 years, but he never again commanded the respect and affection that he enjoyed in the earlier stages of his political career.

The late great editorial cartoonist for the *Toronto Star*, Duncan Macpherson, depicted Joey in the aftermath of the loggers' strike, sitting in royal splendour on a throne. The banner over his throne read: "Better to rule with management than serve with labour."

Breaking the loggers' strike may have had some personal advantage for Smallwood in the short term, but in the long perspective of history it destroyed any chance he might otherwise have had to join the ranks of Canada's true political greats.

He has been acclaimed as the "last Father of Confederation," but revealed himself as well to be the least illustrious.

Child Labour

Most North Americans who are appalled by the use of child labour in Third World countries today are probably not aware that their own history is far from free of the same morally indefensible practice.

In the 1800s, and even in the early 1900s, millions of children in the United States and Canada were forced to work in factories and mines. Most were under the age of 12, and some were as young as six.

As late as 1910, two million children were working in the U.S., many for 12 hours a day, six days a week. In Canada at that time, there were an estimated 400,000 working children.

It wasn't until the 1920s, in fact, that laws against the use of child labour were passed and enforced.

A Canadian Royal Commission on Child Labour in the late 1800s reported that "the employment of children in mills and factories is extensive and on the increase... These children, some as young as 8 or 9 years, invariably work as many hours as adults, and sometimes more. They have to be in the mill or factory at 6:30 a.m., necessitating their being up from 5 to 5:30 for their morning meal, some having to walk several miles to their work... Boys under 12 work all night in the glass-works in Montreal. In the coal mines of Nova Scotia, it is common for 10-year-old boys to work a 60-hour week down in the pits."

The Royal Commission's report disclosed that children were not only fined for breakages, tardiness, and negligence, but that in many factories and mines they were beaten with birch rods. In other mills they were often punished by being shut up for hours in dark, damp, unheated cellars.

Many thousands of children lost their fingers and entire limbs when caught in unguarded gears or pulleys. Many hundreds were killed on the job. The accidents were all blamed on the children's "carelessness," never on the employers' failure to provide safe workplaces.

A newspaper reporter who visited a twine-making factory in 1907 counted nine young girls at one bench alone who had lost either a finger or thumb in the twine-twisting machines. Those who lost a whole hand, of course, were no longer of any use and were immediately fired.

* * *

For those of us who deplore the use of child labour, this sobering look back at our own shameful past may serve to make us more active in the struggle to help the millions of boys and girls in developing countries who suffer the same abuse and misery today.

Chapter 9

My four years in politics

AFTER MY DEPARTURE from the *Western Star*, I took a few months to relax and consider my future career options. My prospects for finding another job as a journalist in Newfoundland were bleak. I had become a pariah for keeping the *Star* from joining the anti-IWA editorial blitzkrieg conducted by other newspapers in the province. Considered little short of a traitor, I was in effect blacklisted.

Of course, even if the other media outlets hadn't ostracized me, I wouldn't have applied to any of them, in any case. I could never have worked for a newspaper or radio/TV station that had so flagrantly violated the fundamental tenets of fair and objective journalism.

It seemed obvious that, if I wanted to continue a career as writer and editor, I would have to move to the mainland. I might even be able to get hired again by the *Montreal Gazette* (though probably, by this time, not without learning French). Alternatively, I was reasonably confident some other mainland city daily would take me on.

I was still pondering my options in mid-June of '59 when I received a phone call from Baxter Fudge, the CLC representative in Western Newfoundland.

After congratulating me for the stand I had taken with the *Western Star* during the loggers' strike, he asked if I had any plans for future employment.

"I've burned my journalistic bridges in this province," I told him, "so I have no choice but to move to the mainland."

"Well, you do have a choice," Bax said. "I'm calling to offer you a job with the CLC. Congress Vice-President Bill Dodge has authorized me to make the offer to you."

"What kind of job?" I asked.

"It would be to help the Newfoundland Federation of Labour and the Congress restore the image of the labour movement in Newfoundland. As you know, it's been badly tarnished by Joey and the provincial media, apart from the *Western Star*. We know what a good writer you are. We know you could help us conduct an effective public relations campaign."

I was intrigued by this offer. It would be a deviation from conventional journalism, but would still exercise my writing and editing ability. It would also enable me to stay home in Newfoundland (later, of course, to be renamed Newfoundland and Labrador).

"Okay, Bax, I accept your offer," I said. "When do I start?"

"You can start in a few days. There's an office vacant in a building on Brook Street. I'll lease it and have it all ready for you by next Monday."

The office was equipped with a desk, chair, bookshelves, filing cabinet, and a new Underwood typewriter. It also had a marvelous copying machine called a Gestetner, which could run off 100 copies of a document from the original master-sheet. High-tech for the 1950s.

Bax and I spent the rest of June and most of July getting acquainted with local labour leaders. I also met with Bill Dodge, who came down from the CLC's Ottawa headquarters to discuss the planned campaign to restore labour's battered post-loggers'-strike image. We were joined at this meeting by Esau Thoms, president of the Newfoundland Federation of Labour (NFL), and Calvin Normore, one of the local labour activists.

Before we could even get started on this project, however, it was pre-empted when Joey Smallwood called a surprise provincial election in late July, to be held on August 20. He announced that this election would give the people of Newfoundland an opportunity to reward him with a vote of confidence for his handling of the loggers' strike. He repeated his vituperative attack on the IWA, calling the union "a subversive outside influence incompatible with the Newfoundland way of life."

This snap election call came as a shock to the labour leaders, who had thought they had ample time to mobilize an effective political challenge to the premier. Instead, they had barely three weeks.

An emergency meeting was called in a small conference room in the Glynmill Inn. I was invited to attend. Bax was there, along with two other CLC reps, Frank Chafe and Cyril Strong. So was Esau Thoms, local labour activists Cal Normore and Wilson Russell, and, surprisingly, IWA leader Harvey Ladd, who had defied Smallwood's expulsion of his union and was still in the province.

I won't try to describe the ensuing discussion in detail, except to say that all the labour officials were convinced they somehow had to contest the election directly instead of just sniping at Joey the strikebreaker from the sidelines.

This seemed to me an impossible undertaking. It would involve forming a new political party; finding and fielding candidates; preparing speeches, posters, leaflets, newspaper and radio ads, and canvassing voters for support.

All this in three weeks.

"That's not even time to organize a new party's founding convention," I pointed out.

"You're right about that," Frank Chafe admitted, "so we'll just have to set the new party up right here and now. It may not be as democratic a process as we'd like, but what choice do we have?"

"I nominate Ed Finn to be party leader," Cal Normore said.

"All in favour — " Bax said.

"Hey, wait a minute!" I protested. "I'm not a politician. I don't want to be a politician, and I'm certainly not qualified to be the leader of a political party, even one created by eight people in a hotel room!"

They all assured me I was the best possible person to lead the new party.

"You're well known in the province as former editor of one of its major daily papers," Ladd pointed out. "You'll give the party a credible image."

"We'll all pitch in help you," Chafe chimed in, "and we'll also have lots of help from the Federation and CLC."

It took them half an hour to overcome my reluctance to become an active politician. It was Bax who put forward the most persuasive argument.

"Ed, you've agreed to help us restore the labour movement's image," he pointed out, "and that means doing all we can to tear down Joey's image. What better way to do that than in an election campaign where you as party leader automatically get media attention and exposure on radio and TV?"

Finally I capitulated and agreed (with deep misgivings) to lead the new party, at least for this election.

I was "elected" by acclamation, eight votes to zero. (Well, I had to vote for myself, too — no one else was in the running.)

RESTORE DEMOCRACY To NEWFOUNDLAND

AN URGENT MESSAGE FROM THE NEWFOUNDLAND DEMOCRATIC PARTY

EDWARD FINN, JR.,
Leader of the Newfoundland Democratic Party

DEAR FELLOW NEWFOUNDLANDERS:

The establishment of the **Newfoundland Democratic Party** is, I am convinced, one of the great events in our recent history. This new party has been launched in this year of turmoil to re-affirm for our people the principles of justice, fair play, honesty and brotherhood which have until recent times been our great heritage and tradition; and to dedicate ourselves to the building of a better Newfoundland, not just for a few people, but for all our people in every section of our great province.

In recent years, and especially this year, the man who has been Premier of this province has ridden roughshod over these principles. He has made a mockery of time-honoured democratic processes, for one-man rule is not democracy. This is why one of our main purposes is expressed in our slogan "Restore Democracy to Newfoundland."

I am proud to be the first leader of this new **Democratic** Party, and to have associated with me a group of candidates dedicated to these worthwhile objectives.

We are, I emphasize, completely devoted to the cause of raising the living standards of our people. Newfoundland is Canada's 10th province, it is true, but we must not be content with remaining the 10th province economically. We must raise our sights. We can and must launch a programme of planned development which will re-invigorate our forest, fishing, agricultural, mining and other industries and vastly improve our transportation facilities.

All this we can do if we work together as Newfoundlanders and Canadians and replace the present conflict among us with co-operation, goodwill and constructive ideas. I and all my fellow-workers urge every one of you to consider our programme carefully because we know that serious consideration will win you to our cause.

Sincerely and fraternally

EDWARD FINN, JR.,

Leader of the Newfoundland Democratic Party.

THE DEMOCRATIC PROGRAMME

1. Restore truly democratic government.

2. Vigorously promote a programme of full employment in the Province.

3. Build up a comprehensive road programme to serve all the people of Newfoundland.

4. Support the proposition that Term 29 is a sacred part of the Terms of Union and cannot be changed by the federal Prime Minister and his Government alone. This matter must be one for proper negotiation, not one-sided decisions by either the Newfoundland or the Federal Government.

5. Establish a programme to assist Newfoundland fishermen, through an organization of the fishermen themselves; for a fish marketing board and the encouragement of producer co-operatives. It will establish support prices for fish and assist in the development of producer-owned fish curing plants.

6. Act immediately to repeal the anti-labour laws passed by the House of Assembly which, if allowed to stand, threaten the welfare of thousands of Newfoundland families and, indeed, the economic welfare of the whole Province.

7. Press for greater control, in the public interest, of the operations of public utilities.

8. Encourage and protect farm development.

9. Provide equal opportunity for all Newfoundland children through grants and scholarships, to get the best possible educational training.

10. Establish a Royal Commission to investigate the spending of public funds on industrial development and fisheries during the past ten years.

11. Make Newfoundland's labour laws the finest of any Canadian Province.

12. Introduce a taxation system based on ability to pay. Investigate methods of removing the sales tax.

Vote DEMOCRATIC on August 20

VOTE for your DEMOCRATIC CANDIDATES:

ST. BARBE .... Jack McCool	GANDER .... James Mullett	BELL ISLAND ..... S. Neary	ST. GEORGE'S .... Gerald Byrne
WHITE BAY NORTH H. E. Richards	TWILLINGATE ..... Ray Rogers	ST. JOHN'S SOUTH Charles Devine	PORT AU PORT ... Ambrose Rice
WHITE BAY SOUTH Jack O'Brien	FOGO .... R. W. Wellon	ST. JOHN'S CENTRE Larry Daley	HUMBER WEST .... Ed Finn
GREEN BAY ...... M. C. Skinner	BONAVISTA NORTH M. K. Pritchett	PLACENTIA EAST .. Esau Thoms	HUMBER EAST ... Joseph Chaulk
GRAND FALLS . J. L. Hannaford	HARBOUR MAIN . A. Dunphy	BURIN .... Cyril Strong	TRINITY NORTH .. S. Drover (Ind.) (we will support)

This message from the leader of the Newfoundland Democratic Party was published in the *St. John's Evening Telegram* on Wednesday, August 12, 1959, during that year's provincial election.

"What's going to be the new party's name?" I asked.

They all looked at one another.

"We could set up a branch of the CCF," Esau Thoms suggested. "That's the most labour-friendly party in Canada, and it has formed the government in Saskatchewan under Premier Tommy Douglas for 13 years."

"True," Ladd agreed, "but I'm sure you all know that the CCF is now dickering with the CLC to jointly found a new national party. They haven't settled on a name yet, but the proposed favourite is the New Democratic Party."

"Yes, that's a great idea, and we could get a head-start here in this province," Bax enthused. "Let's call our new party the Newfoundland Democratic Party. That way we can use the same initials, N-D-P, and Ed would be the first NDP leader in Canada!"

"Well, Newfoundland has been ahead of the other provinces in almost everything else since Confederation," Cyril Strong said. "So it's appropriate that we also be the first to launch this new party."

The meeting adjourned on a high note of optimism, and the next three weeks flew by in a flurry of non-stop mobilizing, door-to-door canvassing, leafleting, press conferences, and dozens of speeches in church halls, schools, and of course on radio and television.

As leader of a party, I was given as much TV time by the CBC as Joey and Progressive Conservative party leader Malcolm Hollett. I wrote all my own speeches, and even had the aid of a newfangled teleprompter for those delivered on TV. (I was glad there were no televised leaders' debates at the time, since I was woefully lacking in the kind of oratorical skill that Joey — and to some extent Hollett — had mastered.)

We managed to field NDP candidates in 18 of the province's 36 ridings, but of course, with just 7.2% of the popular vote, failed to elect even one. The Liberals under Joey swept 31 seats, the PCs won three, and another small pro-sovereignty party, the United Newfoundland Party, captured two seats, even though their share of the popular vote — 8.2% — was only slightly higher than ours.

Still, we were encouraged by the election results. Amassing more than 7% of the ballots from only half the ridings was not an insignificant achievement for a party that didn't even exist when the election was called. In eight seats, our candidates ran second to the Liberals, surpassing the Tories. Clearly Joey's brutal treatment of the loggers and the IWA had alienated thousands of voters and sullied his hitherto impeccable image.

My experience with this 1959 election slightly lessened my disinclination to remain active in politics. I was still determined to resume my career in journalism, but felt I could carry on as provincial NDP leader for a few more years.

Given my aversion to being a party leader, it was ironic that Pierre Elliott Trudeau, in his book *Federalism and the French Canadians* published in 1968, actually credited me with creating the Newfoundland Democratic Party almost singlehandedly. He was writing about the failure of leftists in Quebec to set up a branch of the CCF there. "The Quebec left," he wrote, "were precluded from exploiting the same type of elementary opportunity as that which permitted the launching by Mr. Ed Finn of *a* new party in Newfoundland, even though *the* new party had not yet fired the starting gun."

This "starting gun" was eventually fired in 1961, when delegates from the CLC and the CCF assembled at the Civic Centre in Ottawa to jointly create the national New Democratic Party. I was privileged to lead a delegation from the Newfoundland Democratic Party to this historic meeting, where we officially affiliated with the new federal NDP. I suppose, if I ever get a small footnote in the history books, it will be to have served as an "NDP" provincial leader for nearly two years before Tommy Douglas was elected first leader of the federal NDP.

Tommy and I became good friends after that. He came to Newfoundland shortly afterward to join me in a speaking tour around the province, and later I reciprocated by joining him for a similar speaking tour in his home province of Saskatchewan.

If I needed any other inducement to make my political career a short one, it was the humbling experience of having to address an audience that had been held spellbound by Tommy Douglas for an hour or more. Tommy was the most gifted, eloquent, silver-tongued orator Canada has ever produced. He never had notes. The words just poured out. He laced his speeches with humour and wit. But the message was always forceful, inspiring, even mesmerizing.

I somehow managed not to put the audience to sleep, especially on the Newfoundland tour, where people turned out mainly to hear Tommy, and I could limit myself to a few minutes introducing him. On the Saskatchewan tour, however, I was expected to deliver a speech of at least 15 or 20 minutes myself. In our first stop in Regina, following Tommy's oration, I mumbled and stumbled, and barely got through it. I'd tried to memorize my remarks, as he so easily did, and wound up mangling or forgetting most of them.

Afterwards, Tommy told me, as gently as he could, that, although I was a fairly good writer, I was far from being a good speaker, at least when I tried to emulate him and do it extemporaneously.

He was sympathetic. "Ed, your forte is writing, not speaking," he told me. "So for heaven's sake do put your speeches in writing before you deliver them orally."

This was good advice, which I've followed scrupulously ever since. Had I planned to make politics a long-term career, I would probably have taken courses in elocution and tried to learn how to ad-lib effectively without a prepared speech, but I remained a very reluctant politician. The sooner I could get back to my typewriter on a full-time basis, the better.

This was not to happen, however, for another two years, during which the NDP in Newfoundland, to my dismay, was embroiled in three more elections, the first two federal and the other one provincial. I remained leader of the party during those two years, and ran twice federally as the NDP candidate in Humber–St. George's–Ste. Barbe, the big riding that spanned almost the entire west coast of the island.

These two federal elections were close together because the June 1962 election had reduced the Progressive Conservatives under John Diefenbaker to a shaky minority government. It lasted only eight months before being toppled by the Liberals with the help of the NDP, precipitating another election held in April 1963. The Liberals under Lester Pearson were also held to minority status, but managed to govern effectively for the next few years on a progressive social agenda forged with the NDP led by Tommy Douglas.

When I first campaigned in a federal election, in 1962, I thought that people in the northwest coast outports, although quite intelligent in most respects, were not all that knowledgeable about politics. I soon learned that they knew a lot more about how the political game was played in Newfoundland than I did.

Thirteen years after Confederation, there were still no constituency associations, no selection of candidates through a democratic voting process. Provincially, Joey would call a snap election, without warning, every few years, and all were of just three weeks' duration. He would announce the election on the CBC radio network, and end up by saying, "And here are the names of your Liberal party candidates and the ridings they'll be running in." I suspect — in fact, I'm positive — that some of those Liberal candidates didn't even know they'd be running until they heard Joey mention their names on the air.

Joey never publicly warned, or even hinted, that anyone who dared vote for another party's candidate would be risking their baby bonuses, public pensions, unemployment insurance, or other federal social payments. But his party minions in the outport ridings certainly did. People received these monthly cheques from Ottawa, but everyone knew (or believed) that it was Joey's influence with the federal Liberals that really kept these payments coming. If Joey — heaven forbid! — should ever be toppled from power, goodbye to all that federal bounty.

The other important political fact the outport people knew that I didn't was that a candidate had better have an ample supply of booze to dispense along with a campaign pitch if he or she was to be taken seriously. Liberal candidates in most coastal ridings had schooners to take them from port to port — especially convenient when there was no road on which to drive there. The schooners' holds would be stocked with alcoholic beverages: bottles of scotch or whiskey for the merchants, magistrates, teachers, doctors, clerics, and other eminent citizens, bottles of beer for everyone else. As for us, we couldn't even afford to lease a dory.

I need hardly say how much this put NDP candidates at a disadvantage. We didn't bring any booze on our campaign trail, and not just because we couldn't afford to, but because we were trying to take the high ground and campaign on the issues. But we soon found, to our dismay, that temperance and politics didn't mix, at least not in the west coast outports.

The voters in these small communities (those we could reach by road) crowded around our car when we arrived, licking their lips expectantly, but when they found we didn't even have a few cases of beer in the trunk, they left in disgust. Their comments about the stupidity of a candidate who expected to get elected on empty promises instead of full bottles left us dumbfounded.

* * *

In between these two federal elections, Smallwood sent Newfoundlanders back to the polls provincially in November '62. I ran this time against Joey's minister of labour, Charlie Ballam, in the riding of Humber West. Corner

Brook had previously been one big riding, but Joey craftily gerrymandered Corner Brook in half, split into Humber East and Humber West, and added on Frenchman's Cove, Lark Harbour, Woods Island, and the dozens of other small outports strung along both shores of the Bay of Islands, all of them solidly Liberal.

My election campaign budget was $733, as much as Baxter and other NDP stalwarts could raise on short notice. That was enough to run off a few leaflets and rent a few meeting halls. Still, on election night, November 19, as we listened to the poll results on the radio, I was running ahead of the labour minister for the first few hours.

"By God, Ed," said Bax, my ever-optimistic campaign manager, "it looks like you're going to make it this time!" I had trouble concealing my apprehension. The last thing I wanted was to get elected to a seat in the provincial legislature and be doomed to a prolonged stay in politics. Fortunately for me, if not for the party, when the poll results came in from out the bay, Ballam caught up, overtook me, and won re-election by 240 votes. I managed to appear suitably disappointed when Bax and my supporters commiserated with me, but secretly I was immensely relieved.

We might have made a breakthrough in the 1963 federal election when we persuaded Farley Mowat to run as an NDP candidate in one of the St. John's ridings. A famous writer then living in Newfoundland and very popular there (at least before he wrote *A Whale for the Killing*), Farley might have won this seat for the NDP. But he called me just a few days before we planned to announce his candidacy to say he had to back out. He had signed a new contract with his publisher to start writing a series on the history of Newfoundland, so a political career was now out of the question.

Farley later did get his first (and only) book in this planned series published — it was titled *West Viking* — before public outrage over his book about the bloody slaughter of a whale in a Newfoundland cove impelled him to leave the province.

* * *

The Examiner

One of the highlights of my four years working with the province's Federation of Labour was the publication of a 16-page weekly tabloid which we called *The Examiner*. It was largely subsidized from the residue of the loggers' strike fund, but the Federation also helped financially and provided the editorial staff with space in its offices, then on Bond Street in St. John's.

The editor was Harold Horwood, an eminent journalist, author, labour organizer, and political activist. As a former associate and supporter of Smallwood, and a member of his cabinet before resigning in disgust, Harold had many inside sources of information about the political shenanigans going on at the time. His front-page stories for *The Examiner* often scooped the *Evening Telegram* and other provincial media. So did his *Political Notebook* columns in *The Examiner*.

I was assistant editor of *The Examiner* and wrote a weekly column called *Minority Report*, as well as a page of articles about events in my home town of Corner Brook.

Our sole staff writer and interviewer was Malcolm (Mac) Maclaren, who had worked for the CBC and *Evening Telegram* before being laid off for openly criticizing that paper's one-sided and anti-labour coverage of the loggers' strike. Mac also doubled as our advertising manager.

We launched *The Examiner* in mid-July of 1961 and kept it going until the end of April of 1962. We probably could have continued publishing it a lot longer if the CLC hadn't abruptly cut off its financial support. This happened after Harold wrote a blistering column denouncing the United States for its unprovoked but foredoomed Bay of Pigs invasion.

Never being a writer who toned down his language when he was enraged, Harold upbraided President John Kennedy for "financing and equipping a mercenary army with the aim of overthrowing the Castro government and giving the island back to the corrupt Batista regime, the crooked casino operators, and the brutally anti-labour American fruit plantation owners."

Shortly after Harold's vituperative column reached the office of CLC secretary-treasurer Donald MacDonald, he shot off a stinging letter to rebuke Harold and me. He told us the American unions in the AFL-CIO fully supported the invasion of Cuba, and so did the CLC. This was hardly surprising, since at that time 80% of Congress affiliates were branches of American unions.

Brother MacDonald informed us that all financial aid from the CLC for *The Examiner* would be terminated immediately. This was the paper's death knell, since our meagre local advertising revenue had also dried up because of *The Examiner's* less-than-friendly business news coverage. Just about the only advertisers who kept their ads in the tabloid by that time were the beer companies. Our May 6, 1962 issue was *The Examiner's* last.

(Anyone interested in reading any of the 42 issues of *The Examiner* we managed to publish can access them at either the Memorial University archives in St. John's or the National Archives in Ottawa.)

I learned later that this was by no means the first time Harold had clashed with Donald MacDonald. During the mid-1940s, when Harold was speedily and effectively organizing garage mechanics, brewery workers, garment workers, and other groups for the Federation of Labour, his bold methods and abrasive personality grated on MacDonald, then a leader of the Canadian Congress of Labour to which many of these unions became affiliated.

MacDonald and other conservative union officials were concerned about preserving organized labour's sober and respectable image with the public. In March of 1947, when Harold was escorted at gun-point off the U.S. base at Argentia for trying to organize the labourers there, MacDonald was horrified. He prevailed on the Federation to suspend Harold from his organizing efforts.

The longtime enmity between MacDonald and Horwood makes MacDonald's crackdown on *The Examiner* more easily understood.

Twenty years later, when I was writing a labour relations column for the *Toronto Star,* one of my recurring themes was to promote the breakaway of Canadian branches of American unions from their U.S. parent organizations. Donald MacDonald, by then president of the Canadian Labour Congress, was furious with me, as were other leaders of Canadian sections of AFL-CIO unions. When they convened a meeting to plan ways of blocking union autonomy in Canada, I wrote a satirical column comparing them — not all that biologically accurately, I'm afraid — to the prehistoric dinosaurs attempting to stamp out the first small mammals that evolved to threaten them. I referred to the gigantic raptors' leader as "Donald MacDinosaur." (Was I thinking of getting back at MacDonald for his financial scuttling of *The Examiner* back in 1962? Well, maybe subconsciously.)

Goodbye to Newfoundland

Between 1959 and 1963, my time in Newfoundland was split between helping unions with public relations and, as provincial NDP leader, helping the new party get established in the province. Although I managed to juggle these two roles fairly well, my tenure in both was not meant to last. Bill Dodge made it clear, when he hired me after the loggers' strike, that the CLC's budget wasn't intended to pay indefinitely for a staff person doing PR work in the province. My salary, in fact, was being taken from the residue of the loggers' strike fund, which was close to depletion by the early summer of '63.

I had a phone call from Bill in June of that year.

"There are four unions affiliated with the Congress that are looking for a PR director," he told me. "I've lined up interviews for you with the officers of all four unions. Let's arrange suitable dates that are convenient for both them and you."

Two of the unions were national and two international. I told Bill I didn't want to work for an American union, so we agreed to confine the interviews to the two national unions. One was the Canadian Brotherhood of Railway, Transport, and General Workers (CBRT & GW), the other still really two separate unions that were on the verge of merging: the National Union of Public Employees (NUPE) and the National Union of Public Service Employees (NUPSE). Their merger in September would result in the creation of the Canadian Union of Public Employees (CUPE), with a combined membership of 80,000. It was destined, within the next half-century, to become the largest union in Canada, with over 600,000 members.

I took a plane to Ottawa in early August for the two interviews. The first, for the CUPE position, turned out to be split in two — one with Stan Little, then president of NUPSE, and the other with Bob Rintoul, president of NUPE.

Both officers seemed to be impressed by my application, my experience in journalism, samples of my writing, and supportive letters from the CLC, the Newfoundland Federation of Labour, and from "Lofty" MacMillan, a NUPSE rep I'd helped with an historic strike of hospital workers in Corner Brook.

Little and Rintoul both assured me that the position was mine, and that they would not be interviewing any other applicants. I probably would have become the first Communications Director for CUPE if it had not been for the parting utterances I heard from both of them, in almost identical language:

"CUPE will have only two national officers, President and Secretary-Treasurer. I don't know which office I'll wind up with after the founding convention next month, but, whatever one it is, I expect you to be loyal to me."

This warning (for that's what it was) shook me. I didn't relish the prospect of becoming a punching bag between the two national officers, whose feelings for each other still seemed well short of brotherly love. I was also dismayed by Rintoul's admonishment that I would not be permitted to become as active in partisan politics as I had been in Newfoundland.

My fears about the first CUPE PR director having to tread on a minefield between the two national officers were later borne out by Roy LaBerge, who took the job after I bowed out. He told me he couldn't even go into Rintoul's secretary-treasurer's office without having to explain to Little (the president) what he'd been talking to Rintoul about. The animosity between the two top officers was also replicated among many of the merged staff members from the two founding unions, which made the PR director's duties even more onerous.

If I could have foreseen the circumstances 17 years later that led to my finally taking a job in CUPE's Communications Department, I might have reluctantly accepted the position in 1963. But at the time I had a very attractive alternative: becoming PR Director for the CBRT & GW.

My interview with CBRT president Bill Smith and secretary-treasurer Don Secord went smoothly. Their union had much to offer. It was Canada's oldest and most distinguished national union, dating back to 1908 when it was formed by railway workers in Halifax who broke away from an American union to form their own independent organization. Under its first and long-serving president, the renowned A.R. Mosher, who led the union for half a century, the CBRT was influential in helping build central labour bodies and federations that culminated in 1956 with the founding of the Canadian Labour Congress.

The CBRT also boasted the most durable labour journal in the country — *Canadian Transport* — which had been published by the union in magazine form since 1910. Smith and Secord wanted me to become its new editor and oversee its transformation from a magazine to a tabloid. If I wasn't tempted enough by that offer, they sweetened it by telling me the union had its own printing press in the basement of its national office on Laurier Street. (It was soon to be converted into a printing company, Mutual Press, but would still be wholly owned by the union.)

"We'd be delighted if you would accept our offer," said Bill Smith. "You're just the kind of professional writer and editor with union experience that we were looking for."

"As for your annual salary," said Don Secord, "I'm afraid we can only offer you $10,000, but that's just to start. There will be substantial yearly increases."

Since I'd only been paid $8,000 by the CLC, this was more than adequate, and I told them so.

They asked how soon I could move to Ottawa, and I told them I'd be driving up from Corner Brook in a few weeks.

When I got back home, I wrote a letter to Little and Rintoul, expressing regret that I was withdrawing my application.

I also had to resign as provincial leader of the NDP and bid a sad farewell to the party pioneers who had worked so diligently with me over the previous four years.

I felt guilty as I said goodbye to Cal Normore, Wilson Russell, Mac Maclaren, and the other NDP stalwarts who were left to carry on what I knew would be an uphill struggle for many years. I especially regretted parting with Baxter Fudge, the CLC rep with whom I had worked so closely in both the labour and political fields since the 1959 loggers' strike. Together we had traveled all over the island, mostly in Bax's car, trying to recruit NDP members as well as engaging in many union negotiations and several strikes.

Our adventures together would come close to filling a book on their own, but a few episodes will suffice for these memoirs.

Once, when driving between Grand Falls and Gander, we were engulfed in smoke from a forest fire when the wind suddenly changed. Our vision was reduced to only a few feet. I had to get out and walk in front of the car for more than a mile, a wet handkerchief covering my nose and mouth for nearly an hour before the wind shifted and the smoke dissipated.

On another much more memorable night — October 27, 1962 — while driving to St. John's, we were listening to news of the Cuban missile crisis on the car radio as we entered the Terra Nova provincial park. President Kennedy had put the U.S. armed forces on high alert and Soviet President Nikita Khruschev was refusing to remove Soviet nuclear missiles from Cuba unless the U.S. agreed to remove the missiles it had set up in Turkey. It looked as if the world was on the brink of a catastrophic nuclear war.

So we decided to stop and spend the night in one of the park's guest cabins instead of proceeding on to St. John's. We thought it unlikely that the Newfoundland capital would be on the list of Soviet strike targets, but there was an American base, Fort Pepperrell, right in the middle of St. John's, so, just to be on the safe side, we thought it prudent to stay a few hundred miles away from there that night.

It sounds silly now, and perhaps pusillanimous, but it was the peak of the Cold War, and this underlying threat of a nuclear holocaust was never very far from most people's minds.

As there was no radio or TV in the cabin, we occasionally went out to listen to the car radio; but when the bulletins had nothing new to report by 2 a.m., we reluctantly and fearfully collapsed on our bunks.

We didn't get much sleep that night, but we rejoiced the next morning on learning that a settlement between the two big nuclear powers had finally been reached. There were no radioactive clouds drifting overhead from St. John's on the westerly breeze.

"Another close call for our Western so-called civilization," Bax muttered. "I suppose we have to give thanks," he added with a mischievous grin, "even if it means Corner Brook has probably lost its last chance of ever displacing St. John's as the provincial capital."

* * *

I was saddened, a few years after I moved to Ottawa, to hear that Bax had suffered a fatal heart attack. He had been helping settle a labour dispute in the small mining town of Baie Verte when he suddenly collapsed. With the nearest hospital many kilometres away, he had no timely access to the medical help that might have saved him.

Baxter Fudge left a bountiful legacy to both the labour movement and the NDP in Newfoundland. His pioneering efforts sowed the seeds for the later success of activists in both fields. One of Bax's sons, Derek, has carried on his father's progressive tradition for many years as a staff researcher with the National Union of Provincial and General Employees in Ottawa.

No one can precisely measure the extent to which the efforts of the early NDP pioneers like Baxter may have sowed the seeds that later party leaders and activists have cultivated. But I don't think I'm being immodest when I suggest that we helped get NDP ideas, NDP principles, and NDP policies into the political discourse in Newfoundland and Labrador. They didn't get widely accepted for many years, but they did get sifted through the political mill and greatly nourished the party's roots there.

Trapped on the galactic prison-planet

Many years ago, while still in my early 20s, I read a science-fiction story that I have never forgotten (although I can't remember the author's name). The premise was that, of all the hundreds of thousands of planets with sentient life in the Milky Way galaxy, Earth was the only one whose dominant species was hell-bent on self-destruction.

On every other planet, intelligent species co-operated in sharing available resources. Crime was rare and wars unknown. Care was taken to preserve animal and plant life and to protect the environment. The notion of having to compete for food or water or a decent living was abhorrent.

Not all planets were paradises. On some, a few individuals became greedy or even violent, and, if they persisted, they were sentenced to the ultimate penalty imposed by the Galactic Federation: they were condemned to spend a week or two on Earth.

Having to live on the only planet ruled by a race that was insane by galactic standards — that spent more on weapons than on health care and education, that encouraged greed, tolerated widespread poverty, and suicidally polluted its air and water — this was the worst possible place to serve time, even briefly, for anyone born on a civilized world.

In the story, the interstellar "criminals" were surreptitiously deposited on Earth by spaceships (some unavoidably seen and called UFOs), and retrieved when their sentences were over. Their stay on such a barbaric world — if they survived it and didn't get killed by a stray bomb or bullet — was enough to deter them from any further misbehaviour. Even if they had to spend only a few days here, they left in such a state of shock and horror that they were model citizens on their home planets for the rest of their lives.

* * *

We native Terrans, of course, can't count on being rescued by UFOs. We're stuck on this planet and bound to share whatever fate it will suffer. In the sci-fi yarn, the intelligent inhabitants of other planets assumed that we humans were all congenitally and irremediably mad and that it was only a matter of time before we destroyed ourselves and most other forms of life on Earth (by nuclear warfare, if not by ecological ruin). I recall some of the aliens wondering how they would be able to reform their deviant citizens once Earth, the galactic "prison-planet," became uninhabitable.

Although I've seen little evidence in the many years since I read this story that would invalidate its basic premise (if anything, our species' self-destructive tendencies seem to have worsened), I still have some hope that humankind will come to its senses before it's too late. My main reason for hope is that, contrary to the aliens' belief that all humans are crazy, some of us clearly are not. Some of us recognize, deplore, and want to avert our lemming-like rush to the abyss.

The problem we sane humans face is that we're not the ones in charge of the political and economic systems that are threatening our extinction. That's not to say we're blameless, since it has been our misjudgment, apathy, and weakness that have put the maniacs in control. But it may not be too late to achieve "regime changes" in the halls of power, if we can mobilize and focus our collective sanity effectively in the years ahead.

Signs of significant levels of human sanity can be seen in the spreading worldwide resistance to corporate globalization, in the growth of the anti-war movement, in the upsurge of opposition to American imperialism, even within the U.S. itself. The concept of "power to the people" is often dismissed as an empty cliché, but history — even recent history — has many examples of its validity.

Revolutions don't have to be violent to succeed. Gandhi proved that when the passive resistance he preached led to India's freedom from British rule. His methods also succeeded for dissidents in the Soviet Union and Eastern Europe in the 1980s.

Gandhi believed that all governments — autocratic as well as democratic — ruled only with the consent of the governed, and that the withdrawal of consent was a powerful weapon. "I believe," he wrote, "that no government can exist for a single moment without the co-operation of the people, willing or forced, and if people suddenly withdraw their co-operation in every detail, the government will come to a standstill."

In his essay in *Harper's* magazine — *No More Unto the Breach* — Jonathan Schell argues that, if superior force were always to prevail, "then the British would still rule India, the U.S. would preside over Vietnam, the apartheid regime would survive in South Africa, and the Communist party would rule over the Soviet Union. That none of these things is the case testifies to the capacity of co-operative power to defeat superior force."

The building and deployment of co-operative power, it seems to me, is also an exercise in sanity, and it is desperately needed today on a much more extensive scale and in a far greater cause than simply changing governments. It is needed to change a vicious global economic system that feeds on greed, spawns conflict and misery, and threatens our very survival as a species.

It's a daunting challenge, but not a foredoomed one. Thinking back to that dark sci-fi story, I can envisage a future in which the Galactic Federation can no longer use Earth as a place of banishment — not because it has become a barren and lifeless cinder, as feared, but because it has at last joined all the other planets in becoming civilized.

Chapter 10

The Birth of Medicare

I WAS A WITNESS to the birth of Medicare in Canada, and was privileged to play a very small part in the victorious struggle to bring it to life.

Public health care did not have an easy birth in the turbulent summer of 1962 in Saskatchewan. It was bitterly opposed by the province's College of Physicians and Surgeons, by the Canadian Medical Association (CMA), by most of the big business organizations, and nearly all the newspapers and broadcast media. The anti-Medicare forces were so powerful that it seemed at first they would succeed in killing the Saskatchewan Medical Care Insurance Bill before it could be implemented.

Looking back at that momentous battle, I am always conscious that Medicare in Canada had its inception many years earlier in the mind of Tommy Douglas. When he was a boy, he fell and severely injured his left knee, and a bone disease (osteomyelitis) set in. His parents couldn't afford the services of a bone specialist, so he was put in a Winnipeg hospital as a charity patient.

The doctors decided they had no choice but to amputate his leg. But he was fortunate that an orthopedic surgeon at the hospital was looking for patients he could use in his teaching classes. After examining Tommy's swollen knee, he told his parents he could save the leg if they would permit him to use the boy to help him teach his students. Of course they readily agreed, and Tommy escaped the planned amputation.

"Had I been a rich man's son instead of the son of an iron moulder," he later recalled, "I would have had the services of the finest surgeon and would not have had to depend on chance or charity for a cure. All my subsequent

This photo of Tommy Douglas (seen from behind) was taken during his speech at the Canadian Labour Congress convention in Toronto in 1968. With the help of a magnifying glass, you might be able to see me in the lower right-hand corner.

—Photo by Murray Mosher.

adult life I dreamed of the day when an experience like mine would be impossible and we would have in Canada a program of complete medical care without a price tag."

He took that dream with him into the Saskatchewan legislature when he first became Premier in 1944. "Why should anyone be denied health care because of an inability to pay?" he kept asking the MLAs. "Why should it not be a basic and universal right of citizenship?"

An important first step toward that goal was made in 1947 with the passage of a provincial public hospital insurance plan, but it wasn't until Nov. 17, 1961, that the CCF government felt confident enough to pass the more extensive Saskatchewan Medical Care Insurance Act.

By then, Tommy Douglas had left provincial politics to become the first national leader of the New Democratic Party. But he had fought the 1960 election in Saskatchewan on the central promise of introducing Medicare, had shepherded the bill through its early stages, and felt safe in leaving its implementation to his successor as premier, Woodrow Lloyd.

Passage of the Act, however, ignited a firestorm of opposition that raged for months. It was so fierce and defamatory that Premier Lloyd deferred the Act's planned implementation date from April 1, 1962, to July 1, 1962, in the hope of reaching some acceptable agreement with the dissident doctors.

This was a forlorn hope. Instead of trying to settle the dispute amicably, the anti-Medicare forces launched a vituperative and well-funded propaganda campaign, supported by the Chamber of Commerce and the Liberal and Tory MLAs who formed the opposition parties in the legislature. Patients were told that under Medicare they would lose their personal doctors, a lie that spurred the creation of K.O.D. (Keep Our Doctors) committees across the province. These misinformed committees staged rallies, circulated petitions, and had their protests extensively covered by the province's newspapers, and TV and radio stations.

About 600 of the 900 doctors in the province actively campaigned against public health care, each of them contributing financially to the dissemination of anti-Medicare propaganda. Many doctors wrote angry letters to the newspapers slamming the CCF government — missives that the papers were only too willing to publish — and warning patients that their offices would be closed after July 1 if the Medicare Act was put into effect.

The Canadian Medical Association donated $35,000 to help finance the revolt against Medicare. And, behind the scenes, the American Medical Association was also active in the battle to block public health care in a Canadian province, fearing it would set a precedent that could later threaten private medicine in the United States.

* * *

I was plunged into this maelstrom shortly after it erupted when the Canadian Labour Congress, the Saskatchewan Federation of Labour, and Tommy Douglas himself asked me to hop on a plane to Regina as soon as I could. They were counting on my ability as a writer and editor to help counter the massive wave of anti-Medicare disinformation that was sweeping the province.

My assignment was to assist the province's Federation of Labour and other supporters of the legislation to explain and extol the many benefits to be derived from a public health care system. Those benefits are well-known today and cherished by all Canadians, but at that time the foes of Medicare had full access to the commercial media in perpetrating their fear-and-scare tactics. It was almost impossible to get the favourable side of the Medicare debate covered by the print and broadcast outlets in the province.

One of the pro-Medicare citizens' groups that we helped set up was Citizens for a Free Press, which tried to persuade the province's daily papers to give fair coverage to pro-Medicare voices. The *Saskatoon Star-Phoenix* had even stopped publishing letters to the editor that supported the legislation.

I worked mainly with the Federation of Labour, led at that time by Walter Smishek, who later served as Minister of Health in the NDP government of Allan Blakeney. The important role played by the labour movement in creating Medicare is not widely acknowledged, but should be. The unions were always among the strongest advocates and promoters of Tommy Douglas's health care initiatives. They were active in the establishment of community clinics staffed by pro-Medicare doctors that were so important in consolidating support for Medicare.

After I arrived in Regina and saw how one-sided the public relations battle had become, I knew that a pro-Medicare publication was urgently needed. Walter Smishek shared that view, and, with the Federation's help, we launched our own weekly tabloid paper, *The Public Voice*. It was widely distributed door to door across the province by union members and the many Citizens for Medical Care Committees that had been set up to counter the K.O.D. Committees.

The Public Voice clearly explained the legislation, stressed its obvious superiority to private health care, and rebutted the many lies and distorted claims being spread by the opposing doctors and their business and political allies.

The dispute escalated even more when the doctors carried out their threat to go on strike after the Medicare bill was enacted on July 1. It was a heated and highly emotional period, with attacks on the government and the bill growing ever more wild and hysterical.

The frenzy worsened when dozens of local doctors chose to continue their practice, and even more so when physicians from Britain and other countries began to arrive. They were hired at the community clinics that quickly sprang up to serve patients whose doctors had abandoned them.

Those of us engaged in the furious war of words were appalled by the ferocity of the attacks on the government. We became worried that Woodrow Lloyd and his cabinet would buckle under the pressure. Our fear deepened when Premier Lloyd asked Britain's Lord Stephen Taylor to come to Saskatchewan to act as a mediator. We knew that any settlement emerging from mediation would have to involve some retreat by the government.

We felt there was no need for any compromise with the opponents of Medicare. The polls we took showed that their public support had started to drop sharply after the doctors walked out. This was largely because the doctors and their more fanatical backers turned out to be their own worst enemies. Even their most avid supporters were disgusted by the posters that caricatured CCF leaders as Nazis and communists, and by the burning of effigies of Tommy Douglas.

The turning point in the conflict came in mid-July, when the doctors and the K.O.D. committees called for what they boasted would be a massive public demonstration against Medicare in front of the legislature in Regina. They predicted that as many as 40,000 protesters would participate, but were shocked when the turnout was fewer than 3,000.

The failure of this widely promoted rally eroded the striking doctors' defiance. They had overestimated their public support and underestimated the growing grassroots sentiment that favoured a public health care system.

The strike was then clearly doomed, and the government could easily have enacted the legislation as originally drafted, without weakening it with concessions to the medical establishment. Regrettably, however, Premier Lloyd and his cabinet decided to proceed with the mediation process under Lord Taylor. The ensuing settlement, signed by both parties on July 23, saw the government agree to the doctors' demand to retain fee-for-service as the sole form of payment. The legislation was altered to allow doctors to practise outside Medicare, and to pay doctors under the plan 85% of the College of Physicians' fee schedule.

This compromise satisfied the Saskatchewan Medical Association because it preserved the doctors' fee-for-service system. It even improved it because payment of the fees would come from the government on a guaranteed basis, instead of from sometimes hard-to-collect-from patients.

This retreat by the government was a rollback of public policy that was especially devastating for the community clinics. They had hoped to have a Medicare plan that would encourage (if not compel) doctors to work for a salary in the clinics instead of privately on a fee-for-service basis. The upshot was that a province which had seen 25 community clinics spring up from the grassroots in less than a year eventually ended up with only five such clinics, and those struggling to survive.

This is not to disparage or belittle the truly historic achievement of the Saskatchewan government in implementing the first public health care program in Canada. It was a remarkable breakthrough in the provision of medical care, and one that soon led to its extension across the country and federally over the next five years. We may regret that it could have been a much more beneficial model if the Lloyd government had stayed firm and refused to compromise, but in retrospect the eventual bill was still one that Tommy Douglas could be proud of and approve. His dream had to a great extent become a reality.

Not many Canadians know that the Canadian Medical Association, which did its best in 1962 to block Medicare, elevated Tommy Douglas to its Hall of Fame in October 1998. He is the only non-physician to be so honoured. In giving him this posthumous citation (Tommy had died 13 years earlier), the doctors were admitting publicly that they had been wrong.

The CMA plaque acclaims Tommy as "the Father of Canadian Health Care" who "envisioned, built, and tirelessly promoted our national system of health care. His leadership has provided long-term benefits to medical science in Canada, and a Canadian health care system [that is] a source of envy to other countries."

This glowing tribute from his bitterest erstwhile enemies would be enough to qualify Tommy Douglas as the "greatest Canadian," as a CBC contest found him to be in 2004. What more precious contribution was ever made to all Canadians than providing them with public health care?

I still visit his grave occasionally. He is buried in Ottawa's Beechwood cemetery. He died knowing that his mission in life was not finished — that the public health care system he envisioned would not be completed until it also covered prescribed drugs as well as dental, vision, and aural care.

But from his final resting-place, in the inscription on his tombstone, Tommy passed the torch to us to continue his great crusade. It reads: *"Courage, my friends, it is not too late to build a better world."*

Chapter 11

My TORONTO STAR *column*

IN MID-SEPTEMBER OF 1963, I stowed as much of my personal belongings as I could in my little Fiat and drove to Ottawa to start what was to become
a 17-year stint as communications director of the Canadian Brotherhood of
Railway, Transport, and General Workers (usually shortened to CBRT & GW,
or even just CBRT). I leased an apartment on O'Connor Street, just a few
blocks from the CBRT's national office at 230 Laurier Street. Close enough for
me to go home for lunch.

The officers and staff welcomed me warmly and I soon slipped into the
routine of handling the union's public relations duties, as well as editing and
writing for the union's monthly tabloid journal. *Canadian Transport* had
been published for more than half a century in a magazine format, which
I helped convert into a 16-page monthly tabloid. Bill Walsh, who had been
the previous editor, stayed on as assistant editor, and we soon became good
friends.

My first few years were uneventful, except that I also joined many other
union staffers in becoming active in the anti-Vietnam war movement. In
addition to attending protests and demonstrations, I helped set up and edit a
small tabloid anti-war paper.

One of the other CBRT staff members I worked with closely was research
director Harry Crowe, but he left the CBRT shortly after I got there to
become a research associate with the Royal Commission on Bilingualism
and Biculturalism. After the Commission completed its work, Harry joined
with former MP Doug Fisher to write a column on politics for *The Toronto
Telegram*.

He called me one day in the fall of 1967 to tell me he and Doug had persuaded the editorial board of the *Telegram* to invite me to write a weekly column on labour relations for that paper.

I was not enthused by this prospect, since the *Tely* was such a conservative publication, and I wondered how much freedom I would have with such a column. But after a meeting with one of the editors, Doug MacFarlane, in which he assured me my column would not be vetted or censored, I reluctantly accepted. The column was scheduled to start early the next year.

Just before Christmas, however, I had a phone call from MacFarlane.

"Ed," he said, "you didn't tell us you were so active in the peace movement."

I was stunned. "I didn't think that had anything to do with labour relations," I said.

"Well," he said, obviously embarrassed, "Peter Worthington told us about your putting out an anti-war sheet. It made us re-think whether you would be a good fit as a *Telegram* columnist."

Worthington was an arch-conservative journalist, so it didn't surprise me that he would object to my sharing space with him in the *Telegram*.

"I don't see what my anti-war sentiments have to do with writing on a completely different subject," I said, "but clearly you and your associates in the *Tely's* editorial department think it conflicts in some way. I assume your offer is being rescinded?"

He told me it was.

My reaction was a mixture of regret and relief. I was disappointed not to have a column in a major daily paper, but to some extent I was pleased about not writing for a paper that featured commentators like Worthington and Barbara Amiel.

I was even more pleased a few weeks later when I had a phone call from Martin Goodman, managing editor of *The Toronto Star*.

"I've been reading some of the stuff you've been writing for the labour journals," he said, "and I'd very much like to give you a wider readership. How would you like to write a regular weekly column on labour affairs for *The Star*?"

"Much better than I would writing one for *The Telegram*," I said, assuming he had heard of my abortive experience with the rival Toronto paper.

He laughed. "You'll feel much more at home in *The Star*," he assured me. "And I've seen enough of your writing to know that your column will be fair and objective, and your views solidly argued and supported."

"When do I start?" I asked him.

"We'll have space for you every Monday, and you can start next Monday if you can gear up for it that fast. You should send the columns to our business section editor, Jack McArthur, who is also looking forward to running your stuff."

I told him my first column would get to McArthur on Friday.

That was the beginning of a 14-year association with *The Star* and Marty Goodman and Jack McArthur. In the final two years, 1980-81, I was writing two columns a week, an extra one for the Sunday *Star's* editorial page when it was launched in the early '80s. The total wordage of my columns for *The Star* reached about 800,000 by the time I parted company with that paper early in 1982.

I probably would have continued writing that column for many more years if it hadn't been for Marty's tragic death from cancer just before Christmas, 1981. He was only 46. A few months later, I received a letter from the publisher, Beland Honderich, informing me that *The Toronto Star* would no longer "need" my column, which was to be terminated immediately. I did keep writing occasional opinion pieces for the paper over the next few years, but it was not the same as having a weekly platform.

I had been aware that my column was not popular with either business or union leaders. Marty told me that delegations from both sides of the labour divide would come to see him to complain about something I'd written and demand that the column be scrapped.

"I always tell them your column is fair and well balanced," he said. "Personally, I feel that when you've got both CEOs and union leaders mad at you, there's no doubt about your objectivity."

His approval of my work was obviously not shared by the publisher and probably not by most of the other editors, either. They no doubt felt that publishing a weekly opinion piece by someone who was still a full-time union employee was somehow improper. It certainly was unprecedented for a major newspaper — in this case the paper with the largest circulation in Canada — to give a union PR director exposure to half a million readers every week. It will never happen again, that's for sure.

One of the difficulties of doing a regular column is to maintain minimum standards of quality. I didn't always succeed. Rummaging back recently over the 1,700 or so of those old *Star* columns (which I've kept in six large cartons in the

This shot of me strolling in front of a CN locomotive illustrated a feature I wrote for the *Toronto Star* in 1974 to promote train travel.

—*Photo by Murray Mosher.*

back room under the stairs), I cringed at some of them, even regretted having my byline on a dozen or more, but I found that, on balance, the vast majority of them were passable, and a hundred or so were above-my-average, which I suppose is the best that any columnist could wish for from a self-appraisal.

Much of what I wrote in the late '60s and through the '70s has become irrelevant or outdated, but the central themes that I mined and reworked remain topical. Collective bargaining and the right to strike, anti-labour legislation, unions and the NDP, occupational health and safety, government and business attacks on social programs and the public sector, labour's poor public image, and of course the struggle for Canadian union autonomy — these and other core issues would probably account for nine-tenths of my output. And nearly always, not surprisingly, the views I expressed conformed with those of the labour establishment. I wouldn't have been PR-flacking for unions if I didn't agree with what they stand for and what they seek to accomplish for their members.

But occasionally — maybe one column every four or five months or whenever I disagreed strongly with the labour leadership — I ventured to express a conflicting opinion. For this unforgivable sin of treason (which is how any kind of internal dissent was perceived by the top labour brass), I was usually ranked very high on their hit list. Sometimes I made it all the way up to No. 1.

Let me give you a few examples.

When Pierre Trudeau decided to patriate Canada's constitution and enact a charter of rights and freedoms, the Canadian Labour Congress decided not to participate in the national debate. I was appalled. Here is part of what I wrote in *The Star* at the time:

The CLC has decided to sit out the constitutional crisis. Its rationale is that the debate over the constitution is not really all that important. Not as important as unemployment, oil prices, interest rates, and freedom of information, on all of which the Congress has taken strong stands.

The fact is that the CLC's hands-off approach to the constitution and the proposed charter of rights has more to do with internal discord than with any feeling that the constitution is not momentous enough to merit organized labour's attention… It was the Quebec Federation of Labour's opposition to patriation and the Bill of Rights and Freedoms that kept the constitutional issue off the floor at the last CLC convention. It has been fear of offending the

QFL that has dictated the CLC's subsequent silence, and its pretense that the whole thing is not worth bothering with.

It's sad to observe this exercise in self-censorship by the country's labour leadership. Unions have a stake in the nation's future, as well as their own. Their members will all be affected by whatever happens to the federal government's constitutional package, and especially by what happens to the Bill of Rights and Freedoms.

Well, I was soundly rebuked and reviled by many union officers at the time, but most of them sheepishly admitted later that their decision to sit out the constitutional debate was a serious mistake. Trudeau later claimed that he would have liked to strengthen the unions' right to freedom of association and to strike in the bill, but was discouraged from doing so by the CLC's apparent indifference. Whether this is true or not, the labour movement has likely paid a steep price for the CLC's failure to take a strong and principled stand on this issue.

In fairness, I should acknowledge that a few labour unions and organizations — notably the B.C. Federation of Labour and the National Union of Provincial Government Employees — defied the CLC's do-and-say-nothing policy and presented well-argued briefs to the Special Joint Commons and Senate Committee during hearings on patriating the constitution.

I also got in trouble with many union leaders when I presented my annual list of the Top Ten of them — those whom I perceived as being the most competent and influential. The ones I left off the list were always quite miffed, to say the least, but even those ranked near the bottom resented being relegated there. Given their rivalries and jealousies, and their not inconsiderable egos, it would have been impossible, in any case, to draw up any such list without offending all except those listed at the top.

In one year's list, I had Bill Dodge, who was then the CLC's secretary-treasurer, in the No. 4 spot, and CLC President Donald MacDonald in the No. 7 position. MacDonald was quite put out. Dodge told me later that, the morning after the list was published, he got a frosty call from MacDonald on the office intercom: "Would the No. 4 labour leader in Canada deign to come to the office of No. 7 for a few minutes?" And he wasn't trying to be facetious.

My relations with the top labour leaders — especially those heading the Canadian branches of American unions — probably sank to their nadir during the early '70s when I churned out reams of columns and articles calling for

Canadian union autonomy. I wasn't alone by any means in this struggle for an independent Canadian labour movement — many other courageous union staffers as well as national union officers joined the crusade — but I was the only one who had an ongoing public forum: a column in the country's largest newspaper in which to harangue the CLC and the international unions. And I kept at it for six or seven years, until the trend toward national unionism swelled from a trickle to a flood.

I don't want to inflate my contribution to this development, but of all the causes I championed as a *Star* columnist, I'm proudest of that one. I'll discuss it in more detail in a later chapter.

My relations with the top union leaders, hardly ever cordial, fell into a deep freeze after I wrote a long introspective article on labour for *Maclean's* magazine just before the 1974 CLC convention in Vancouver. Now, 90% of that *Maclean's* piece was a defence of unions and a call for better labour laws and pro-labour government policies. But in the section on the labour movement's leaders and structure, I lapsed once more into less than fulsome praise.

Following are a few pertinent quotes from that article:

Labour leaders suffer from what might be called a siege mentality: a conviction that they are beset on all sides by hostile forces in business, in government, in the media. Like a nation at war, they expect blind adherence within their ranks to their leaders' decisions and actions. Anyone who raises questions and offers alternatives is denounced as a troublemaker or even a traitor. The persistent emphasis on the need for solidarity is a convenient excuse to avoid self-criticism and to perpetuate obsolete ideas, methods, and structures.

The goals of organized labour are admirable and its function of redistributing the nation's wealth indispensable. But its internal conservatism is appalling. Its sentries patrol the ramparts of Fortress Labour, ready to repel attackers armed with Dangerous New Ideas. Inside, its "Holy Office" keeps a vigilant eye on suspected heretics, ready to send them to Coventry if they deviate too far from official dogma.

Industries, schools, churches, political parties, and most other institutions have been changed beyond recognition since I joined the labour movement in 1959. But a labour leader who went into a coma in 1959 and recovered today could step back into his old job without missing a stride.

> This organizational stupor stifles creativity and delays a long overdue tuneup
> of labour's creaky machinery.

That critique, written nearly 40 years ago, is no longer applicable to most labour organizations. But at the time it had substance, and I was surprised when I could still walk on a dark street at night without fear of encountering a union-hired hit man.

The closest I came to any physical retaliation was perhaps on an Air Canada plane taking me to the 1974 CLC convention in Vancouver. It was packed with delegates to the convention, including several beefy staff reps of American union branches, several of whom were reading my article in *Maclean's* and muttering angrily.

They didn't notice me back in a rear seat with a newspaper hiding my face — not until Tommy Douglas (who was to be a guest speaker at the convention) noticed what they were reading.

"Oh, I see you're reading Ed Finn's *Maclean's* article," he said, smiling wickedly. "If you'd like to talk with him about it, he's back there in seat 84-A."

There was no immediate rush to get at me, and even while leaving the cabin after landing and waiting at the luggage offramp, I suffered only dirty looks. Not nearly as many, though, as the friendly nods from delegates who secretly agreed with me.

The labour movement has survived the organizational flaws I wrote about so long ago. Most unions have grown with the expansion of the work force, and, despite the hostile anti-labour antics of governments and corporations, continue to do what they do best: represent workers at the bargaining table and strive to keep their living standards from being seriously lowered. There have been important breakthroughs in such areas as pay equity, health and safety, and parental leave. So many labour leaders have been doing and saying the right things.

We mustn't forget, either, that they are politicians, and that, in the house of labour, as in the House of Commons, politics truly is the art of the possible. They may still be convinced that everyone outside the labour movement is out to get them, but that doesn't necessarily mean they're paranoid.

Working for a union in any capacity, for that matter, is not the easiest occupation in the world, and especially not in North America, the last bastion of the adversarial system of labour relations in industrial nations. Those who work in a union's communications department, as I did for more than three decades, if judged by the low level of public esteem in which unions are held, would probably be rated the most ineffective PR flacks in Canada. But, as I used to point out, making unions look good to the non-union public is not quite the same as shilling for the Boy Scouts or the United Way.

Strikes in particular are almost impossible to popularize in an economic system that endows employers with all power and profits except those that the unions can wrest from them. The right to strike in such a system is indispensable for unions because it's the only leverage they have for dealing with intractable employers. But the best PR campaign that Madison Avenue could devise would never be able to justify or sugarcoat a strike, especially one that disrupts transportation, the mail, the schools, garbage collection, or any other vital public service.

In one of my satiric *Star* columns, I wrote about a fictional union president, Percival J. Pickett, who was so disturbed about his union's bad public image (after his union's first strike in three years) that he went to see a slick advertising specialist.

"Is there any way," he asked, "that my union can become popular?"

The ad-man, Horace Hardsell, assured him that there was.

"All you have to do is renounce your right to strike and accept whatever wage increases, or even wage cuts, that the employers propose. Never go on strike. The public hates strikes."

"But," Pickett protested, "that would take away all our bargaining power."

"Precisely," said Hardsell. "You would announce that from now on your union will accept arbitration as a means of settling contract disputes. Your popularity rating will shoot up immediately."

"Except with the union's members!"

"Yes, well, it's the public we're concerned about, not your members," Hardsell reminded him. "You must realize, too, that the public doesn't distinguish between one union and another, so continuing strikes by other unions will soon nullify any gains in public esteem that *your* union will achieve."

"You mean," said Pickett, "that strikes by other unions will reflect unfavourably on mine, no matter how meek and well-behaved we may become?"

"Yes, of course," said Hardsell. "Unions are all lumped together in the public mind. To aspire to lasting popularity, you must prevail on all other unions to follow your example."

"I never realized that improving my union's image involved improving the image of the entire labour movement," Pickett mused. "But let's suppose I could get all the other unions to agree never to go on strike, would my union's good public image *then* be assured?"

"Not automatically, no," Hardsell told him. "Forgoing strikes is just the main precondition that's required to guarantee the success of your PR campaign. You will also need an ongoing advertising program to remind people how submissive, co-operative, and public-spirited your union — and organized labour as a whole — has become."

"I see. And how much will this advertising cost?"

"Well, let's see." Hardsell scribbled some figures on a pad. "My estimate is that an effective ad campaign in all the media — TV, radio, newspapers and magazines, plus billboards, of course — will run to about $30 million a year."

"Thirty million? Every year?"

"Oh, yes, people have such short attention spans. One-shot publicity projects are practically useless. You have to keep propagandizing the public continuously, and that's not cheap."

"I see. Well, thanks for your advice. It has certainly put my mind at rest," Pickett told him.

"Ah," said Hardsell, smiling, "then I've convinced you to make use of my Bay Street PR firm to improve your union's poor public image?"

"No," Pickett said glumly, "you've convinced me that I've got to learn to live with it."

That column may have done a disservice to union staff communicators. None of us, of course, were laid off by union leaders who might have mistakenly deduced from the column that external PR was futile. But it might have led to some slight downgrading of our worth and a tendency, during periods of financial restraint, to regard PR as the most dispensable of a union's services.

We had more success, however, with internal PR — informing our own members — than we had with the general public. I always regarded my *Star* column more as a medium of reaching union rank-and-file members than the paper's non-union readers. That's why I devoted so much space to issues such as pensions, on-the-job safety, labour history, political action, the need for union mergers — things that an informed membership could put to good use.

There's no way to assess the impact of my columns in these areas. I know for sure that some of my efforts failed — trying to persuade unions to demand a co-management role in the administration of pension plans, for example, or my proposal to set up one gigantic labour strike fund instead of having hundreds of smaller funds. But I believe the seeds I planted in some other fields bore fruit — crabapples rather than Macintoshes, maybe, but better than complete crop failure.

Some of my columns and articles have gotten into university and school textbooks; my *Ten Labour Myths* became something of a perennial best-seller; and several union staffers have even credited me with converting them from non-active members of their locals into union activists.

Personally, I got a lot of satisfaction from doing the *Star* column. When you have to express your views on paper once or twice every week, it forces you to put your thinking machinery in gear more often than you otherwise might — sometimes with unexpectedly happy results. My many columns favouring Canadian union autonomy and supporting the union leaders and members who pursued that goal, often against heavy odds, were especially rewarding. So were those that explained, defended, and extolled the activities of labour organizations striving to improve the quality of life for all Canadians, not just their own members.

Looking back over the more than a million words I wrote since the 1950s for *The Toronto Star*, *The Montreal Gazette*, *Canadian Labour*, *Canadian Dimension*, *Canadian Forum*, and other publications (even a few articles in *Maclean's*), I see that time has debunked and trivialized some of that output, but most of it has stood the test of the passing years.

That's mainly because most of the social, economic, and political problems I wrote about are unfortunately still prevalent. The same challenges still face us, the same blights of poverty and inequality are worse than ever. During the 1970s, I naively hailed the "humanization" of capitalism, and its apparent acceptance of the welfare state, workers' rights, and a relatively fair distribution of wealth and income. In later columns, of course, I deplored the return of the ruthless "robber baron" form of economics, and today, witnessing its brutal and destructive power, I realize that keeping capitalism alive in the post-war years — even in what seemed a relatively benign form — was not something we should have been happy about.

Chapter 12

The struggle for Canadian Union Autonomy

THE CANADIAN MEMBERS of the United Auto Workers (UAW) severed the umbilical cord with their parent American union in September 1985 and gave birth to the Canadian Auto Workers (CAW). They were one of the last large union groups in Canada to break away from a parent U.S. organization, the culmination of a long struggle for Canadian labour autonomy that started in the late 1960s.

That was when I started writing a column on labour relations for the *Toronto Star*, and, as an ardent Canadian nationalist, I used this newspaper "soapbox" to encourage and promote the trend to nationalize the labour movement. At the time, nearly 70% of all organized workers in Canada were members of locals chartered by U.S.-based unions, and, of the 1.5 million workers represented by the 117 unions affiliated with the Canadian Labour Congress, 80% belonged to unions headquartered in the United States. Clearly, emancipating Canada's labour movement from this overpowering American dominance would be a daunting and difficult task.

And yet, year by year, union by union, progress was made over the next 20 years, with the transformation of the UAW into the CAW one of the most significant milestones on the road to independence.

The CAW's founding convention was seen as evidence that organic ties to labour unions in the U.S. were no longer essential for a viable union operation in Canada. It was not surprising that the auto workers were relatively late in going international. If there was one industry where continental unionism seemed to make sense, it was the auto industry. After all, the workers were employed by the same big companies on both sides of the border, so why not have the same union?

That appeared to be a mutually beneficial arrangement for many years. But in the early 1980s, when the North American auto industry ran into tough competition from Europe and Japan, along with a major recession, severe strains were put on the international ties. In effect, the American-based union started to negotiate how wage and benefit concessions, rather than gains, should be allocated between members in the two countries. Bob White, who had succeeded Dennis McDermott as the union's Canadian director, balked at what he considered an unfair — and unnecessary — share of the pain being put on the Canadian workers.

It had become evident, years earlier, that unions with members in both countries, if forced to choose between them, would almost always favour their U.S. membership majority. This in fact happened repeatedly during the 1970s and during the recession of the early '80s, when most of the big American unions adopted strongly protectionist policies. They pushed for more tariffs to block imports from Canada, even though they knew the result would be to throw many of their Canadian members out of work.

The chief American lobbyist for the Steelworkers' union at the time, Ray Dennison, frankly admitted an "America first" outlook. "The U.S. is in trouble," he said, "and every nation has a right to act in its own self-interest."

To which I responded in my *Star* column: "Okay, but let's have a Canadian labour movement that is also free to act in *its* members' self-interest."

The defenders of international unionism fell back on the argument that it was still needed to counteract the growing power of transnational corporations. But this, too, was a specious claim. Co-operation between unions in different countries — even multi-nation bargaining — is possible without having organic unity.

Progress in that direction had already been made with the creation of such global bodies as the International Metalworkers' Federation and the International Federation of Chemical Workers. Operating out of Geneva, these multinational labour organizations encompass unions in more than 60 countries. But — and this is very significant — of all these countries, Canada was the only one that did not have a wholly independent labour movement.

A few years before, at a conference of the Metalworkers' Federation in Montreal, I asked its Canadian-born secretary-general, Charles Levinson, whether in his opinion multinational unionism should be patterned on the U.S.-Canada model.

"Certainly not," he replied. "Coordinated union activity involving several countries can best be achieved by and between autonomous labour movements, each of which may be seeking different national objectives."

That's a crucial point. The main issue, in dealing with corporations having plants in two or more countries, is the distribution of jobs among those countries. Canada, I argued in my *Star* column, needed its own sovereign unions for these negotiations, as much as it needed its own national government.

It's possible, of course, that adequate autonomy may not necessitate complete secession. The Steelworkers' and Machinists' unions in Canada, for example, still remain branches of their larger American organizations because they have been given the freedom to operate in this country as if they were virtually independent. They elect their own leaders, control their own finances, conduct their own bargaining with employers, and adopt policies that meet the needs of the Canadian members. And, in the case of the Steelworkers, two Canadian officers in succession — Lynn Williams and Leo Gerard — have been elected president of the entire continental union.

Most American unions, however, have not been nearly so accommodating to their Canadian branches, forcing them to break away to achieve the levels of autonomy that were not voluntarily granted by the U.S. leaders.

The CAW's secession was peaceably arranged with the UAW, and all the structural, financial, and other elements of the separation were mutually agreed upon. The same was true of the earlier separation of the Canadian sections of the Papermakers, Chemical Workers, and other U.S. unions. The Papermakers' Canadian branch actually polled its members and was able to show the American leaders that a large majority favoured separation.

At the historic founding convention of the CAW, Bob White was elected its first national president. Before the confrontation with the UAW over concession bargaining, he had been a strong supporter of international unionism, as had his predecessor, Dennis McDermott, who shared the spotlight with White at the birth of the CAW.

As I watched McDermott raise White's arm in triumph, my mind flashed back 14 years to a union hall in Toronto, not far from the convention site. I had been challenged to a debate there on the pros and cons of Canadian union autonomy, with McDermott as my formidable adversary.

That was in 1971, when any attempt to sever (or even weaken) Canada-U.S. labour links was viewed by the labour hierarchy as malicious and subversive.

McDermott, I recall, was at his vitriolic best. He called me "a phony nationalist," and accused me of wrapping myself in the Canadian flag. He charged that I was trying to divide and demoralize the country's labour movement.

I had become the target of many such attacks by international union leaders after I wrote an article for *The Labour Gazette* — the official journal of the federal Department of Labour — on "The Prospects for an Autonomous Canadian Labour Movement."

I had pointed out that over 70% of organized workers in Canada then belonged to American unions. "It is as necessary to repatriate Canada's labour movement," I argued, "as it is to regain control of our industries and resources, if Canada is to be saved from a complete American takeover."

To say that McDermott and other Canadian officers of U.S. unions were outraged by that article, as well as my *Star* columns on the same subject, would be an understatement. I got challenged to other debates, and was verbally flayed at union gatherings from coast to coast.

I persevered — not just because I believed that union self-government was as feasible as it was desirable, but also because I knew my nationalist sentiments were shared by most rank-and-file union members in Canada, by the leaders of the national unions, and even by some Canadian officials of American unions. This was one issue on which the proponents of continental unionism had lost touch with the majority of their members. I was so confident that the campaign for independence would prove irresistible that I predicted in *The Labour Gazette* that "a fully autonomous Canadian labour movement, maintaining only fraternal ties with the U.S. unions, will emerge within 15 years."

The following brief summary of this November 1970 *Labour Gazette* article may be of some interest.

The Canadian Labour Congress, at its biennial convention last May, adopted three minimum standards of autonomy for its American-based affiliates. They called for the election of top Canadian officers by the Canadian membership, their investment with decision-making authority in Canadian affairs, and provision of services appropriate to the Canadian milieu.

This code, although a significant advance, omits several key proposals made by reform nationalists at the convention. One was the retention in Canada of sufficient dues revenue to finance distinctively Canadian services; another would have given the Canadian branches the right to amalgamate, without having to wait for initial mergers of their parent U.S. unions. Even in their diluted form, the CLC's autonomy standards are not enforceable on the internationals. They are merely voluntary guidelines that each American union is free to observe or ignore.

The extent to which the internationals now dominate the Canadian labour movement can be gleaned from the latest (1967) statistics released by the Corporations and Labour Unions Returns Act (COLURA). They disclosed that, of the 1.5 million workers represented by 117 unions affiliated with the CLC, 79.1% belonged to 82 international unions affiliated with the AFL-CIO; 13 of the 20 unions in Canada with memberships exceeding 25,000, six of the nine unions with memberships over 50,000, and two of the three unions with 100,000 or more members were headquartered in the United States; of the 15,676 collective agreements existing in Canada, 12,620 — 81% — were held by U.S. unions; and 25 of the 30 executive officers of the CLC were representatives of American-based unions.

In the three years since this COLURA report, the pervasive influence of U.S. unions in Canada has not diminished; they remain by far the most dominant force in the Canadian labour movement. Their top officers are Canadian citizens, and they claim the Canadian branches already enjoy adequate autonomy. This claim is not supportable. As John Crispo has pointed out, in his recent definitive study of international unions, "only 20 internationals — one in five — have actually established a Canadian organization in the sense of a separate and distinct national structure."

It is true that the locals of most American-based union exercise considerable autonomy in collective bargaining, but even here it is far from complete. Many internationals still reserve the right to approve or disapprove the terms of agreements negotiated in Canada. It is not unknown for American head offices to veto contracts endorsed by the members of their Canadian locals, or, conversely, to exert pressure for contract settlements not acceptable to the Canadian members.

The officers of some Canadian branches can claim, correctly, to have received much more in strike assistance from their U.S. parents than they have contributed to the international strike funds. The Steelworkers are the most notable example of this largesse. Since 1968, their locals have put $4.1 million into the union's strike coffers in Pittsburgh, and have taken out $12.3 million, a "subsidy" of almost $55 for each Canadian member. It should be kept in mind, however, that the Steelworkers in the U.S. have a stake in maintaining a wage level in Canada that is at or near par with the American rates. If the Canadian locals are not fully supported financially in their struggle to keep their wages up, the result could be a transfer of business and jobs from the U.S. to Canada, and mass layoffs of American steelworkers.

The total figures on international union revenue and expenditures in Canada indicate that the American unions, in the aggregate, are now taking considerably more out of this country than they are putting back. In 1967, $35 million in Canadian members' per capita dues were paid to U.S. headquarters, while the internationals' expenditures in Canada for salaries, strike benefits, and pension and welfare payments amounted to $18 million. In the six years, 1962-67, for which records have been kept, the internationals are reported to have collected $166,322,000 in Canada, while pumping back $98,253,000.

Granted, there are other expenses not recorded in the COLURA reports that some internationals incur in this country, such as the costs of education and research projects and the publication of separate Canadian journals. But, apart from the large industrial unions, few U.S. parent organizations provide extensive services of this kind to their Canadian members.

Of course, even with this net outflow of Canadian union money to the U.S., it would not constitute an indictment of the internationals. As Prof. Crispo has noted, "they could not be accused of engaging in a kind of profiteering. At least, an economist would not take that view. By his reasoning, international unions would have a right to a fair return on their past investment, and that return would have to be relatively large to compensate for the risks involved."

From a nationalist perspective, however, the disclosure that the internationals are now reaping an annual net surplus of $10 million or more from their operations in Canada would effectively demolish the argument that the Canadian labour movement cannot be financially self-supporting.

The hand that holds the purse-strings also controls to a great extent the ability of the Canadian branches to implement new ideas or programs, or to give aid to other unions in trouble. Chronic financial malnutrition is a characteristic of most sections of American unions in Canada. The latest illustration was provided by the appeal of the postal unions for monetary support in their battle for fair pay from the federal government. Most of the national unions made prompt and generous donations, with the CBRT, for example, forwarding a cheque for $35,000 within a few weeks. In comparison, the U.S. branch unions' response was a bare trickle while their Canadian directors and vice-presidents began the labourious process of trying to wheedle contributions to the Canadian posties from their U.S. head offices.

Nothing in the past history of the Americanization of Canadian labour encourages the hope that the majority of U.S.-based unions will willingly yield self-governing rights to their branches in Canada. But if they continue to refuse providing this freedom voluntarily, the buildup of pressure from their increasingly nationalist Canadian members will become irresistible. I am now convinced that we can look forward with some optimism to the emancipation of the Canadian labour movement before the end of the 1970s at the earliest, by the end of the 1980s at the latest.

The Canadian leaders of U.S. unions, however, had a long tradition of U.S.-Canadian integration behind them. American unions had begun moving into Canada as early as the mid-1800s — mainly because of the dearth of national unions here — and they seemed solidly entrenched.

But their tight grip on the Canadian work force was not unbreakable. That was first demonstrated in 1908, when a large group of U.S. railway union members in the Maritimes split away and formed a Canadian union. It grew and flourished, serving as tangible proof that national unionism could succeed.

That pioneer breakaway union was the Canadian Brotherhood of Railway, Transport and General Workers, which for the next six decades was the pre-eminent non-American union in Canada. Gradually other national unions sprang up, but not in significant numbers until the upsurge of patriotic fervour that accompanied Canada's Centennial celebrations in 1967.

Union nationalism flared up in earnest in the late 1960s and throughout the '70s. In rapid succession came major breakaways from U.S. unions — by electrical workers and carpenters in Quebec, by iron workers in British Columbia, by retail store employees in Saskatchewan, by brewery and distillery workers across the country.

In the 1970s, the swing to Canadian unionism gained momentum. The big Papermakers' Union went independent. So did the Communications Workers. Other Canadian branches of U.S. unions, though stopping short of disaffiliating, harnessed their growing nationalist sentiment to push for and acquire much greater degrees of self-rule.

Paralleling and reinforcing these developments was the phenomenal growth of indigenous Canadian unions, mostly in the burgeoning public sector. As more and more government employees decided to unionize, they invariably turned to national unions to represent them. National unions such as the Canadian Union of Public Employees (CUPE), the Public Service Alliance of Canada (PSAC), and the National Union of Provincial Government Employees (NUPGE) rapidly overtook and surpassed most of the American branch unions in size and stature.

Even before the UAW split, the American unions' Canadian membership had shrunk from 80% to less than 40% of the country's organized work force. It has since dropped even further, to less than 25%.

The success of Canadian union nationalists in establishing a self-governing and self-sufficient labour movement — a process in which I can say without immodesty that I played a small role — set an example for other groups and sectors: for our politicians, academics, artists, even national business leaders. If the working people of Canada can stand on their own and learn to run their unions without American help or intervention, then so can other Canadian groups and institutions.

This "quiet revolution" in the labour movement, by the way, was not motivated solely by national pride, nor by the insensitivity of U.S. union leaders to Canadian interests. There was also a realization that American unionism did not conform to the Canadian way of life.

The Americans, in the main, want to confine their activities to what they call "business unionism," or the basic collective bargaining and contract policing functions. In Canada, union people are not content with these bread-and-butter activities. They want their unions to get involved in the broader social and economic issues — to push for laws, policies, and programs that benefit their members and all working people, not just as workers, but as consumers, as parents, as retirees, as citizens in the fullest sense.

This explains why Canada's unions have been in the forefront of all the campaigns for major social programs, from publicly funded Medicare to public education, from workers' compensation and unemployment insurance to the Canada Pension Plan. These services make up the social fabric that holds our country together, and beyond that, to make Canadian society distinctively different from — and, I would add, qualitatively better than — American society.

Ours is far from a perfect country, but, compared to the American system, it is arguably a more humane and civilized place to live. Unfortunately, the quasi-American ultra-conservative government of Stephen Harper now in power in Ottawa as I write these words seems bent on transforming Canada into a U.S. colony with all its flaws and inequities, but surely most Canadians are not going to let that happen. I can't believe they will abandon the proud Canadian collectivist approach to embrace the brutal American cult of individualism and privatization.

Canadian union members can certainly be counted on to resist the Americanization of our country's traditions as fervently as they opposed (and eventually terminated) the Americanization of their unions. I would go so far as to say that, if other Canadian organizations were as active as the unions have been in defending the Canadian way of life and national identity, the prospects for preserving these values nationally in the years ahead would be a lot brighter than they now seem to be.

Chapter 13

The Labour Gazette

SHORTLY AFTER I STARTED writing my weekly column for *The Toronto Star*, I had a phone call from Jack Nugent, editor of *The Labour Gazette*, official journal of the federal Department of Labour. He invited me to lunch, and it was the start of a long and mutually beneficial friendship.

Jack became editor of *The Labour Gazette* in 1965 — the ninth editor since Mackenzie King — and over the next few years transformed it from a dreary chronicle of facts and figures into a lively, informative, and eminently readable magazine. This was in sharp contrast with other government house organs, which confined their contents to dry, statistical material and the fawning puffery of ministerial sayings and doings. Under Jack's editorship, *The Labour Gazette* sought out and published hard-hitting and often provocative essays on all aspects of the world of work.

William Lyon Mackenzie King might well have approved of Jack Nugent's innovative makeover of the journal he started and edited for eight years. King quit in 1908 only to run as a Liberal candidate and win election in the riding of Waterloo North. Prime Minister Wilfred Laurier had been so impressed by King's editorial success with *The Gazette* that he appointed him the first full-time Minister of Labour in his cabinet.

As the first *Gazette* editor, King had filled the journal with more than dry facts and figures, exploring issues such as labour organizing, contract negotiations, minimum wages and benefits, and especially his favourite subjects: mediation and arbitration. Under successive editors and governments, however, the journal was converted into just another dull and unreadable government publication.

December 1971

The Labour Gazette

The struggle for Canadian labour autonomy

by Ed Finn

The Labour Gazette had me pose for this photo that appeared in a long essay I wrote for the Department of Labour's monthly journal in December 1971.

Jack Nugent revitalized *The Labour Gazette*. He assigned staff writers to cover all important developments in the labour field, and coaxed first-rate interpretive articles from well-known practitioners and specialists.

So, when he told me over lunch that he would like me to become a *Gazette* contributor, I leaped at the opportunity. It would give me a chance to write longer and more detailed articles on complex issues than my 800-word limit in *The Toronto Star* allowed.

"But, you know, Jack," I warned him, "that some of my views will not be popular with either business or labour leaders — or even politicians."

"That's what I expect from you," he assured me, grinning. "I want *The Gazette* to be a forum in which the most radical opinions can be expressed and exchanged. And you should know, as well, that I'll be running articles by writers who will dispute and challenge your views."

I assured him that this would be quite acceptable, and congratulated him on turning *The Labour Gazette* into such a refreshing and stimulating journal. "I'm surprised," I said, "that you were able to go so far to buck the usual bureaucratic caution and conservatism that's so evident in other government publications."

"It hasn't been easy to open up *The Gazette* to discussion of contentious issues," Jack admitted. "It horrifies most of the civil service mandarins. But I've been supported and even encouraged by the past two Ministers of Labour, Bryce Mackasey and John Munro. They both want *The Labour Gazette* to be the prime journal for fresh thinking and dialogue in labour affairs — even if that means ruffling a few feathers or stirring up controversy."

Over the next 10 years, I wrote more than a dozen essays for *The Labour Gazette*, on a wide range of topics, including the right to strike, workplace safety, industrial democracy, private and public pensions, and of course the struggle for Canadian union autonomy.

The extent to which Jack continued to brighten and revitalize the Labour Department journal was evident to anyone who was a regular reader. It featured articles on worker alienation, flextime, mediation techniques, working women, voluntary arbitration, profiles of labour leaders, and dozens of other labour-related issues. Thanks to his imaginative and daring style of editing, *The Labour Gazette* became "must" reading for anyone who wished to keep abreast of the latest trends and happenings in a vital but little known part of our society.

Unfortunately, despite the support of the two labour ministers, Jack did not have the backing of the government bureaucrats or of many other cabinet ministers. He was denied funding to promote *The Gazette*. All complimentary copies to journalists and unions were terminated, and Jack's proposal to launch a drive for more subscriptions was flatly denied. It was as if the

Department (perhaps the whole government) was ashamed of *The Gazette* rather than proud of it, as they should have been.

Because of these ongoing restraints, which were directed straight from the PMO, the journal's circulation slowly declined from a high of 20,000 to a low of just over 2,000. It was reaching only a small fraction of the people who were — or should have been — interested in labour matters.

Jack was able to keep circulation from declining further, and even managed to attract an extra 2,000 readers, but his budgets were trimmed, his staff reduced, and all efforts to further boost the journal's circulation stymied by Prime Minister Pierre Trudeau. Jack resigned in disgust in 1974, and shortly thereafter won a Canada-wide competition for a senior editorial post with the British Columbia Department of Labour.

He was fortunately succeeded as editor of *The Gazette* by one of his most highly regarded staff writers, George Sanderson, who courageously retained the same fresh, probing format that Jack had pioneered. But the internal harassment continued and intensified, and Sanderson's efforts were finally crushed in 1978 when *The Labour Gazette* was callously terminated.

Writing about the journal's demise in *The Toronto Star*, I reported that *The Gazette's* loyal readers — the people who make our labour relations system work — had reacted with shock and dismay to the news that the November 1978 issue would be the last. Letters of protest poured in from loyal readers across the country and even from some foreign subscribers.

Typical was a letter from Prof. W.D. Wood of Queen's University in Kingston. "*The Labour Gazette* filled a vital need in the labour relations field," he wrote. "In addition to its factual information, it provided a unique forum for different viewpoints and analysis of current developments in the world of work."

Many of the *Gazette's* readers, as well as staff writers, believed it was this very open editorial policy and the publication of "controversial" essays such as mine that led to its termination.

The saving of $225,000 in publishing costs that the government cited as justification for axing the *Gazette* was described by Senator H. Carl Goldenberg, a respected labour mediator, as "false economy.

"To deprive those of us involved in maintaining and promoting industrial peace of such a valuable and unbiased source of information at this time," he declared, "does not serve the public interest."

Senator Goldenberg also pointed to a clause in the Labour Department's official charter that required the department to "issue at least once a month a publication to be known as the *Labour Gazette*." He said that terminating the journal before amending or rescinding this clause or seeking parliamentary approval was to ignore a legal obligation to keep publishing it.

To which one of the department's top mandarins was quoted as sneering, "Who's going to sue us?"

The Trudeau government rejected all appeals to reprieve the journal's death sentence, claiming that *The Gazette* was only one of the many casualties of Ottawa's current spending cuts. But readers dismissed this excuse, arguing that the money was well spent to preserve a unique journal, one whose passing would leave an irreplaceable void in the country's communications network.

Granted, the readership was by then comparatively small, but it was comprised of union and company officials, labour law administrators, mediators and conciliators, and labour contract negotiators — the people who were actively involved in some aspect of labour-management affairs. *The Labour Gazette* gave them the news, views, and data about their specialized field that they either couldn't get anywhere else, or could obtain only with great difficulty.

Moreover, *The Gazette* supplied them with the only national forum in which business, labour, government, and academic writers could regularly exchange views on labour relations topics. This was undoubtedly one of its most useful functions.

Several other labour publications were available, but they all had a much narrower focus, being published by and for unionized workers, by and for managers, by and for educators. Only *The Labour Gazette* solicited and published articles and essays from all sections of the labour relations community, so that its pages provided a vital cross-fertilization of ideas.

Jack Nugent and George Sanderson also firmly rejected the government's cost-cutting excuses. They were convinced that the decision to axe *The Labour Gazette* was motivated solely by a desire to get rid of an embarrassing department journal — one that deviated sharply from other government publications. It even (horrors!) committed the heresy of occasionally publishing articles by writers (including me) who dared to disagree with government policies.

"There was no need to trim departmental costs," Jack told me. "Clearly the magazine was silenced for having permitted authors like you to question federal government handling of problems such as inflation and unemployment."

The void in in-depth coverage of labour relations left by the loss of *The Labour Gazette* has become even deeper and broader in the nearly three decades that have elapsed since its brutal execution.

Chapter 14

Three strikeouts, one hit

DURING THE YEARS I wrote for the *Toronto Star* and other newspapers and magazines, I waged a few other editorial crusades besides the battle for Canadian labour autonomy. Three of these ongoing efforts — to promote labour-business-government cooperation (or tripartism), to create one big strike fund, and to give workers and their unions joint control in the management of their pension funds — proved to be the proverbial quixotic tilting at windmills. On the other — opposing the Meech Lake Accord and the Charlottetown Accord — I wound up on the winning side.

Co-operation vs. competition

Today, the idea that labour and management in Canada could agree to conduct their relations in a co-operative rather than adversarial system (with or without government involvement) is laughable. It would be ridiculed and dismissed as a bizarre fantasy.

But in the 1960s and early '70s, this kind of economic collaboration had been widely established in most European countries and in Japan. It had minimized labour strife and greatly increased productivity. So why wouldn't the same co-operative system work in Canada? This question was asked by prominent academics, politicians, editorial writers, and even by some labour leaders and business executives.

I have copies of dozens of studies, reports, magazine articles, and speeches that abounded 40 or 50 years ago, all extolling the merits of industrial democracy and co-operation — including several that I authored myself.

Professor John Crispo of the University of Toronto spent a year in Europe studying the tripartite system of labour relations practised there. In his report, he warned that, unless employers and unions in Canada learn to co-operate in the same way, Canada's economy would keep losing ground to European producers.

"The notion of collective bargaining functioning almost oblivious to national economic and social priorities," he wrote, "is becoming increasingly untenable." He continued:

> Yet neither employers nor unions in North America are really prepared
> for anything else. Instead they engage in a largely uncoordinated and
> unrestrained free-for-all over the spoils of different plants, companies, and
> industries. A more intelligent way must be found to bring some degree of
> compatibility between labour/management wage and price-setting proce-
> dures and government fiscal and monetary policies [as is the case in Europe].
> The two sets of mechanisms involved cannot continue on their often distinct
> and separate courses without setting the stage for more frequent and serious
> collisions between them.

Another unlikely proponent of European-style labour relations was CLC President Joe Morris, who had also spent some time in Europe in the early '70s as a delegate to meetings of the International Labour Organization and other international labour bodies. He even introduced a pro-tripartism manifesto at the 1976 CLC convention in Quebec City, where incredibly it won the support of most delegates. Its passage was all the more surprising because it came just a few months after the Trudeau government imposed its much-resented "6-and-5%" wage controls.

It soon became evident, however, that most labour leaders did not share Joe Morris's enthusiasm for any kind of co-operation with a government that had outlawed free collective bargaining — or with employers who agreed with Trudeau's imposition of wage controls. The CLC's tripartite manifesto was repudiated by most of its affiliated unions and was quickly rescinded at the next Congress convention.

The manifesto, significantly, was also denounced by all the major political parties, even by the pro-labour New Democratic Party, which feared that a tripartite system would somehow bypass Parliament. Business leaders, too, saw it as a threat to their "divine right" to run their companies in the proper profit-maximizing manner.

A few years later, when the same government lifted wage controls, it unveiled its own "Agenda for Co-operation," a Green Paper that drew the same blasts of criticism and ridicule as had the CLC's manifesto.

I wrote a retrospective think-piece on this subject in 1985, published in a Lorimer book called *Doing It Right: Eminent Canadians Confront the Future*. It was flattering to be included in this collection of essays by truly eminent Canadians such as George Ignatieff, Walter Gordon, Frank Stronach, Mel Hurtig, and Bishop Remi De Roo, but I managed to hold my own. Following are a few quotes from my dissertation, which the editor — Labour Minister John Munro — titled: "Co-operation is Not a Dirty Word":

> We turn a blind eye to the flaws and failures of the present labour relations system, attributing them to everything except the very nature of the system itself. We look for scapegoats and villains in our midst. The corporations blame militant unions and overspending governments. The unions blame profiteering companies and underspending governments. The governments blame militant unions and tax-evading companies. And they all accuse one another of being greedy, of taking more out of the economy than they are willing to put back in.
>
> But really, aren't we all — no matter into which of these categories of villains we happen to fall — merely following faithfully the precepts of private enterprise? Everyone for himself, everyone looking out for Number One, everyone striving to take the biggest possible slice of the national economic pie? And somehow, we tell ourselves, all this rivalry works out for the common good. Our whole society is rooted in competition. We are educated (indoctrinated) from birth to regard one another as adversaries against whom we will have to struggle all our lives — in school and university, in the workplace, in all our dealings with one another.
>
> The late John Holt, in his book *Why Children Fail*, eloquently deplored an educational system that discourages co-operation among students, and instead pits them against one another. "We destroy the love of learning in children," he charged, "by compelling them to work for petty and contemptible awards — gold stars, or papers marked 100%, or honour rolls — in short, for the ignoble satisfaction of feeling they are better than someone else."

It seems clear, in assessing the outright hostility to co-operative arrangements in Canada, that it stems more from an ideological than a practical outlook. After all, the entrepreneurs, business executives, and managers in Europe are just as profit-motivated as those in Canada. But their brand of private enterprise is much less doctrinaire than ours. It is pragmatic and flexible, concerned only with results, adaptable to any social, political, or economic system that will demonstrably increase efficiency and profits.

In Canada, on the other hand, the tension and conflict that is created by the adversarial system permeates the country's plants and offices, spreading antagonism and impairing productivity. Workers forced to compete instead of co-operate with one another are unhappy, resentful, and much less efficient than they could be. Absenteeism, malingering, alcohol and drug addiction become much greater problems. Pride of workmanship declines. The fanatical emphasis on competition, ironically, makes Canadians less competitive with their overseas rivals who have learned the value of co-operation and teamwork.

Prof. Crispo, after his tour of Europe, went on a cross-country tour of Canada during which he talked with dozens of CEOs of major corporations. His main purpose was to assess their willingness to give European-style industrial democracy a chance. The response he got was strongly and unanimously negative.

"I should have expected nothing less," Crispo told me later. "The combined effect of the free trade deals and the new communications technologies was to enhance corporate power enormously. Now equipped to outsource their operations and jobs to low-wage, low-tax, low-regulation countries in Asia, Africa, and Latin America, they could now reject the contract demands of even the largest domestic industrial unions. They could even force the unions to relinquish many of the previous gains they had won."

These employers relished wielding their new power in the adversarial system that still prevailed in Canada. To them, it was a labour relations Utopia.

"Why on Earth should I switch to a system that gives unions more power instead of less?" one CEO asked Crispo.

The answer, of course, is that there was no reason for a fighter suddenly armed with an arsenal of new weapons to show any mercy to a disarmed foe.

The results of this enormous power conferred on corporations are all too evident today — not just in the country's workplaces, but in the shameful disparities of income and living standards that have so degraded our whole society.

The One Big Strike Fund

In retrospect, my idea of pooling all the unions' strike funds into one huge financial resource was impractical and foolishly idealistic. But I was convinced — still am, for that matter — that all the difficulties involved could be overcome.

Here's what I wrote on this subject over 40 years ago during a prolonged strike by Steelworkers Local 6500 against Inco in Sudbury:

> Like most members of other unions, I made my donation to the Sudbury miners' strike fund, and last Christmas I sent along some food and toys to their families.
>
> Such contributions helped supplement the Steelworkers' dwindling strike fund and enabled Local 6500 to sustain its strike through a long, cold winter. They also, as displays of solidarity, gave donors like me that gratifying glow that comes from assisting fellow unionists in trouble.
>
> But this kind of "pass-the-hat" strike aid is a poor substitute for an effective union strategy against powerful transnational companies. No union, no matter how large its strike fund or how militant its members, can hope to prevail against a global giant like Inco — not unless it can command financial resources far beyond those to be derived from ad hoc appeals to other unions.
>
> The ideal situation, of course, would be for unions to schedule their clashes with transnationals so that they would take place when the union, rather than the company, had an edge in bargaining leverage. That would be feasible, however, only if union-management showdowns were exercises in tactical logic, in which the "generals" could coolly plan all their moves. But this is seldom the case. Most strikes are initiated as much by emotional and political forces as by economic ones. They occur when workers' anger and frustration reach a level where the strike becomes their only outlet.
>
> That seems to be what happened in Sudbury last September. From a tactical standpoint, the strike couldn't have been called at a less opportune

time. The nickel market was in a slump, and Inco was sitting on a huge stock-pile. The strike actually came as a welcome relief to the company, eliminating its labour and operating costs while it got rid of its surplus stock.

The union's "generals" — its top officers in Toronto and Pittsburgh — would never have started a strike under those adverse conditions. In fact, they did everything they could to avert it. But, contrary to the widely held image of "dictatorial labour bosses," the decision to launch a strike is almost always made at the local level. In this case, the majority of Inco's employees in Sudbury voted for strike action.

That was more of an emotional than a carefully reasoned decision. The company had aroused its workers' wrath by mass layoffs, as well as by its petty contract offers. Although they knew they were the underdogs, the members of Local 6500 felt they would be losing their pride and self-respect if they knuckled under.

These human feelings can often override purely economic self-interest. Any company, if it wishes to push its employees beyond their limits of tolerance, can provoke them into a strike, no matter how hopeless it may appear to be.

So it's useless, in most cases, for union leaders to plan any grand strategy against the large transnationals based on the best timing for strike action. What they need is a bargaining lever that's long and strong enough to counteract the power of global corporations at any point in their business cycles, or in the seesawing union-company relationship.

The utopian answer you hear at labour conventions is the development of true international unionism — co-operation among unions in all countries to prevent the transnationals from singling out any one union in any country to exploit and overpower.

That may happen some time in the far future, but it is not a practical solution for today. We have to assume, then, that union-company showdowns will remain confined within national boundaries, and that the key to an effective strike will be the union's ability to outlast the company.

Local 6500 may well manage to outlast Inco in its current prolonged contest, but if so it will be at a disastrous economic price to its members, to the Steelworkers' treasury, and to the city of Sudbury. This will continue to be the main drawback in an endurance strike, as long as each union is left to build up its own resources, supplemented, if at all, by donations from other unions and workers.

But what if all unions in the country — or even the majority of them — decided to pool their strike money and create one enormous common strike fund, from which each could draw if necessary, and under tightly monitored and verifiable conditions?

Administered, perhaps, by the Canadian Labour Congress, such a gigantic fund could serve to redress the current imbalance of power between individual unions and the transnationals. It would have to be closely regulated to ensure that strikes were not called frivolously, or without first exhausting every effort to get a peaceful settlement. Unions and their locals would have to surrender some of their bargaining autonomy in order to justify tapping the central fund.

In practice, such an immense financial reservoir would serve far more to avert than to sustain strikes. On the union side, it would induce local union members to consult with their top officers on contract demands and strategy, in order to qualify for more generous and long-lasting strike pay. On the company side, it would discourage management from provoking strikes intended to starve the workers into submission.

The lesson of the Sudbury strike, surely, is that no one union, no matter how big or well-heeled, can singlehandedly finance a lengthy strike against a much larger and richer corporation.

By extending the insurance principle on which any group protection plan operates — i.e., by pooling all unions' strike funds — the Canadian labour movement would be forging that bigger and better bargaining lever it so desperately needs.

* * *

That column was written a long time ago, when the transnational corporations were much less financially endowed than they are today. The One Big Strike Fund didn't materialize then, and is not likely to become a reality now, even though the need for it is so much more urgent.

My proposal was either ignored or derided by union leaders 40 years ago. They called it a pie-in-the-sky daydream of someone who never had to administer a union's strike fund. Others were kinder, telling me it would be a good idea if it didn't involve so many changes in the union's constitution, or a surrender of internal financial control that their members would never approve.

I felt then, and still do, that these were weak and unfounded excuses — that they could be overcome by union leaders with the courage and vision to put such a strong bargaining weapon in the arsenal of any union genuinely in need of it. And today that means all the industrial unions — and perhaps even the big public sector unions, too.

Co-management of pension funds

My argument that unions and their members should have more say in the management of their private pension funds was a recurring theme in my *Toronto Star* columns and *Labour Gazette* essays.

I didn't think it was all that radical to suggest that the management of pension funds should be taken out of the hands of private employers altogether. After all, if pension monies are considered as part of the workers' compensation package — as a form of deferred wages — then a union representing the workers covered by a pension plan could quite legitimately demand that the plan come under the *exclusive* control of the union. After all, the employees' contributions to the plan — and those contributed to the plan on their behalf by their employer — cease to be the employer's money. It becomes the employees' money at the time they earn it, not at the time they receive it upon retirement. So, if a company retains any "right" to control the management of pension funds, it is only on the sufferance of its employees and their union.

I didn't push this view because, although I thought it quite logical and defensible, it was regarded as "extreme" and "impracticable," even by most union leaders and rank-and-file members. So I took a more moderate position: that employees, through their unions, should have at least an *equal* voice in the management of their own pension funds. If that modest advance could be made in the more than 20,000 private pension plans that then existed in Canada (in the 1970s when I was writing my column), I thought it would be a significant leap forward in labour relations. At the time, fewer than 500 of these plans were subject to collective bargaining in unionized plants or offices, and the "negotiations" dealt only with the improvement of benefits, leaving control of the funds' management and investments entirely in company hands.

What follows are some excerpts from a *Labour Gazette* article I penned on pension funds in the late 1970s.

So what's wrong, you might ask, about leaving private pension funds to be administered by employers? Can't they be trusted to manage the funds in the best interests of their employees? My answer is an unequivocal "No." As Jack McArthur, financial editor of *The Toronto Star*, recently charged in his column, "Too many private pension plans are a mess of unethical conduct, unsafe investment, and unfairly treated employees." To lend more substance to my opinions on this subject, here are the views of Douglas Fullerton, former stock broker, financial consultant, and chair of the National Capital Commission:

"Many pension funds are run by company executives lacking professional investment experience. Conflicts of interest abound. Many firms use the buying power of their pension fund to strengthen their business connections; governments use theirs as a convenient dumping ground for their bond issues. Bad management is able to conceal its mistakes, hindering corrective action.

"Improving investment performance, however, will mean little unless some mechanism is established for translating increased yield into higher benefits for retiring employees. Most corporate funds are now set up so that better performance simply allows the company to reduce its own contributions to zero, with a little jiggling around of the actuarial assumptions.

"In other words, companies tend to regard the management of the pension fund as just another part of their business operations, with all benefits accruing to the company and none to the employees — however large the employees' own stake in the fund. This is a pernicious and paternalistic approach, and is perhaps the strongest of all reasons why employees should have a say in pension fund management. The fund must be treated as a trust, with employees sharing in improved performance. The company obligation can no longer simply be that of undertaking to meet contractually set payments to retired employees."

Fullerton's criticism of sole pension fund administration by companies and governments was actuated in part by the revelation that the pension funds of Toronto and Montreal police were being put mainly into low-yield municipal bonds — being used, in other words, to subsidize the municipalities instead of being invested in high-yield stocks and mortgages to earn the best possible benefits for the police pensioners.

The interests of employees and retirees, however, will never be a priority in pension plan administration so long as the unions maintain what amounts to a "hands-off" policy on this issue. I would go so far as to say that Canadian unions have been derelict in failing to push for joint control status in the management of their members' pension funds. The companies have been pleasantly surprised that a strong union campaign for such joint control has never materialized. Management consulting firms have been warning every year since the early 1960s that a concerted drive by unions for pension fund co-management was imminent, as well as a demand that pension plans all be non-contributory — i.e., to have them fully financed by employers.

No such union initiative, however, as ever been launched. Why not? Basically, there are three reasons for this timidity. First, most union officers tend to be overawed by pension plan complexities and are content to leave such abstruse financial matters to the company's hired experts. Second, most union leaders don't want to accept the added responsibility that pension fund co-management would entail. They have trouble enough, they feel, in satisfying their members' expectations on the bread-and-butter issues of wages and other major fringe benefits without taking on the added burden of pension fund performance as well. Thirdly, there is the conflict of interest that pension improvements sometimes generate among union members, with older workers — especially those over 45 — rating pensions much higher on their priority list than do the younger workers.

None of these three disincentives to a demand for co-management of pension funds excuses the unions' long inertia. Union leaders could hire their own pension experts, as they do specialists in other fields. They could have these experts do most of the co-managing on their behalf and make sure investment choices were made mainly to benefit the retirees. And the potential rift between the older and younger workers could be overcome by effective education and persuasion, as are other differences between various groups of members. (The fact that even the youngest workers will eventually reach retirement age is surely the most telling point to make.)

I concluded my essay with this short summation: "The case for a union role in pension fund management is strong, the need is great, and all that is missing is the unions' resolve to start pushing hard for the expanded role to which they are clearly entitled."

That drive, unfortunately, was never launched. A few unions did ask for and were given a token seat or two on their company's pension fund board, but very few actually achieved full co-management status.

Today, of course, private pension funds have been reduced well below the numbers that existed in the 1960s and '70s. Many have been dissolved with the bankruptcies of companies or their flight from Canada to low-wage developing countries. Most of the remaining plans have been converted from the much preferable defined benefit (DB) plans to the far inferior defined contribution (DC) plans.

The DB plans guarantee employees a monthly retirement payment based on their contributions and length of service. Any shortfall in the plan's investment yield has to be made up by the employer. Under a DC plan, on the other hand, employees have no guarantee of the size, security, or continuity of their pension benefits. The amount they receive is decided by how the pension fund contributions are invested and how much the investments generate in returns. The DC plans put all the investment risks on the employees, none on the employer.

Much of this pension misfortune, I believe, could have been averted or at least moderated if the unions had a co-management role in the funds' administration. Certainly the widespread conversion of DB to DC plans could not have been effected if the workers through their unions had gained co-management status. Having declined that role, the unions now have no defence when employers make pension changes unilaterally. I make this observation retrospectively and sadly, not snidely or in an "I-told-you-so" manner.

Meech Lake and Charlottetown Accords

Over a five-year span between 1987 and 1992, the federal Conservative government headed by Brian Mulroney made two concerted efforts to radically amend the Canadian Constitution. The alleged objective was to "bring Quebec into the Canadian constitutional family" by granting it "distinct society" status. This would have required a devolution of federal powers — not just to Quebec, of course, but to all the provinces, which would be given exclusive jurisdiction over resources and culture. The federal government would also be stripped of its power to override any provincial legislation that would be deemed injurious to the national interest.

The Meech Lake Accord was adopted in principle by the federal government and all 10 provincial premiers in 1987. It was also supported by the Liberal and New Democratic parties and by most national organizations, including the Canadian Labour Congress.

Ottawa and the provinces were given three years to formally approve and implement the Accord. The deadline for this overall endorsement was June 23, 1990.

It seemed certain of gaining the required unanimous support, but opposition to the accord started to build when its adverse implications for national unity began to leak out. Former Prime Minister Pierre Trudeau campaigned against it, as did constitutional expert Senator Eugene Forsey. Provincial support cracked in Newfoundland after a provincial election put a Liberal government headed by Clyde Wells into power. He had spoken out against the Accord during the election campaign. And in Manitoba, MLA Elijah Harper vowed to vote against the Accord and deny it the unanimous support it would need there.

My opposition to the Accord was not, of course, a significant factor in its defeat; but an opinion-piece I wrote for the *Ottawa Citizen* a week before the June 23 deadline did get published in other newspapers across the country as well. This was on the eve of a scheduled vote on the Accord in the Newfoundland legislature.

Here's a summarized version of my article:

As an expatriate Newfoundlander living in Ottawa, I'm hoping — along with most other mainlanders — that next week's vote in the Newfoundland House of Assembly will result in the salvation of Canada. In other words, we're rooting for a majority vote to reject the Meech Lake Accord.

Why? Because the most shattering blow that could be delivered against national unity before June 23 is not the defeat of this odious document, but its adoption. Meech is a formula for the eventual disintegration of Canada.

The vague promises and cosmetic add-ons produced last week don't change a comma in the original 1987 agreement that poses such a dire threat to the federal nature of the country.

The provinces would still gain control over immigration, and would still be able to opt out of federal programs. The Gang of Eleven — the First Ministers' conferences — would still be entrenched as the real centre of power and decision-making, superseding the House of Commons. The provinces would still be free to spend federal money as they wish, instead of having to meet national standards of health care, education, and other social needs.

Nor would all these concessions appease Quebec, whose nationalists have only had their appetite for independence whetted by this accord. They would soon be back to escalate their demands for full autonomy, armed with the power to veto the Triple-E Senate or anything else the other provinces were seeking.

Most Canadians understand this grim reality. That's why the polls indicate that most of us disapprove of this deal.

So who was speaking for Canada at last week's first ministers' con-job in Ottawa? It wasn't Mulroney. It wasn't Bourassa or Peterson or Buchanan or Ghiz or Devine or Getty or Vander Zalm. It wasn't McKenna after the third day, and it wasn't the Filmon-Carstairs-Doer troika after the sixth day. It was, finally, only Clyde Wells, who decided to leave the ultimate fate of the accord to the elected representatives of his fellow Newfoundlanders in the House of Assembly.

Patriots are thankful for this last chance to avert a national calamity. It is the best result we could hope to come from such a cynical exercise in the politics of intimidation. It was a week of infamy — secret, manipulative, devoid of any genuine effort to correct the myriad flaws in the accord. Instead, it was unscrupulously designed to ram the accord through, unaltered, by clubbing the dissident premiers into submission.

"Sign," they were told, "or be responsible for the break-up of Canada. Sign or Quebec will separate."

The heavy burden of guilt that was piled up had no substance in truth or morality, but it was onerous enough to subdue all of Wells's provincial allies. One by one they succumbed, leaving him isolated in his opposition.

But he was isolated only among the other first ministers and their toadies. He had — still has — the support of a clear majority of Canadians. That is the single and most important fact that the people of Newfoundland should keep in mind during the crucial days ahead, as they convey their thoughts, feelings and wishes to their MLAs.

It would be eminently fitting for Canada's newest province to save Canadians from the folly of their first ministers. The makeshift vessel that is Meech, with its loathsome cargo, has been adrift on the seas of political expediency and internecine bickering for three years. It's time it was sunk, and what better place for it to founder than on the rugged shores of Newfoundland.

As it turned out, it wasn't necessary for such a vote to be held in the Newfoundland legislature. All Wells had to do was defer a vote until the June

23 deadline ran out. The Accord then automatically died. It would probably have failed, anyway, since Elijah Harper's refusal to cast a vote for the Accord in the Manitoba legislature denied it the unanimous consent it would have required there. Harper therefore shares with Clyde Wells the credit for saving Canada from a constitutional catastrophe.

The powerful pro-Meech forces, however, refused to concede defeat. Under Mulroney, they quickly forged another version of Meech — the Charlottetown Accord. It was almost identical, with the same proposed constitutional amendments that would devolve much of the federal power to the provinces. The only substantial change was that it would be put to a national referendum.

The federal and provincial leaders believed the main reason they lost the Meech Lake battle was because of the secrecy of the negotiations and the autocratic process of requiring only élite political approval. They were confident that, with massive and unanimous federal and provincial political support for the Charlottetown Accord, they could win the propaganda fight that would precede the referendum scheduled for October 26, 1992.

All three main political parties — Conservative, Liberal and NDP — were again backing the new deal, as were most national groups, again including the Canadian Labour Congress and of course big business organizations like the Chamber of Commerce.

Now, normally, the political, business, and labour élites would have prevailed, particularly with the firepower of the big corporations which owned or controlled the mass media. They could afford to mount the most elaborate pro-Charlottetown propaganda campaign, as they had in the national free trade fight five years earlier.

In the Charlottetown Accord battle, however, they miscalculated. They forgot that the memory of Meech Lake was still fresh in the minds of most Canadians, as was its planned decentralization of political powers and rights to the provinces. Such a threat to national unity could not easily be covered up.

Still, the leaders of the political parties and the major corporations and unions were so confident of their superiority in debate and persuasion that they agreed to give the opponents of the deal equal time and space in the media.

Now, think about that! The effect was the same as if the foes of Charlottetown had their own mass media! The people of Canada — for the first time in my lifetime — got to hear both sides of a major issue in equal proportions. They truly were given the opportunity to make up their minds in full knowledge of both the pros and the cons.

The result was that the political, business, and labour establishments went down in flames. It wasn't a complete rout, but the anti-Charlottetown Accord voters won a decisive victory, 54.3% to 45.7%.

That was the last attempt to dismantle the federal structure of Canada. It was also the last time our corporate rulers gave us equal space and time in their media. Of course, we now have our own virtual media in the form of the Internet and its various spinoffs, a development that goes a long way toward counteracting corporate control of the commercial print and broadcast outlets.

* * *

The decision by the Canadian Labour Congress and the New Democratic Party to throw their support behind the Meech Lake and Charlottetown Accord efforts to split the country into 10 autonomous fiefdoms was deeply disappointing to their supporters. And also to constitutional experts such as Senator Eugene Forsey.

Senator Forsey wrote the *Toronto Star* to commend one of my columns on these abortive attempts to disempower the federal government. Here are a few excerpts from my column:

> We probably would not have a national Medicare program, a national public pension plan, or a national unemployment insurance scheme if complete jurisdiction over these matters had been invested in the provinces in the Constitution. It was only because the federal government was able to use its spending and redistributive powers to knock provincial heads together that these vital social programs were established.
>
> It is precisely because Ottawa has relented on its preconditions for sharing the cost of Medicare that Ontario, Quebec, and some other provinces have been able to get away with doctors opting out, extra-billing, and other departures from the basic principles of universal public health care. The same deterioration will take place in public pensions and UI if the proposed constitutional changes are ever implemented. In that event, it is difficult to imagine the federal Parliament functioning as anything more than an impotent debating forum.

The federalist option of One Canada — perhaps with some special status for Quebec — surely must be the appropriate alternative to provincial empire-building, under whatever guise.

Senator Forsey, in his letter to the editor, said that I had "hit the nail right on the head. I hope that what Ed Finn has said will get through to the powers-that-be in the Canadian Labour Congress and the NDP. People need to have thrust under their noses the very practical, down-to-earth consequences of these airy-fairy constitutional proposals of fanatics and 'intellectuals.' Ordinary citizens are too apt to think that all this 'constitutional stuff' is of no importance to their daily lives. They could have a rude awakening.

"Family illness has put an almost complete stop to my public activities. But if I ever manage to do a dissection of the current proposals to amend the Constitution, I shall certainly quote Ed Finn's column, and with whoops of approval."

My favourite (original) puns

I have a reputation, deserved or not, as an inveterate punster. Most of my puns have been eye-rolling groaners, but the occasional one has been funny and perhaps even witty. The following examples are among my favourites.

While a few friends and I were visiting New York, we strolled past that city's magnificent public library on Fifth Avenue at 42nd Street. At each side of the library building stands the huge statue of a lion.

"What's with the lions?" one of my friend asked. "What have lions got to do with a library?"

"Surely the answer is obvious," I said. "The statues are there for the benefit of library patrons who like to read between the lions."

* * *

While working with the *Montreal Gazette* in the mid-1950s, I covered some baseball games at the old Delormier Stadium, home of the Montreal Royals, then a farm team of the Brooklyn Dodgers.

For some reason, the stadium was being extensively renovated in the middle of the baseball season, necessitating the temporary closure of more than one-third of the washrooms. Fans forced into long lineups at the toilets still open were understandably furious. They were missing key hits and plays.

Writing my story on one of the games, I referred to the toilet shortage in these words: "The fans can easily rectify this problem. All they have to do when they go to a game is bring their own relief pitchers."

* * *

Also during my time at the *Gazette*, I was assigned to do a story on the perennial problem of persuading passengers to move to the back of the bus or streetcar.

I put the problem in a historical perspective, pointing out that Noah even had trouble getting the animals to move to the back of the ark.

And when the Greeks rolled their wooden horse to the gates of Troy, the soldiers jammed inside balked at moving to the rear end. The crush became so awful that one soldier was accidentally stabbed by another warrior's spear.

His captain saw how badly he was bleeding, and yelled out: "Is there a doctor in the horse?"

* * *

While working in CUPE's Communications Department, one of my associates was Bozica Costigliola. Of course we all called her "Biz" for short.

Several months after she got married, she arrived at the office sporting the telltale protuberance of early pregnancy, which she proudly displayed to us.

"Wow," I said, "that's show, Biz!"

* * *

The condominium of garden homes where I live with my family is self-managed by residents elected to its board of directors. I served as vice-president for a few years. One of my duties was to write a bi-monthly newsletter.

Several of the owners had dogs, which they walked around the condo grounds every day. Most did the required poop-scooping, but some didn't; so other residents who inadvertently stepped in a pile of excrement bombarded the board with their complaints.

I wrote an editorial in the newsletter scolding the culpable dog owners and urging them to clean up after their pets. The editorial had the desired effect, but maybe it was because of the heading I put on it: "We're having too many close encounters of the turd kind."

Chapter 15

The Waffle and the Pancake

DURING THE LATE 1960s and early '70s, a small reformist group within the New Democratic Party launched a campaign to move the party back to the socialist roots of its founders in the CCF. It adopted a manifesto calling for an independent socialist Canada, one that was opposed to foreign business ownership and in favour of more public control of key sectors of the economy such as energy.

Why this group was named the "Waffle" is unclear. Economist Mel Watkins, who was one of its leaders, says the name was applied to the group because of its failure to call for an independent Canadian labour movement as well as an independent economy. Its members "waffled" on this issue and didn't even include it in their manifesto.

Even so, the movement to pull the NDP more to the left infuriated most of the party's hierarchy, and especially the leaders of the Canadian branches of American unions. They were incensed by the media attention it attracted, and particularly by the sponsorship of a Waffle candidate, Jim Laxer, in the party's leadership convention in 1971.

The establishment candidate, David Lewis, would normally have won easily, perhaps even on the first ballot. But Laxer pushed the election to a fifth ballot before finally losing to Lewis. This was the limit of the NDP brass's tolerance, and over the next few years the Waffle's members were in effect purged from the party. As Watkins put it, "We were too weak to win and too strong to be tolerated."

The failure of the Waffle group to push for trade union autonomy, however, prompted some of its labour supporters to form a sub-group committed to that cause. They were active at subsequent conventions of the CLC and provincial federations of labour, and succeeded beyond their expectations in making "self-government" gains for Canadian sections of U.S. unions.

Members of the labour reform group that split off from the Waffle were unsure what to call their group. At a meeting shortly after its formation, one of them, Fred Tabachnick, who was then with me at the CBRT & GW, suggested waggishly that we call it "the Pancake," and this appellation stuck.

I was active in both the Waffle and Pancake groups. My first contribution to the Waffle was to join with Jim Hayes, then handling communications for the federal NDP caucus, in writing a series of articles for the party's newsletter. The articles didn't openly support the Wafflers, but expressed nationalist and socialist views that were similar to theirs.

It was remarkable that the NDP MPs permitted such heresy to appear in the federal party's newsletter, but somehow they did — at least until the Waffle became more of an irritant to the party brass.

Jim Hayes credits me with helping to promote the Waffle's manifesto and give it some credibility with the broader party membership. Whether or not I deserve that accolade, I certainly participated in all stages of the Waffle's subsequent campaign, helping write its press releases and resolutions at party assemblages, and supporting Waffle leaders such as Laxer at NDP gatherings.

Like Mel Watkins, I don't consider the Waffle to have been a foredoomed flop. It did invigorate the budding Canadian sovereignty movement and was an inspiration for later nationalist organizations such as the Council of Canadians and the Polaris Institute.

The Waffle was also a great model and stimulus for the country's reform-minded young people. In fact, university students were prominent in its ranks, including many in the New Democratic Youth (NDY). In 1972, I accepted an invitation from the NDY to address its convention in Banff and to advise them how they could forge closer ties with young people in the labour movement.

The convention was not held in the Banff Springs hotel, but in the large Banff Centre there. I arrived a day before the convention opened, and, as the only person there over the age of 30, I drew suspicious glances from many of the delegates. When I was introduced as the keynote speaker the next morning and identified as a union PR director and *Toronto Star* labour columnist, one delegate piped up, "We all thought you were here as a spy for the RCMP."

"Not only am I not a spy for the RCMP," I assured them, "but I'm not even a spy for the NDP!" This got me a good laugh, one of the few I generated in my hour-long speech. But of course I was there to inform and advise, not entertain them.

I concluded my address with these words:

"Don't underestimate the NDY's role as the NDP's most reform-minded group in making the NDP a more attractive party to young people in all walks of life. It is not enough to be a political party with progressive policies: the NDP must *appear* to be a progressive party in the eyes of the voters.

"The NDY's role as gadfly, as pusher and prodder and vitalizer of the party is of immense value in preventing the NDP from suffering a hardening of its ideological arteries. In fact, I see the NDY as the party's left wing, counterbalancing the political conservatism of trade unions on the right. The more success you have in keeping the NDP a genuine party of reform and social betterment, the more success you will have in attracting to your ranks and to the party those young people in the labour movement and elsewhere who are seeking a constructive outlet for their energy and ideals.

"Unlike many others of my generation, I admire today's youth in general, and NDYers in particular. I admire your refusal to accept unquestioningly the traditions and shibboleths of a bygone era, and your determination to shape and adopt new policies, new attitudes, new methods more suited to a rapidly changing world. If Canada is ever to become the kind of country we would like it to be, you are the Canadians who will make it so."

This reliance on youth was not appreciably justified in the closing decades of the 20th century, and in fact the NDY itself quietly disbanded a few years after its Banff conference. But the confidence in the young that I expressed in my speech was validated in the early years of the 21st century by the rise of the mainly youth-driven Occupy movement and the street protests by university students, mostly in Quebec but later in other provinces.

The Pancake initiative, however, was primarily led by older union professionals, such as Gil Levine, CUPE's research director. I was the CBRT's legislative director in the early '70s when I got active with the Pancake. Both Gil and I were not allowed to attend the 1970 convention of the CLC in Edmonton, largely because of pressure from the Canadian branch officers of U.S. unions. They resented our outspoken endorsement of the rank-and-file rebels in their locals who had submitted pro-autonomy resolutions to the convention.

In my *Star* column prior to the May 1970 CLC convention, I was not optimistic that the Pancake "manifesto" would get enough support from delegates to be adopted as official CLC policy. In fact, I described the CLC as being "as susceptible to change as a glacier. Its conventions are tightly controlled exercises in 'guided' democracy... Anyone who bucks the administration is by definition a communist, a political agitator, a wild-eyed utopian, or just a plain troublemaker."

None of these disparaging labels could correctly be applied to the Pancakers who did make it to the convention. They were comparative moderates. Their manifesto was solely designed to change the Congress into a more effective, democratic, and truly Canadian central labour body. Granted, it did call for the granting of full autonomous status to the Canadian sections of U.S. unions, and for the establishment of an orderly procedure whereby inadequately serviced members of one CLC union could transfer peaceably to another union; but it also called for unions to get more actively involved in projects for broad social and community betterment, and for an intensified CLC campaign to facilitate union mergers and encourage more multi-union bargaining with employers.

Gil and I, watching from afar, were pleasantly surprised when, far from being spurned, the Pancake's key proposals were widely acclaimed by delegates and then grudgingly endorsed by the CLC hierarchy. Adoption of the relatively strong policies on Canadian union autonomy, social unionism, and industrial democracy were especially gratifying to the Pancake group and their many allies at the convention.

It was a rarity within the labour movement to have any serious challenge to the administration emanate from appointed staffers, who are generally considered to have little or no political influence. Those hired as technicians by the entrenched officers (especially those with the American union branches) were vulnerable to retaliation, even dismissal from their posts. None, to my knowledge, were canned, but some were chastised in other and more petty ways. It may well be that they were saved from serious punishment by the enthusiastic (and unexpected) acceptance of their reform proposals by the convention delegates. To suspend, dismiss, or otherwise discipline them after that achievement could have unpleasant political consequences for the union leaders themselves.

In my post-convention *Star* column, I reflected that, in retrospect, the Pancake group had obviously underestimated the spread of nationalist sentiment in labour circles, as well as rank-and-filers' dissatisfaction with the internal status quo and their thirst for newer, fresher, even more radical ideas.

"The collective brainpower of the reformers," I noted, "also went a long way toward offsetting their numerical weakness. (One reporter at the convention even flatteringly termed them 'labour's thinkers.') Their convention strategy was well planned, and they were more than able to match the eloquence of establishment speakers at the mikes.

"The magnification of their role and activities by the media, as well as their comments in interviews, garnered twice the media coverage given to the CLC leaders, much to the latters' chagrin. The result was that the Pancake caucus received credit for all the progressive policy changes, even though — to be fair — the Congress brass had intended to move voluntarily to some extent on social action and industrial democracy.

"The big break for which the Pancake reformers deserve full credit was the establishment of minimum standards of autonomy and service for the Canadian sections of U.S. unions. The CLC's executive board members had not planned to go nearly that far. But, after the Pancake victory in forcing a more militant stance on social unionism, they hastily rewrote their own autonomy resolution to incorporate most of the Pancake proposals."

I remained skeptical, however, that the Pancake's apparent success at the Edmonton convention would be translated into effective action. This concern was shared by a Pancake delegate, who told me about his astonishment at seeing an American union officer seated near him raise his hand to vote for the pro-autonomy resolution. Knowing the man was an ardent anti-nationalist, the Pancake delegate asked him how he could support such a resolution.

"Why not?" was the smug reply. "It's not as if the Congress can force us to comply with any resolution adopted here."

True enough. All the CLC could do was appeal with them to comply.

The resolution as revised by the CLC executive was much weaker, anyway, than the Pancake's originally worded one. It omitted two key Pancake proposals: that sufficient dues revenue be retained in Canada to enable Canadian officers to finance distinctively Canadian programs and services; and that the Canadian branches be given the right to merge, without having to wait for initial mergers of their parent organizations in the U.S.

The question of finances was crucial because, no matter how extensive other guarantees of autonomy may appear, they would not be worth much without the necessary funds to put them into effect. The autonomous right to merge in Canada was also essential, if the fragmented structure of Canadian labour was to be rationalized.

However, the autonomy standards approved at the Edmonton convention did provide for the election of the Canadian officers by Canadians, which was a big first step. The Steelworkers, the United Auto Workers, and some other U.S. industrial unions already granted their Canadian members that right. But most of the internationals at that time, particularly the craft unions, did not.

The Pancake group kept a close watch on the Congress over the next few years, and, as expected, found that progress toward labour self-government was disappointingly slow. But by the time the 1974 CLC convention rolled around, the tide of autonomy had quickened from a sluggish stream to a rapidly rising tide.

This trend was accelerated by two developments. First, the leaders of the big public sector unions — CUPE, PSAC, and NUPGE — became more actively committed to the battle for a free and sovereign Canadian labour movement. So much so that their chosen candidate for one of the CLC vice-presidents' posts — CUPE's Shirley Carr — was placed on both the administration and reform caucus election slates and won in a landslide.

The other pro-autonomy factor was the patriotic upsurge among Canadian members of U.S. branch unions. They were not satisfied with a mere slackening of control by the American head offices, but were clamoring for complete independence. Even as the 1974 CLC convention was getting under way in Vancouver, members of the big Pulp and Paper Mill union were voting by a large majority to break away from their U.S. organization to set up an entirely independent Canadian union.

This growing "separatist" movement soon became an unstoppable force that neither the CLC nor its U.S. labour counterparts could withstand. Over the next two decades, most of the Canadian branches of the big American industrial unions — including the auto workers — severed the organizational ties with their U.S. parents and established wholly Canadian operations. The big exception was (and still is) the Steelworkers, whose ongoing international integration was due to the extensive self-governing status the Canadian sections already enjoyed. It also helped that two top Canadian officers in a row (Lynn Williams and Leo Gerard) were elected to head the big international union on both sides of the border.

Looking back at the three-decade struggle for a free and democratic Canadian labour movement, I would not give undue credit to the small Pancake contingent. But I think they did play a key role in fanning the first sparks of Canadian union autonomy and helping to cultivate the pro-independence fervor that followed.

Chapter 16

Hired and fired by the CBRT

FROM 1963 to 1981, I was on the staff of the Canadian Brotherhood of Railway, Transport, and General Workers, the oldest national union in the country. For most of those 18 years, I served as its director of public relations, and for a few years as research and legislative director.

At my "job interview" in September 1963, I was impressed by both CBRT president Bill Smith and secretary-treasurer Don Secord. They were both capable and dedicated union leaders who assured me I would have the freedom to perform my PR and editorial duties without interference.

"We're confident, based on your past performance as a journalist and PR staffer with the CLC in Newfoundland," said Smith, "that you will more than meet our expectations as PR director and editor of our monthly journal."

Canadian Transport was the longest-running union publication in Canada, having been launched in 1910, shortly after the union itself was founded by a group of railway workers who broke away from an international rail union. They called their new union the Canadian Brotherhood of Railway Employees (CBRE), but changed it to the CBRT & GW after organizing other "transport and general workers."

The fledgling union's first president, Aaron Roland Mosher, became one of Canada's most outstanding labour leaders. He kept winning re-election for an amazing 44 years, until 1952, a tenure unmatched in the labour movement before or since. Under his leadership, the CBRT became the largest national union of transport employees, embracing truckers, bus drivers, city transit, and seaway workers.

At the time of its creation in 1908, the union Mosher led was unique in two important respects. Firstly, it was a wholly Canadian union in an era when the country's labour movement was largely an extension of the American Federation of Labour (AFL). The big upsurge of union nationalism was still 60 years away.

And secondly, it was a union dedicated to an industry-wide rather than a craft structure. Before the founding of the CBRE, workers were organized strictly on craft lines. Each trade had its own union. Indeed, this remained the predominant union framework in North America until the emergence of the United Mine Workers, the Steelworkers, and the other big industrial unions in the 1930s.

But it was Mosher who first argued that all workers in an industry should be in the same union, regardless of their different skills and occupations. And he was the first union leader to prove that industrial unionism was not only viable, but could also be more effective and beneficial to working people.

Little wonder, then, that A.R. Mosher is the only Canadian labour leader who has ever been honoured with his own stamp by the Post Office. It was issued in 1981, and the tribute was probably more for his influence and leadership in establishing two multi-union labour organizations that predated the Canadian Labour Congress.

The first was the All-Canadian Congress of Labour (ACCL), which Mosher was involved in setting up in 1927 to promote national unionism. The second was the Canadian Congress of Labour (CCL), formed in 1940 when the ACCL united with the Canadian branches of the new American industrial unions. Mosher was elected its first and only president until the historic merger of the CCL and the craft unions created the present CLC in 1956.

I cite this brief history of the CBRT and its first superb leader to explain why I was so delighted to join its staff.

The other significant aspect of the CBRT that impressed me was its internal democracy. It maintained a separate fund that defrayed all the expenses of delegates to its biennial conventions, including lost wages. So, unlike most other unions whose small locals often couldn't afford to send delegates to conventions, every local in the CBRT from coast to coast was represented at its national gatherings. These delegates not only elected their national officers and adopted policies that set the union's future course, but also set the officers' salaries. To make sure they remained in control between conventions, the delegates also elected a National Executive Board the majority of whose members were rank-and-filers.

Many additional safeguards were built into the CBRT's constitution and long tradition. Appeals against decisions by the officers or executive board, for example, could be carried all the way to a convention; and I witnessed several such appeals upheld at the conventions I subsequently attended. Between conventions, several other wage and policy meetings were held at the regional level, and all contract demands had to be submitted from the locals and all proposed settlements had to be ratified by the workers they covered before they were finalized.

Perhaps the extent of this internal democracy was best exemplified by the freedom given to all CBRT members to express their views in *Canadian Transport*. Rarely was an issue of the union's journal published while I was editor that did not contain at least one letter from a member objecting to some action or decision by the union's leadership. Often there were several such letters from dissidents published. I know of no other union in Canada (or anywhere else) whose elected leaders so readily allowed their critics space in the union's official journal.

The CBRT officers' reasoning made sense. First, they realized that it was the members' dues that paid all the costs of publishing *Canadian Transport*, and that it was the members' only public forum to express their views between conventions. Secondly, the officers were aware that *Transport* was an outlet for dissent that, if bottled up, would almost certainly erupt more explosively later at the convention. And thirdly, they knew that their supporters far outnumbered the dissenters among the locals and would spring to their defence with their own letters to the editor. And this in fact was what developed — a lively exchange in the union's journal between membership critics and backers of the administration. It was *Transport's* most popular feature.

Another bonus for the officers was that their most vituperative detractors, through intemperance and the failure to support their verbal attacks with evidence, soon discredited themselves. Most such fault-finders, when they came to the mikes later at a convention, were greeted with derisive hoots and groans.

I was quite comfortable working for a union that practised as well as preached democracy at every level of its operations. In 1967, after I'd been with the CBRT for four years, I was asked to write a weekly column on labour relations for *The Toronto Star*, and I told Bill Smith and Don Secord about the invitation before accepting it. I made it clear to them that I would sometimes be critical of the CLC and its majority of U.S.-based unions on the lack of autonomy provided to Canadian branches, and might occasionally disagree with the CLC on other issues as well.

If I had been working for any other union at the time, I very much doubt that its top officers would have given me their blessing to write such a column while still remaining on its payroll. But Smith and Secord had no such misgivings. On the contrary, they were delighted by *The Star's* offer. They urged me to take the opportunity to become a columnist for the newspaper with by far the largest circulation in the country.

Later, when my *Star* columns in the 1970s supported the growing campaign for Canadian union independence, the Canadian officers of American unions were furious. They first tried to persuade *The Star's* managing editor, Martin Goodman, to terminate my column. When he refused, they tried to pressure the CBRT leaders to threaten me with dismissal if I didn't quit my *Star* "moonlighting." Of course, Smith and Secord, being ardent union nationalists themselves, told the Canadian officers of U.S. branches they agreed with my sentiments on union autonomy. "We may disagree occasionally with his views on other labour matters," Smith said, "but not with his democratic right to express them wherever and however he chooses."

So my years with the CBRT were quite interesting and rewarding. I did have some initial trouble as editor of *Canadian Transport* because of a running feud between my two assistant editors, Bill Walsh and Fred Tabachnick. Bill was an old-time newspaperman who had been the journal's editor before I arrived to help convert it from a magazine into a tabloid. He and I got on quite well, but when Fred was hired in 1968, he and Bill clashed almost from the start. Fred was a gifted editor, writer, and PR specialist who had formerly been a reporter with *The Calgary Herald* and a PR staffer with the federal caucus of the NDP. But he was young and well-versed in modern PR techniques, and his bright ideas, all of which had merit, rubbed Bill the wrong way. For the next few years, until Bill retired, I seemed to spend more time as their referee than their colleague.

Without Bill's griping, however, Fred and I developed a solid teamwork approach that grew into a close and lasting friendship. Fred left the CBRT in 1974 to join CUPE as a senior communications officer. It was ironic that, seven years later, when I also departed the CBRT to take a PR job with CUPE, Fred had become that union's director of communications, and was now my "boss." We had reversed roles, but nothing had changed in the teamwork relationship we had established at the CBRT.

I probably would have stayed with the CBRT to continue and complete the labour part of my career if it had not been for the union's lockout of its national office clerical employees early in 1981. By that time, Bill Smith had been replaced as president by a former staff rep, Don Nicholson, and Don Secord by the union's former education director, Dick Gingerich. It's safe to say that, had Smith and Secord still been in those leadership positions, the dispute with the clerical staff's local of the OPEIU (the Office and Professional Employees' International Union) would have been peaceably settled. It would certainly not have escalated into a lockout. Nicholson and Gingerich, however, despite their purported dedication to basic union rights, tended to be less inclined to practise them when dealing with unionized staff.

I was shocked when the clerical employees were locked out in the late spring of 1981. It seemed so alien to the CBRT's principles and traditions. Other senior staffers — Education Director Dewey Merrett, Legislative Director Jack Wynter, Organizing Director John McNevin, and Office Manager Jack Mollins — were equally disturbed by the lockout.

The clerical workers, of course, immediately strung picket lines around the CBRT's national office on Carling Avenue, so Nicholson rented space in a downtown hotel to serve as a temporary CBRT headquarters. We were expected to continue our normal work there as long as the contract dispute lasted, to the extent it was possible to do so without secretarial and other clerical help.

However, we still had concerns that I relayed to Nicholson.

"Don," I said, "we can still make phone calls, type notes and press releases, even use the copiers to the extent we did before the lockout, but I hope it's safe to assume we won't be expected to perform any work that normally falls solely within the jurisdiction or the secretarial and clerical staff."

I was dismayed by his noncommittal response. "You'll be asked," he said, "to do anything that is essential to the service we are obliged to provide the union's members."

"That's fine," I said, "as long as it doesn't involve scabbing."

He was angered by such a blunt warning, but turned and walked away without saying any more.

If there hadn't been a national postal strike going on at the same time, the dispute with the clerical workers might have been settled eventually without provoking another dispute with the senior office staff. But the mail delivery had been interrupted for several weeks by a CUPW walkout, and its settlement came while the CBRT's clerical employees were still locked out.

A few days later, about 30 bags of mail were delivered to the CBRT's temporary office in downtown Ottawa.

We were appalled when Nicholson ordered us to open the bags, then sort, open, and distribute the envelopes they contained.

We refused to become scabs. Nicholson insisted that the mail had to be processed, arguing that the imperative to respond to membership needs superseded any concern we might have about performing what would normally be clerical duties.

Of course we disagreed. The stark choice Nicholson gave us was either to become scabs and lose our self-respect, or refuse to become scabs and lose our jobs.

The next day, Nicholson, Gingerich, and the other national officers fired all five of us.

It was a black day in the history of the CBRT & GW, and one of the blackest in the history of the Canadian labour movement.

The "fired five" met several times in the next few weeks to consider our future prospects. We intended to appeal our dismissal to the union's National Executive Board, as we were entitled to do under the CBRT's constitution and bylaws, but, correctly assuming that would be a fruitless exercise, we also filed unjust dismissal charges with the Canada Labour Relations Board (CLRB).

Neither of these avenues of redress proved successful. The union's executive board listened to our presentation, asked a few hostile questions, then summarily rejected our grievance. The CLRB also dismissed our charge of unjust dismissal, not because it lacked merit, but because the board felt such a case should be made to the Ontario Labour Relations Board (OLRB), not the federal board. This decision came as more of a shock and disappointment than that of the union's board, because, after all, the CBRT itself, as a railway union, definitely came under federal law, so why not the union's staff?

It turned out that, because the members of the national office staff were located in Ontario, this was also ruled (as bizarre as we found it) the appropriate jurisdiction for resolving staff dismissals at the union's head office in Ottawa.

We probably would have re-submitted our unjust dismissal case to the provincial labour relations board if it had not been for the time that had elapsed since our firing, and the financial pressure that had built up by four months without a pay-cheque. Indeed, a member of the OLRB admitted to us later, that had the case come before that board, our dismissal would have been ruled unfair and unfounded and the CBRT would have been compelled to re-hire us with full back pay.

For two of us, however, the further delay such a procedure would entail was not tolerable. Jack Mollins was able to take an early retirement; I had been offered a PR job with CUPE; and Jack Wynter was being considered for employment as a mediator at the federal Department of Labour. But for Dewey Merrett and John McNevin, employment prospects were still bleak, so we decided not to pursue the OLRB appeal route. Having a wrongful dismissal ruling served on Nicholson, Gingerich, and the other CBRT officers would have been satisfying, as would the reimbursement of lost back pay, but none of us would really have wanted to resume our careers with the CBRT under its current leadership. As it turned out, Dewey Merrett soon had a job offer from the Manitoba Department of Labour, and John McNevin snagged a good position as an organizer with the New Democratic Party in B.C.

The CBRT, on the other hand, never lived down the disgrace of locking out its clerical workers and then firing five of its senior staff for refusing to become scabs. Nicholson, who used to boast of garnering the most votes in elections for the CLC's executive board, received so few votes at the next CLC convention that he was turfed off the board and replaced by CUPW President Jean Parrot.

This was the beginning of a slow but steady decline for a union that was once the brightest star in the Canadian national union firmament. The CBRT & GW was ignominiously swallowed up by the Canadian Auto Workers in 1992, and disappeared. It was a dismal end for a union whose beginning heralded such a proud and distinguished record of accomplishments for most of the ensuing century.

Challenging the aristocrats

> "There is the multitude, and there are the natural leaders. Wealth, birth and culture mark out the man to whom a community looks to undertake its government. These men have the leisure and the fortune... They are the aristocracy, and the rulers of a country should be taken from among them."
>
> —*Lord Salisbury, 1894.*

When Lord Salisbury uttered this tribute to the ruling class in Britain, he was the Prime Minister of a government almost entirely comprised of MPs who enjoyed inherited wealth, land, and titles. They were all men, of course, and all opposed to women's suffrage.

Historian Barbara Tuchman, in *The Proud Tower*, her brilliant book about the late Victorian era, graphically describes the rigid class structure that prevailed in the British Isles at the time—and which remains more or less intact today.

"The ruling families," she writes, "had no doubts of their inborn right to govern and, on the whole, neither did the rest of the country."

Eventually, the British aristocrats were forced to moderate their more blatantly élitist ways. They had to extend the right to vote to women and to men without property. They had to allow ordinary people from "the multitude" to run for office and even sit beside them in the House of Commons. But they never considered such commoners to be "gentlemen" like themselves. They maintained most of their power and privilege, even though they did not display it quite so openly. And the squalor and misery to which they consigned the "lower classes" continued to blight the lives of millions who had the misfortune to be born outside the ruling families.

Ruling classes, of course, have not been confined to Britain. They have emerged in almost all countries, in all ages. Sometimes, as in Britain, they comprise the nobility, but more often they are the entrepreneurs and landowners, sometimes the military, occasionally the priesthood. Whatever their status, however, they are always the holders of the greatest wealth.

In the past, such rulers—whether kings or dictators or warlords or high priests—governed with an iron fist. They ruled by fear and force, deploying their police and military to crush dissent. But invariably, sooner or later, their harsh rule seeded violent revolutions that sent them to the gallows or the guillotine.

The ruling classes learned from these sobering lessons that, to preserve their domination, they had to share at least a bit of their wealth and give the masses some measure of freedom. And so "democracy" in its various forms replaced absolute rule by the rich and powerful.

But make no mistake: the aristocracy continued to flourish in most countries, and still ruthlessly held and extended their economic sway. Not as openly and brutally, of course, but just as effectively. Today it is almost entirely a corporate aristocracy. The world's 500 or so billionaires don't have titles; there is no King Gates or Grand Duke Buffett in the United States, no Baron Thomson or Count Weston in Canada. But the power wielded by the world's most affluent remains virtually unabridged. It masquerades as "democracy," but is really plutocracy: government by the wealthy.

Such power cannot be exercised without inflicting immense harm on the powerless, on their communities, on the environment. Poverty, hunger, income disparities, homelessness, illiteracy, slave labour, air and water pollution—these and other grave social and economic malignancies multiply as the corporations that serve the plutocrats continue to plunder the planet's finite resources on their behalf.

As in the past, however, more and more people are starting to rebel against their opulent oppressors. They are protesting at summit meetings; they are campaigning against industrial pollution, deforestation and strip-mining; they are boycotting companies whose sweatshop products are made by overworked, underpaid women and children. They are calling for a truly democratic form of government.

It's an uphill struggle, to be sure, but there's much more at stake today than there was in any previous revolution—perhaps even the very survival of life on Earth. The British aristocrats, for all their pride and arrogance, had natural constraints imposed on their greed. So did all the monarchs, czars, emperors, and dictators. Their depredations were limited by geography. They couldn't conquer and pillage the entire world.

But the transnational corporations can—and do. Freed from legislative as well as geographic limits on their power, answerable only to their acquisitive major shareholders, equipped with the financial and technological weapons of global conquest, armed with the sweeping rights conferred on them by international trade agreements, their hordes of executives, bankers, lawyers, and administrators overrun country after country. Servile politicians do their bidding. Media toadies praise their iniquitous "free market" system and ridicule its critics.

Despite their awesome power, however, the plutocrats are not invulnerable. As their unconstrained pursuit of profit becomes more visibly disruptive, as they hurt more people and communities, as they befoul more of the ecosphere we all share, growing numbers of people will join the uprising against them. And eventually—let's hope before it's too late—their business and political and military and media bulwarks that now seem impregnable will be shattered.

Remember: there was a time, not so long ago, when people thought the Berlin Wall would never come down. When it did fall, the hammers were not swung by the billionaires or free-marketers, but by average citizens who saw the wall and all it stood for as an abomination they were no longer willing to tolerate.

Chapter 17

The 1973 railway strike

DURING THE 17 YEARS I did communications, research, and legislative work for the CBRT & GW, the union was involved in many difficult contract disputes with employers of its members. I sometimes provided public relations support that helped the union's bargaining reps to reach settlements that averted a strike or lockout.

One such dispute I still recall was a breakdown in negotiations between the CBRT local that represented the staff of the Chateau Montebello in Quebec and the hotel management. The staff rep, Laurent ("Butch") St.-Pierre, had given up trying to wring a decent offer from the hotel manager and was on the verge of calling a strike.

I asked Butch to wait while I explored some way of putting public pressure on the hotel, which was owned by Canadian Pacific Railway. I learned that it was a popular place for conventions and other gatherings of major business groups.

I asked him to find out if any such events were scheduled at the Montebello. He phoned me back with a list of seven big corporate conclaves that had been booked over the next few months. Just what I was hoping to hear.

Next I phoned Wilf List, the outstanding labour reporter for the *Globe and Mail*. I told him about the breakdown of negotiations with the Chateau Montebello and the imminence of a strike that would shut it down.

The next morning, the front page of the *Globe's* business section featured Wilf's story of the dispute and the probability of a strike that could last for weeks and perhaps months. The news of this threatened prolonged shutdown appeared below a three-column photo of the Chateau.

That afternoon, an elated Butch phoned to tell me he'd had a call from the Chateau's manager, almost pleading with him to return to the bargaining table. The manager was sure that an agreement could be reached that would be satisfactory to management as well as the hotel's employees.

"I don't know how many frantic messages he received from business firms and groups that were planning to meet at the Chateau," Butch said, laughing. "But there must have been quite a few of them after this morning's *Globe and Mail* hit the desks on Bay Street."

* * *

The labour-management dispute that highlighted my years with the CBRT, however, was the 1973 railway strike by the 56,000 non-operating employees of both Canadian National and Canadian Pacific. These "non-ops" — the clerks, baggage handlers, warehousemen, ticket sellers, truck drivers, and other employees not actually working on the trains — were in a restive and militant mood as negotiations for a new contract dragged on through 1973. Their average wage was only $142 a week and their last raise, a year and a half earlier, hadn't even made up for the steep rise in inflation.

Of course, labour contract "negotiations" in the railway industry were always a farce. The companies knew that the federal government would never tolerate a national railway strike that lasted more than a week or 10 days. With so many industries dependent on the rails for raw materials and the transport of their finished products — especially the grain farmers — the pressure to end a rail strike was greater and felt much earlier than for any other strikebound service under federal jurisdiction.

So the two big railroads never bargained in good faith. They knew that a strike would be either averted through last-minute government arm-twisting and "mediation," or soon halted by the enactment of back-to-work legislation and imposed arbitration. In either case, the eventual settlement, whether by mediation or arbitration, invariably awarded pay and benefit increases that fell significantly below those sought by the unions.

Most mediators and arbitrators appointed by the government were Supreme Court justices who were predictably conservative in recommending or imposing settlement terms.

Given this customary refusal by company negotiators to engage in genuine bargaining, and beset by their increasingly irate and impatient members (many of whom were already staging brief illegal local walkouts and slowdowns), the union leaders had no choice but to call a strike as soon as they could legally do so. This was in early August, seven days after they rejected a conciliation board report.

In addition to wages, several other contentious issues on which the parties were far apart included job security, sick leave, and especially the companies' relatively meagre pension plans. In previous negotiations, the pension issue was always sidetracked, but this time rising pressure from an aging membership — the average age of both CN and CP workers at the time was in the mid-40s — compelled the unions to insist on substantial pension upgrades.

The CBRT was only one of 17 non-op unions, and the only Canadian one. But its leaders always played a key role in contract talks with the railroads. In the 1973 showdown, CBRT secretary-treasurer Don Secord shared the main negotiating role with Dick Smith, Canadian vice-president of the Brotherhood of Railway and Airline Clerks (BRAC).

They knew, of course, that any national rail strike would soon be terminated by legislation, but the rising rank-and-file ferment left them no choice. They were wrestling with this dilemma when I joined a strategy session in the temporary strike headquarters in a downtown Montreal office building. I had been asked to handle public relations for the duration of the strike.

"Are we all agreed," Dick Smith asked, "that we have no alternative but to launch a national strike seven days after the conciliation board report?"

"Yes, of course," said Don Secord. "But does it have to be a nation-wide strike? As you know, CUPW (the Canadian Union of Postal Workers) had some success when they conducted a series of rotating strikes last year. They would shut down all the post offices in a city, province, or region for several days, then resume service there, but move the strike to some other location for a while. The Post Office had a lot of trouble coping with that strategy."

Secord's idea appealed to the rest of the strike leaders. Even if it didn't force the railways back to the bargaining table, it would at least avoid a nation-wide transportation crisis and delay government intervention.

So the 1973 railway strike did begin as a series of rotating provincial or regional shutdowns. But it was not a tactic that could be maintained for more than five or six weeks. It had two major flaws. First of all, the engineers and other operating staff were not on strike, so the companies could have them run the trains up to the border of the affected strikebound region; then, when the strike was rotated elsewhere, they could move as far as the next struck region.

Eventually the freight would reach its destination — several days late, of course, but that was a delay that both shippers and their clients could tolerate.

The second problem that arose for the strike tacticians was even more serious: a growing dissatisfaction with the rotating strike strategy among their rank-and-file members. It called for provincial two-to-five-day shutdowns that involved losses of pay by the workers involved. This would have been acceptable if the shutdowns were all of the same duration and resulted in the same wage losses by all the employees. But of course, to be effective, the rotating strikes had to last for varying lengths of time and had to jump unpredictably across the country, with some provinces being hit two or three times and others just once or not at all. Otherwise, the companies' movement of trains across the country would have been even less obstructed.

When the workers in some provinces saw their pay cut more often and more deeply than that of their co-workers elsewhere, their protests to the non-ops' strike committee became too vociferous to ignore. Reluctantly, after a six-week stratagem that did nothing more than delay strike-breaking legislation, Smith and Secord and the other non-op leaders had to stop "rotating" and resort to calling an all-out national strike.

Everybody knew, of course, that an emergency bill to terminate the strike would soon follow. It would be introduced in the House of Commons by the newly appointed Labour Minister, John Munro.

The day the full-blown national strike started, I had a phone call from Munro. "Ed," he said, "I want to talk with you about this rail strike. I've rented a temporary office in a downtown hotel where we can meet in private with no one else knowing about it."

I was only too eager to have this talk with Munro, so I agreed to come down to see him that afternoon. He had only been given the Minister of Labour post in the Trudeau government's cabinet a few months earlier, having served before that as Minister of Health and Welfare. I had pegged him as a progressive and enlightened politician, probably the leading small-l liberal in the federal cabinet. He was ideally suited to the labour post. Genuinely supportive of organized labour and working people, a persistent champion of basic union rights, he had won the grudging admiration of many union leaders, as well as many of their rank-and-file members.

At our meeting, Munro expressed his deep regret that all his efforts to mediate a settlement to avert a national railway strike had failed. He blamed the companies much more than the unions, but said that strike-ending legislation was unavoidable.

"If I didn't bring in such a bill," he said, "the Minister of Transport certainly would. But that would be shirking my responsibility, as distasteful as it may be. At least, my shepherding the bill through Parliament will give me a decisive say in the arbitration process."

"The rail union leaders know you have no choice in this matter," I assured him. "They won't hold the legislation against you personally."

"There is something quite important that I do have control over," he reminded me, "and that's in the appointment of the arbitrator chosen to draft the final settlement."

I nodded. "In the past, it's almost always been a current or former Supreme Court justice."

"It may well be this time, too, but not if the union leaders prefer someone else."

I stared at him. "Are you actually suggesting they make the choice of arbitrator?" I was incredulous.

"Well, I'll make the appointment," Munro said, "but it will be greatly influenced by their preference. I'd like you to go back to Smith and Secord and suggest that they give me a list of two or three persons in the order of which they would like to see arbitrate this dispute. If the first one is not available, I'll try the second, then if necessary the third."

I'm sure this was the first time (and undoubtedly the last) that a Minister of Labour allowed union leaders, in effect, to pick the arbitrator who would impose the final settlement of their contract dispute.

"I'd appreciate it," Munro added, "if you would confine this matter to Smith and Secord, and get their assurance that it will never become public knowledge."

I promised him I would do that, and we shook hands on it.

The next day I met with the two strike committee leaders. They were as surprised and elated as I was by Munro's offer.

"Okay," said Smith, "now who would we really like most to be the arbitrator?"

We proposed and discussed several possible candidates, including professional arbitrators who had shown fairness and objectivity in drafting their awards.

"What about Emmett Hall?" I said.

"Not another Supreme Court justice, surely," said Secord. "Their record in arbitrating rail strikes can hardly be considered encouraging."

"Emmett Hall could be an exception," I argued. "He's no longer on the Supreme Court, and his performance in heading the Royal Commission on Health Care in the early '60s shows him to be quite progressive. In his 1964 report, he not only praised Tommy Douglas and the government of Saskatchewan for introducing the first public health care program in Canada, but he also recommended that it become a national program and be extended to cover other health needs such as prescription drugs and dental care for children."

"Yes, but just because he supports public health care doesn't necessarily mean he'll be sympathetic to railway workers," Smith pointed out.

"You could say the same about the other prospective arbitrators you've considered," I argued.

He and Secord weren't convinced that Hall would be the best possible arbitrator, but agreed to put him at the top of the list they presented to Munro. And that's who he appointed.

For the next two months, Emmett Hall convened meetings of the union and railroad negotiators, listened to their arguments, and carefully studied the details of previous arbitrated settlements. Smith and Secord were impressed by his probing questions and objectivity.

He released the terms of his imposed collective agreement in early January of 1974. It hit the railway industry like a bombshell. Acclaimed by the unions and their members and stridently denounced by the two big companies, it was a landmark in Canadian labour relations history.

Hall not only agreed with the unions' position in nearly all the major issues in dispute, *but in some cases — including pension improvements — actually awarded them more than they'd asked for.*

He declared in his opening statements that railway workers (and by implication all workers) are entitled to "complete protection from the income-eroding effects of inflation" and provided a cost-of-living clause to ensure that protection.

He confirmed the unions' contention that workers should share proportionately in the benefits of rising productivity.

He endorsed the principle that the pay level of workers providing essential services should correspond to that of comparable workers in the private sector.

Of major significance was his statement that public sector workers should not be penalized by their employers' alleged inability to meet the cost of otherwise justified wage demands.

"The use of the railways as an instrument of national policy," said Hall, "requires that it should be the nation as a whole, not the employees of the railways, which must absorb any deficit that may occur. . . The employees cannot be asked to subsidize the carrying out of a commitment made in the national interest."

Based on this precedent-setting principle, the monetary gains Emmett Hall awarded the railway workers totalled 24% over two years, far exceeding any settlement the rail unions could ever obtain at the "bargaining" table — or even the pay increases they had requested.

This was no reflection on the union negotiators. They had no way of defying the companies' "inability to pay" claims, as Hall was free to do. If indeed such claims had any validity, the companies could only offset the cost of the arbitrated wage hikes by asking for increased government subsidies — something they could not do if they had freely yielded them in negotiations.

Reduced to simple terms, this meant that the unions had a better chance to win a satisfactory settlement if it were imposed on them than if it were negotiated. Assuming, of course, that the arbitrator was not bound by the companies' alleged profit-and-loss figures, and that he was as humane and enlightened as Mr. Justice Emmett Hall proved to be.

Not surprisingly, no arbitrator of subsequent railway labour disputes has emulated Hall's principles and precedents — or been allowed by a government to do so.

A week after Hall handed down his revolutionary arbitration award, the non-ops' leaders held a celebratory wine and cheese party. The sent an invitation to Hall that they never expected him to accept, but he was one of the first to show up.

He was greeted by Smith and Secord, who thanked him effusively for the generosity of his imposed settlement. I tagged along with them.

"We never expected even to be awarded as much as we asked for," said Smith, "let alone more!"

The tall, silvery-haired jurist smiled as he waved off their compliments. "I only did what previous arbitrators should have done, which is to completely disregard the companies' so-called inability-to-pay excuse," he said.

Then he added a remark that was so unexpected that it shocked us. I can't remember the exact words, but this is roughly what he said: "My father worked for the CPR for more than 30 years, and when he retired they gave him a pension so low that he could barely afford the basics of life. I've been waiting ever since for an opportunity to make that company pay at least some small penalty for treating its long-serving retired employees so shabbily."

As we stared at him, our jaws dropping, he added: "Gentlemen, it's I who should be thanking you for whatever influence you may have had with the Labour Minister to get me this arbitration appointment."

Later, after the party was over and Hall had left, Secord said to me, "If we'd known Hall's father was a CPR pensioner, we wouldn't just have put him on a list of our preferred arbitrators — we would have told Munro he was our one and only choice!"

Chapter 18

From Bachelor to Bridegroom (belatedly)

I WAS MARRIED ON April 25, 1970, just a few months before my 44th birthday, to Geraldine (Dena) Pelletier at the Holy Name of Jesus Church in Montreal. We've been happily married ever since.

I'm glad that I waited so long to end my more than four decades of bachelorhood. My two brothers and all my male school chums and co-workers got married and started raising families much earlier, usually by their mid-20s, as was customary in those days. In the late 1930s and early '40s, when I was a teenager growing up in Corner Brook, a boy upon reaching puberty was expected to start asking girls for dates, take them to movies and dinners, and eventually propose to one of them and "tie the knot."

Had I followed that traditional date-mate-and-propagate routine instead of remaining single for so long, my life would have unfolded much differently. I would probably still have become a journalist and editor of the *Western Star*, but I would not have gone to Montreal to work with the *Gazette* in the mid-1950s and thus would never have met the girl I eventually married.

Having a wife and children would also have made it more difficult for me to resign as editor of the *Western Star* in 1959 rather than bow to the publishers' orders to slant and distort the paper's coverage of the loggers' strike. I would still have refused to violate the fundamental principles of journalism, of course, but I would have been forced very quickly to find another source of income to support my family instead of waiting several months to get a job offer from the CLC. It's possible, I suppose, that I would still have been unemployed when offered a PR job by the Congress, but even so, with my family responsibilities, I could never have agreed to become provincial leader of the NDP. A prolonged political career would have necessitated being away from home and family for much too long.

If I had still been employed by the CLC strictly as a communicator, it's also possible, if not probable, that I might have later moved out of Newfoundland with my family to some other part of Canada. I might even have taken a PR position with a union. But the chances of my ever working with the CBRT & GW or CUPE, or the CCPA, or writing a column for the *Toronto Star,* would have been remote, and so most of the other experiences I've written about in these memoirs would never have occurred.

So why did I remain single until I was nearly 44 to marry a beautiful girl who was 20 years younger? The simple factual explanation is that Dena was the first woman I fell in love with who also came to love me. Never before had I been attracted to a woman who reciprocated my affection.

Two other factors kept me single. One was my lack of physical qualities that might appeal to a girl or woman. As a teenager and in my 20s, I was homely and pudgy (10 to 15 pounds overweight), and wasn't earning nearly enough to be considered a good "provider."

My second defect as a potential beau and husband was even worse: I had a seriously underactive libido. I didn't know I was afflicted by that disability when I was a teenager and young man, especially since boys at the time in puritanical Corner Brook were denied even the most elementary sex education (unlike the girls, who I'm sure were fully enlightened by their mothers.) My condition was probably the result of hypothyroidism, which can strongly inhibit the libido and also make it difficult to avoid weight gain. I was indeed found to suffer from an underactive thyroid during a medical checkup while in my late 30s, and had it remedied with a daily dose of synthetic thyroid extract.

In my mid-teens while in high school, I was attracted to girls, but not in the obsessive, hormonal-driven way that other boys my age were. I got up nerve enough to make the traditional overtures, if only because they were expected, but I was shy and inarticulate. Most of the girls I went to school with were comely, smart, and self-assured. The two I managed to approach were not impressed by my clumsy, tongue-tied, and admittedly half-hearted advances. But they were careful to turn me down — *let* me down — as gently as they could, even with sympathetic smiles. I appreciated their kindness, if not their pity. And I knew by then that none of the other girls would be any more receptive.

My reaction to their rebuffs was an odd mixture of regret and relief. On the one hand, although I had been fairly certain I lacked even the minimal male attributes that might appeal to a girl, it still hurt to have that assumption so decisively confirmed. On the other hand, since I also lacked the powerful post-puberty sex drive that excited other boys my age, I was grateful to be spared the complex, confusing — and terribly time-consuming — ritual of dating and courtship. I was free to concentrate on my reading and writing, free to tap the wellsprings of knowledge at the local library to compensate for being deprived of a formal higher education.

I was bereft of romantic attachments all the way through my 20s and 30s, but I don't want to leave the impression that these were joyless or unreward-ing years. Though sexually dormant, I was productively active in other ways. I read a lot, wrote a lot, traveled a lot, even laughed and punned a lot. I worked closely and harmoniously on many projects with both male and female col-leagues. Those 25 years were a period of fulfillment and satisfaction, intellec-tually if not emotionally.

My libido started to show some signs of flickering to life, especially after my hypothyroidism was diagnosed and treated in my late 30s, and I was attracted at various times to unmarried young women I worked with or met socially. But I could never muster the courage to make advances I was certain would be unwelcome. By the time I reached my 40th birthday, I had resigned myself to a life of permanent loveless bachelorhood.

But I had reckoned without Dena.

* * *

I first met Dena Pelletier in 1956 while in Montreal working as a reporter with the *Gazette*. She was 10 years old. She lived with her parents and two brothers in a house across from the one in which I was a boarder. I'd been invited to board there by Sylvia Rhind, a sister of my sister-in-law who was married to my brother Mike. They made room for me with husband Murray, their two young daughters, Linda and Janet, and son Jimmy.

The Rhinds were good friends with the Pelletiers as well as neighbours. Dena's parents, Gerry and Betty, socialized with Sylvia and Murray, and Dena played with Linda and Janet. She often came over to watch TV with them, and I soon became her adoptive "uncle," as well as the avuncular family friend of her two brothers and the Rhind children. I treated them all as I did my many nephews and nieces, "spoiling" them with birthday and Christmas gifts, and occasional dimes and quarters and chocolate bars.

When I left Montreal in the fall of 1957, I promised to correspond with them all, but only Dena and Janet sent me letters for a while, until they reached their teens and became interested in boys. I then lost contact with the Pelletiers, only dropping in on them once in the early 1960s when I was in Montreal to attend a CLC conference. Dena had grown into a beautiful blonde teenager by then, with beaux aplenty and a busy social life of dates and dances. I didn't see much of her during this visit, but was very surprised to feel a twinge of envy and regret when her most recent boyfriend arrived to pick her up.

The turning point came in 1968 when Dena phoned to invite me to the celebration of her parents' 25th wedding anniversary. It was the first time I had ever talked with her on the telephone. She told me later that it was while chatting with me during these festivities that her perception of me, despite the age gap, started to change from that of an old family friend into a pro-spective "boyfriend" and even husband.

It helped, I suppose, that during the previous year I had exercised three times a week at an Ottawa gym and had kept to a strict 1,700-calories-a day diet. It was a regimen that brought my weight down to a trim 170 pounds. I was as fit and healthy as I had ever been. The improvement in my appearance was not consciously undertaken to impress Dena, but it may have been one of the factors that apparently caused her affection for me to blossom into some-thing stronger. Like most women in assessing a man's ardor, she had abso-lutely no doubt by then that I had fallen in love with her. It was equally clear to her, however, that, although the age disparity between us didn't bother her in the least, it had all but extinguished any faint hope I may have had to move beyond friendship to courtship. She realized I would need encouragement.

Over the ensuing year, I received more invitations to visit the Pelletier family, and always Dena was there to talk and socialize with me. Boyfriends were nowhere to be seen. On one such occasion, in the afternoon of a day in late autumn of 1969, she mentioned wistfully that a movie she especially wanted to see — the musical *Oliver!* — was playing at a downtown theatre. Emboldened, I offered to take her to the movie, and to a dinner afterward.

Her face lit up. "Oh, Ed, that would be splendid!" she said. My heart racing, I called a taxi to take us downtown to the theatre on St. Catherine Street.

Dena and I cut our wedding cake at the reception that followed our marriage in Montreal on April 25, 1970.

Later, after the movie, which we both enjoyed and remains our favourite musical, we had dinner at a nearby Italian restaurant. But I was still not convinced that this was a "date," or that Dena considered it to be anything other than a pleasant outing with an old family friend. However, as we were finishing the dessert and the conversation was still about the movie and the Montreal Canadiens, she felt she had to take the initiative.

"Ed," she said, "forgive me for being so blunt, but I've always wondered why you never got married."

I looked into her shining hazel eyes, and shrugged. "It's simple: I never met a woman I could love who could ever love me."

"But what about me?" she asked, taking my breath away.

I blushed. "You were much too young when I was at the marrying age, and now I'm too old for you to marry, even if you wanted to."

Dena gave me a fond but reproving look. "Surely that's for me to decide, Ed," she said, "and I have decided that the age difference between us is immaterial. You're still young enough for us to have a long and happy married life, and of course children."

I was stunned by her confidence and by the affection reflected in her eyes and voice. I gazed at her silently for a full minute, before I could say the words.

"Dena Pelletier," I said hoarsely, "will you do me the very great honour of becoming my wife?"

"I will, I will, with all my heart!" she declared, beaming. I will never forget the brilliance of that smile.

"I'm sorry I don't have an engagement ring to put on your finger," I apologized, "but I never expected that one would come in handy tonight."

Dena laughed. "We can shop for my engagement ring when you come back to Montreal next weekend," she said. "You can put it on my finger then."

We kissed for the first time in the taxi that drove us back to Dena's home, where we broke the news of our betrothal to her parents. They were delighted, and promised to treat us to an engagement party the following weekend. (The cake that Dena's mother baked for that event had just one word enscrolled in chocolate on the top: GOTCHA!)

The night we got engaged, after returning to my apartment in Ottawa, I was in such a state of exhilaration that I was unable to fall asleep. I picked up a pen and pad and, for the first and only time in my life, wrote a short verse. Strangely, I was never stirred to express myself in rhyme before or since. This was what I scribbled on the pad:

> The glacier melted at her touch
>   and set me free,
> But it took her dazzling smile to melt
>   the ice inside of me.

The news of our impending wedlock was greeted with mixed elation, shock, and skepticism by family relatives on both sides. The 20-year age gap was cited as a formidable impediment to a long and happy marriage. Fathering a family in one's forties and expecting to live long enough to raise children and finance their education through university — that was considered an unrealistic prospect by some. So was the ability of an older man to keep his much younger wife satisfied in all the ways that a marriage entails.

To the consternation (and relief) of the skeptics, we have enjoyed a long, compatible, and productive marriage. We have been blessed with two bright, marvelous, talented children — Kevin and Kerri-Anne — who have also been fortunate to find and wed outstanding partners, Gwynneth and Arun. Our lives have been enriched by their love and companionship, and by Kevin and Gwynn's two delightful children, Garrett and Heather. I've been doubly fortunate to share the same reading tastes with Kevin and to share the CCPA's national office in Ottawa with my daughter Kerri, who became the Centre's director of communications.

* * *

It was during the five months of our engagement — between November 1969 and April 1970 — that any lingering doubts I may have had about the viability of our impending married life were swept away. I traveled to Montreal as often as I could to meet with Dena, and we enjoyed more restaurant meals, movies, and even a few hockey games.

At the Pelletier residence, however, when her parents and brothers were home, the only place we could have any privacy was in Dena's bedroom. I was allowed to be in there with her, but parental approval was conditional on leaving the bedroom door ajar at all times. It was the 1960s and early '70s, after all, and the pre-marital proprieties had to be observed.

On one occasion, however, while we were in her bedroom discussing plans for a honeymoon in England and Scotland, Dena suddenly asked me to shut the door.

I was surprised, but could see from her expression that she meant it. So I walked over to the door and, slowly and carefully, closed it.

But when I turned around, I saw she was frowning at me.

"Why did you shut the door?" she asked.

"Because you told me to, of course," I replied, bewildered.

"I certainly did not," she protested. Then understanding dawned on her pretty face, and she burst out laughing.

"Ed, you're going to have to learn some basic French," she giggled. "I didn't ask you to shut the door. What I said to you was 'Je t'adore!'"

And she translated it for me with a kiss.

Since then, I must confess, I haven't added much more French to my vocabulary, but that Gallic term of endearment has gotten a lot of usage.

Still does.

* * *

Looking back, I can better understand that the personal and gender-relation setbacks I sustained as a young man were in fact fortuitous — that they opened the door to a more lively, productive, and satisfying future than I would otherwise have experienced.

I joke sometimes that I have had the best of both worlds: two-and-a-half decades of safe, independent, ostensibly carefree bachelorhood, the next forty-plus in the more challenging but much more gratifying bliss of wedlock and parenthood.

Chapter 19

The Bank of Canada

ONE OF MY STRANGEST experiences was serving on the board of directors of the Bank of Canada for three years, from 1979 to 1982. I was an unlikely appointee to the Bank's board, nearly all of whose directors are loyal supporters of the political party that forms the government. The exception was to have one director nominally representing organized labour. Bill Dodge, then secretary-treasurer of the CLC, was the first of these non-political board members, and I followed him.

John Munro, who was then Minister of Labour in the Trudeau government, asked me to take the director's post vacated by Bill Dodge.

I was not at first disposed to accept this appointment. "I don't know anything about banking or financial matters," I reminded Munro. "I doubt if I can contribute anything to the Bank's policies, other than disagree with them."

"But it will be fun to have another dissident like Bill Dodge in the Bank of Canada boardroom," Munro said. "It will be like putting the cat among the pigeons."

"No, John," I said, "It will be like putting the pigeon among the cats." And that's basically what it turned out to be. I agreed to take the post knowing I could never change the Bank's fixation with controlling inflation or its underlying belief that inflation was mainly caused by "excessive" wage increases. But I thought the experience would be interesting, even enlightening, and it was.

Before my first board meeting, I read as much as I could about the Bank of Canada's origin, history, and operations. Like most Canadians, I knew very little about this mysterious and secretive institution. I was vaguely aware that

166   Ed Finn

the central bank set interest rates and had something to do with the value of the dollar, but not much else.

My ignorance was shared by the vast majority of Canadians, which was regrettable, because no other non-government agency exerts more influence on the economy — or on our daily lives. Its decisions — which are increasingly made by one man, the governor — can plunge the whole economy into recession, drive thousands of firms into bankruptcy, and destroy hundreds of thousands of jobs. And that's what happened in the early 1980s, and again in the early 1990s.

When the Bank of Canada was founded in the 1930s, it was intended to be (and was even called) "the People's Bank," because its primary purpose was to help alleviate the widespread unemployment, poverty, and misery of the Great Depression. Indeed, its mandate called for it to be just as concerned about unemployment as it would be about prices, production, and inflation.

In 1961, however, this mandate was radically changed by an open clash between Bank of Canada Governor James Coyne and the Conservative government of John Diefenbaker. Coyne openly defied Diefenbaker by making speech after speech claiming that Canada was living beyond its means and declaring that the Bank's top priority should be to battle inflation, even at the expense of higher unemployment and higher interest rates.

Dief was not amused. He used his majority in the House of Commons to pass a bill declaring the Bank governor's position "vacant," essentially firing Coyne. But that was the last time a Bank of Canada governor lost a contest with the elected politicians. Ironically, Coyne's ouster had the unintended effect of establishing the Bank's autonomy, not its subservience to government direction.

This happened when Coyne's successor, Louis Rasminsky, persuaded the government to amend the Bank of Canada Act to provide that, in the event of a dispute over monetary policy, a directive would be sent to the governor ordering him to comply with the government's wishes. His only alternative then would be to resign.

Instead of making the Bank more accountable, however, it gave the governor even more independence. Why? Because the threat of a governor's forced resignation, inciting the wrath of the financial markets and possibly precipitating a foreign exchange crisis, had the effect of deterring all successive governments from repeating Diefenbaker's interference with Bank behaviour. None has since dared to issue such a directive, even supposing they wanted to do so.

Coyne's firing thus further empowered the Bank to take independent decisions on monetary policy, even if the government disagreed with them. It was a sweeping expansion of the role of a central bank that was soon emulated by other central banks around the world, making them rivals, not servants, of ruling governments on financial and even broad economic matters.

The result was to transform "the People's Bank" to "the Governor's Bank," and beyond that to "the Private Banks' Bank," an institution that since the 1960s has operated outside the democratic system, virtually removed from any effective government influence. The Governor of the Bank of Canada, unelected, secure with a seven-year appointment, unilaterally controls the levers of monetary policy, deciding how high interest rates will be and how much our dollar will be worth.

This awesome power over the economy wielded by one man can be devastating if he (so far never she) becomes obsessed with a single objective that he feels must be pursued at all costs. In the case of Gerald Bouey, who was the Bank's governor while I was on the board of directors in the early 1980s, that objective — it could even be called a *jihad* — was to "wrestle inflation to the ground." Price stability was to be the Bank's all-consuming preoccupation, even if it meant pushing the economy deeply into recession and abandoning the rest of the Bank's mandate to maintain jobs and production.

Inflation soared to double-digit levels, even reaching as high as 17% at one point despite (if not because of) the Bank's anti-inflation crusade. Interest rates ballooned above 20%, and unemployment soared to 12.8%, the highest since the Great Depression. In their 1995 book about the Bank of Canada, *Where The Buck Stops*, business journalists Michael Babad and Catherine Mulroney described the ensuing period as "a season of despair, of massive layoffs and plant shutdowns, of hundreds of thousands of people being thrown out of work, of Canadians being forced to simply walk away from their homes because they could not pay the indecently steep mortgage rates."

This was the time when I was on the Bank's board of directors, the proverbial skunk at the anti-inflation (and consequently anti-labour) picnic. I'm restrained by having signed the Official Secrets Act from divulging details of the Bank meetings I attended, except to say that they were excruciatingly difficult to sit through. Votes were seldom taken, but if they had been, they would be 10 to 1, 11 to 1, 12 to 1, depending on how many directors showed up for the meetings.

The interesting thing about my being on the Board at that time was that I was also still writing my *Toronto Star* column, and in that column I would take occasional pot-shots at the Bank. I was careful not to make use of any of the inside information I was privy to as a director, but I was able to take issue with the Bank's public policies, particularly its incessant ratcheting-up of interest rates and putting most of the blame for inflation on "exorbitant" union-negotiated wage increases .

I was also getting flak myself from my union pals.

"What in blazes are you doing on the board of the Bank of Canada?" they would angrily demand. I would assure them I was doing my best to keep interest rates from rising, and (tongue in cheek) that, if I hadn't been on the Bank's board, interest rates would have shot up to 30% instead of "just" 20%; but for some reason they didn't believe me.

My fellow directors, of course, were even more upset by my *Star* columns than my labour associates were with my inability to change Board decisions. In fact, most of the other directors were furious. Eventually I came to a Board meeting at which they tabled a motion to have me kicked off the board. I might have voted for that motion myself if it had come to a vote, but Governor Bouey was a lot smarter than the other people around the table.

He told them it would be neither prudent nor justified to terminate my director's status prematurely just because I was disagreeing, in public and in print, with Bank policy. "Mr. Finn is as free to express dissenting opinions in his *Toronto Star* column as he is here at our board meetings," he told the other directors. "He is simply exercising his freedom of speech, and in doing so has scrupulously refrained from using information that is not publicly available."

Several directors disagreed, arguing that my status as a Bank director should in itself be sufficient to deter me from venting my dissatisfaction with Bank policy in the largest circulation newspaper in the country.

"And what do you think the result of his having that platform would be if we threw him off the board before his term expires?" Bouey retorted. "I put it to you that it would make him a martyr and cause more trouble for the Bank than would allowing him to stay and serve out his term."

The directors reluctantly bowed to Bouey's argument against turfing me out, and so I stayed around for another year or so. I failed to convince the

Bank of Canada to return to its intended role as the People's Bank instead of "the Private Bankers' Bank," but I gained some invaluable insights into the workings of the nation's financial inner sanctum.

I'll close these memories of my stint with the board of the central bank by quoting from the conclusion of *Where the Buck Stops*:

> "The Bank of Canada has become an institution that is largely beyond our control, a power unto itself. It is secretive, aloof, and at times has treated us with disdain. We did not consciously give the Bank of Canada this ultimate power — it somehow grabbed it, and various governments participated either actively or passively. Whether a central bank governor likes it or not, we live in a democracy, and this institution's unbridled power must somehow be brought into line."

These words were written in the mid-1990s, and no government since then has mustered the courage to challenge the Bank of Canada or try to bring its operations back under parliamentary control. We no longer live in a genuine democracy, so the chance of democratizing the Bank has become even more remote. One thing is certain: the political pressure needed to change "the Private Bankers' Bank" back to the "People's Bank" will never be mounted unless the 95% of the people now unaware of the Bank's intended role and purpose become enlightened.

The economic costs of poverty

The main arguments raised for reducing the appallingly high rate of childhood poverty in Canada have mostly focused on its social costs — on the misery and deprivation inflicted on our youngest and most vulnerable citizens.

This is indeed the most compelling reason for ending the impoverishment now blighting the lives of one in every eight children in Canada. The moral case for lifting them out of poverty is so strong that it should have impelled our political and business leaders to take the necessary remedial action long ago. Their continued indifference to this moral outrage suggests that appeals to their conscience are never likely to work.

But there's a powerful anti-child-poverty case to be made on economic grounds, too. Politicians and CEOs may be heartless, but any proposed action that would boost the GDP should appeal to their business-first bias. At least, it should unless they lack brains as well as hearts.

It shouldn't take all that much intelligence, surely, to realize that people mired in poverty when young are likely when grown up to engage in criminal activities, to be less skilled and productive workers, and to be ill more often and thus require more costly health care treatment.

The Center for American Progress (CAP), a progressive think-tank in Washington, recently did a study on the economic costs of child poverty in the United States. Their researchers' estimated figures are staggering. They calculated that Americans who were poor as children — and there are now 40 million of them — are much more likely than other citizens to commit crimes, to need more health care, and to be less productive in the workforce.

One CAP researcher, Harry J. Holzer, described the results of their study to a House Ways and Means Committee hearing last year. *He told the stunned Congressmen that the costs to the U.S. in crime, health care, and reduced productivity associated with childhood poverty amount to an estimated $500 billion a year.* This breaks down to about $170 billion a year in increased crime, $160 billion in increased health care costs, and another $170 billion in decreased productivity.

We have to be careful about applying these U.S. statistics to Canada. We can't just make a demographic projection and assume that, because our population is one-tenth that of the U.S., the overall economic cost of child poverty in this country amounts to one-tenth the U.S. figure, or about $50 billion a year. It could be less, it could be more. On the one hand, there may be a lesser propensity for poor kids in Canada to become criminals when they grow up, but on the other hand, because of our universal public health care system, the per-capita costs of treating the sickness-prone poor in Canada is probably higher.

Even if the economic costs of child poverty in this country were as "low" as $40 billion, that's still an awful lot of money being wasted — billions spent, in effect, to *maintain* a scandalously high child poverty rate rather than reduce or eliminate it.

Are our politicians and CEOs really this stupid? Can't they see that investing $40 billion a year in poverty reduction would save the same amount or more in crime, health care, and low-productivity costs? The money is being spent (mis-spent), anyway, so why not divert it into a constructive channel? It would fund an effective campaign to give every Canadian child a decent upbringing — free from poverty and hunger, free to get the best possible education, free to live in adequate comfort and security.

How many break-ins and robberies in Canada are committed from desperation by people deprived of the legitimate means of earning money? How many violent crimes are committed by people so embittered by a poverty-stricken youth that they vent their rage in anti-social behaviour? Such crimes, of course, are inexcusable, but they could also be preventable. If we provided everyone with a safe, secure, and happy childhood, we'd have a much safer and secure society.

The same rationale applies to health care and incomes. Poor people tend to have poor health because they're denied proper nutrition, hygiene, and preventive care as children. Poor kids are also denied the physical and mental (and emotional) potential to acquire the best education, and so many of them end up with low-waged, dead-end jobs — or no jobs at all.

A recent UNICEF report ranked Canada in a dismal 21st place among 26 rich nations in its rate of child poverty. It's shameful, it's unpardonable — and it's as much an economic as a moral disgrace because the financial means to end child poverty in this country is so readily available.

The specific measures to achieve this goal would include a national child care program to allow poor parents to get waged work; big improvements in welfare rates and other subsidies; more and better low-cost housing; lower tax rates on the working poor; greater access to job training; higher minimum wages; and more unionization and collective bargaining.

And if the moral imperative for taking these initiatives is not enough to persuade the skinflints in our boardrooms and legislatures, the enormous economic benefits certainly should be.

Chapter 20

A decade with CUPE

THE DAY AFTER I was fired from my PR post with the CBRT & GW (along with four other senior staff members) for refusing to scab on the union's locked-out clerical workers, the story of our dismissal broke in the local papers. CBRT President Don Nicholson blamed me for leaking his purge of the senior staff, claiming he might have "reconsidered" firing us if it were not for the quick media outburst. But I hadn't said a word to any journalist, and neither had any of the other fired staff members. We later learned our dismissals had been leaked to the media by one of the locked-out secretaries.

In any event, I had a phone call the next day from Eddie McAllister, executive assistant to Grace Hartman, president of the Canadian Union of Public Employees. He was shocked to learn of Nicholson's harsh reaction to our refusal to do any work normally performed by the locked-out clerical staff.

After discussing the likely fallout from this unprecedented breach of labour principles by union leaders, Eddie asked me if I had any plans for finding another job.

"I'm still trying to recover from the shock," I told him, "but no doubt I'll have to explore other employment prospects pretty soon. Of course CUPE would be my number one choice, but NUPGE or PSAC might find a spot for me if there's no opening in your PR department. I was going to call Fred [Tabachnick] in a few days."

After working with Fred at the CBRT in the early '70s, and knowing how closely we agreed on how best to communicate in and for the labour movement, I was hoping to renew our working relationship. The only difference was that our roles would be reversed, since Fred had become director of

CUPE's PR department after Norm Simon left. That would be no problem, of course, because we both preferred a teamwork approach rather than the top-down, boss-subordinate system.

"Fred's away on vacation right now," Eddie said, "but I'm sure he'll be delighted to have you join his department team. I've already talked with Grace, and she's keen to have you working with CUPE, too."

This was comforting to know, but not surprising. In my *Toronto Star* column, I had often had occasion to write favourably about Grace Hartman, who had an outstanding 30-year career as a labour activist. A long-time fighter for women's rights and a pioneer in seeking pay equity for female workers, Grace had risen from carpet weaver to clerk typist to union officer with a CUPE local in Toronto. In 1975, she was elected national president of CUPE, becoming the first woman to serve as the top officer of a Canadian national union.

My highest praise for Grace came in a column I had penned just a few months earlier in 1981, when she was sentenced to a month in jail for defying a court order to end a strike by Ontario's non-medical hospital workers: orderlies, cleaners, janitors, clerical and other support staff. The strike should not have been illegal, but was ruled to be because the Ontario government had deprived the province's hospital workers of this fundamental union right. The hospital boards and the government ruthlessly exploited CUPE's enforced bargaining impotence to grossly underpay the workers and deny them the levels of benefits and working conditions they deserved.

This callous mistreatment stoked the employees' anger and frustration to the point where they rejected the hospitals' paltry contract offer by an over-whelming 91% vote. Grace and other CUPE leaders then really had no other option but to lead a province-wide walkout, even knowing it was illegal and would be mercilessly crushed.

As it turned out, the jailing of a prominent female union president aroused a great deal of resentment among the citizens of Ontario. The growing public antipathy to the government's blatant mistreatment of the hospital workers was probably a key factor in the subsequent arbitration ruling on the dispute. The imposed settlement produced a significantly better contract than had come from previous arbitrators. It still fell far short of the improved pay and benefit levels the employees deserved, but it made the strike and the jailing of the union's leaders a worthwhile endeavour.

This caricature of me by "LAF" from the Canadian Cartooning Company shows me holding a copy of the *CUPE Facts* and wearing a Montreal Expos button. It was presented to me during a dinner held on the occasion of my retirement from CUPE in 1991.

As for Grace, then 63, she came out of her prison cell even more honoured and acclaimed than ever within the labour movement. I looked forward to working for the union she now headed, and also to joining the top-notch team of communicators Fred had put together. There were four of them at the time — Mark Belanger, Dennis McGann, Ron Verzuh, and Bozica ("Biz") Costigliola — but later in the 1980s they were joined by several other first-rate communicators, including Tracey Morey, Diana Rienstra, Doreen Mayer, Sandra Sorensen, and Dave Blaikie.

One of my first assignments, after joining this gifted group, was to take over editorship of *The Facts*, CUPE's research-oriented monthly journal. This involved working closely with the union's Research Department headed by Gil Levine. Gil was no stranger to me, since we had co-operated in helping mobilize the anti-Vietnam War movement in Ottawa and working with other national unionists in the struggle for trade union autonomy. Like Fred, Gil had also assembled a superb team in his department, arguably the best and most talented group of research specialists in the labour movement. They included assistant director Larry Katz, John Calvert, Richard Balnis, Tony Wohlfarth, Jane Stinson, and Randy Sykes.

It was a pleasure working with these facts-and-figures experts, who were also proficient writers. They were busy with their own research projects, of course, as well as contributing to *The Facts*, so they couldn't always meet the copy deadlines I set for them. No matter. I filled in with my own articles or with pieces from my PR colleagues, and so every issue went to the printers on time.

It's difficult to reminisce about this CUPE research journal without seeming to boast; but I was far from alone in giving it high marks for the quality of the "facts," analysis, and commentaries it presented every month. *The CUPE Facts* became so admired and sought after in the labour movement that we were soon sending more copies to other unions than we were distributing within CUPE.

One of the highlights of my 10 years editing *The Facts* was a special issue we published early in 1988: *The Facts on Free Trade*. It was CUPE's contribution to the national debate then raging over the free trade deal the Conservative government of Brian Mulroney was negotiating with the Ronald Reagan administration in the United States. What was missing from the debate was a comprehensive analysis of the wording of this trade deal, showing how it threatened Canada's social programs, culture, and sovereignty.

I co-edited this 130-page special *CUPE Facts* with John Calvert and Duncan Cameron, a professor of political science at the University of Ottawa who later served as president of the Canadian Centre for Policy Alternatives (CCPA). The authors of the articles and essays in this issue were all highly knowledge-able and informed. Not all were authorities on international trade, but they did know how damaging this agreement would be in their respective fields.

They included Margaret Attwood, Eric Kierans, Stephen Clarkson, Hugh Mackenzie, Rick Salutin, Ian Scott, Bob White, Tony Clarke, Shirley Carr, and John Warnock. So impressive was this collection of incisive and informative critiques of this first U.S.-Canada trade deal that it was broadly considered to deserve a wider readership. A month later, it was converted into a book — *The Facts on Free Trade* — published by James Lorimer & Company.

I remained editor of *The CUPE Facts* until I left CUPE in 1991 at the man-datory retirement age of 65. Other PR and research staff took on the editorial role for a while, but for some reason this important research journal stopped being published soon afterward.

Grace Hartman reached her retirement age in 1983, stepping down from her position as president at that year's national convention in Toronto. One way Fred and I paid tribute to her splendid record of leadership was to have a weekly opinion column by her published in the *Globe & Mail* during the six months prior to her farewell at the convention. I ghost-wrote these columns (for which we had to pay *The Globe* the equivalent of advertising space). This arrangement occasionally caused Grace some embarrassment. She did a lot of traveling, so it wasn't always easy to let her know what she would be writ-ing about in her current weekly column. This was well before the advent of emails or any other kind of electronic messaging — even before the invention of the fax machine — so the only way to reach someone quickly in another part of the country was by telephone. With cellphones also far in the future, Grace had to be somewhere near a regular phone, and once in a while, if she was on a long trip in a plane or bus, she was unreachable.

When she arrived at a hotel and found she had a dozen calls waiting from reporters eager to ask her to elaborate on her latest column in the *Globe* that morning, her frantic phone calls to me or Fred were memorable, to say the least.

But Grace had a great sense of humour. We all got a chuckle out of such unavoidable failures by communicators to communicate, when we got together later.

I was sorry that I had only a year-and-a-half working for Grace. She was one of the best union leaders I had the good fortune to serve under. The same could be said for the other national officer at the time, secretary-treasurer Kealey Cummings. They shared one of the finest attributes of good leadership: trusting the staff to perform their duties effectively without undue supervision, surveillance, or interference. Grace and Kealey operated on the assumption that the qualified people they had hired as communicators, researchers, educators, and other specialists didn't need a Big Brother (or Big Sister) continually checking on them, or second-guessing them.

This trusting, hands-off approach to leadership pays off in the highest levels of staff morale and productivity. Grace and Kealey knew we always had the best interests of the union at heart. They gave us general guidelines occasionally, of course, but also sought and heeded our ideas and suggestions. It was the ideal relationship between elected officers and their aides. Unfortunately, not all union leaders are so wise and considerate in dealing with their staff.

* * *

I had plenty of other writing and editorial work to do during my decade with CUPE, often in collaboration with Fred or other associates in the department. Looking back, I marvel at the sheer volume and variety of work that came from just a half dozen of us. We turned out two other regular publications besides *The Facts*: a monthly tabloid, *The Leader*, later transformed into a weekly CUPE news bulletin; and a quarterly magazine, *The Public Employee*. We also had to write pamphlets, posters, and radio spots for national or provincial campaigns. We wrote speeches for the national officers. We put out copious news releases. We offered and taught at "schools" for local members wanting to learn how to become better writers and newsletter editors. We frequently had to travel around the country when locals or regional divisions in trouble asked for PR help. Once in a while, we wrote longer booklets on urgent developments, such as free trade, cuts to Medicare, and anti-labour legislation.

I tended to write my booklets as series of "10" — *Ten Labour Myths, Ten Medicare Myths, Ten Public Sector Myths*. For some reason, this format seemed to make the booklets more readable and popular.

CUPE during the 1980s was steadily increasing in size and influence on its way to becoming the largest public sector union in the country — indeed, the largest Canadian union, period. This rapid growth strained the union's resources and put pressure on all the staff, both at the national office and in the field. Adding to this pressure was CUPE's super-democratic structure, which gave the locals more autonomy than those of most other unions.

It was not uncommon in those days, for example, for Fred to get a phone call from a local anywhere in the country that went something like this:

"Hey, Fred, our local went out on strike yesterday and we're getting a lot of flak from the local press. Could you please send one of your staff here right away to help with the bad public image we're getting."

Fred had to make an effort to stifle his frustration. In vain, he had been trying for some time to explain to the locals — and to the staff reps assigned to service the locals — that the best time for pro-union PR was *before* going on strike, not afterward. Post-strike PR was almost always swept away by public and press reaction to the walkout. Too late then to sell the notion that the workers had good, solid reasons for hitting the bricks.

Fred and I had tried to persuade the union's National Executive Board to make it a condition for receiving strike pay that a local had to ask for PR services *before* going out, not afterward. But that, apparently, was considered a politically unpopular infringement on local autonomy.

As the '80s wore on, all of us in the communications department, at various times, were faced with the onerous task of trying to make a local look good after it had interrupted public services. But once in a while, a local did call us in before walking out, providing at least a fighting chance of averting a strike.

One such occasion I remember well involved Local 1068 which included the garbage collectors in Kentville, Nova Scotia. The town council had announced it was going to turn over the garbage collection to a private contractor, and the workers were furious. Their collective agreement had expired, they were in a legal position to strike, and they were champing at the bit. Fortunately, the local president, whose name escapes me, was able to persuade them not to do anything hasty until he called the national office for PR help.

Fred was elated to get such a pre-strike request and asked me to get down to Kentville as fast as I could. As soon as I arrived, the next day, I met with the workers and staff rep, and was filled in on the details of the town council's decision to privatize their jobs. I learned two very interesting things:

- First, the council had contracted out the garbage collection once before, about 15 years earlier, and it lasted only seven months before being brought back as a public service.
- Second, the town's garbage dump was located near an army base on land that was owned by the military and leased to the town council — on condition that garbage from the dump be kept from blowing onto the base.

Upon further discussion with the workers, I was told that the private firm that was given the contract previously had set an unpopular two-bag limit on collections per household, and was often late and sloppy in its pickups.

The contractor also failed to keep the dump "tidy" and free from blowing debris, exposing the town council to a threatened cancellation of its lease by the army.

This was all the information I needed to launch a strong "keep-the-garbage-collection-public" campaign. In leaflets, newspaper ads, radio blurbs, and press conferences, I reminded citizens of the unpleasant consequences of the previous privatization exercise. "The same problems with your garbage collection are bound to be repeated," I warned. "What private firm is going to be able to afford the cost of picking up an unlimited amount of garbage and keeping a couple of its employees permanently at the dump to satisfy the army's clean-dump conditions?"

I also warned any prospective firm planning to bid on the garbage contract not to count on lowering its labour costs by paying its collectors less than the unionized workers were getting.

"One of CUPE's top priorities," I announced, "if the town council goes ahead with this misguided decision, will be to organize the contractor's employees. And once they become CUPE members — and they will — we'll demand they be provided with the same level of pay and benefits that the members of our Local 1068 are now getting. There will be no profit gained from exploiting cheap labour."

This PR campaign had to be crammed into the eight days that remained before the council's deadline for submitting bids.

The morning after this deadline, the mayor went to the post office and opened the box into which the bids were to have been placed. When he came back out of the post office, the press and radio reporters were waiting.

He waved his empty hands at them, shrugging. "There wasn't a single bid made for our garbage collection contract," he reported. "So I suppose the council has no alternative but to continue having this service provided by the municipal workers we employ for that work."

The workers, who had also gathered around the post office, burst into loud applause, and some of them gave me hugs and back-pats of gratitude.

"It's you who deserve the credit," I told them. "You called the national union for PR help when there was still time left to mount a PR campaign to save your jobs."

I don't mean to imply that every such pre-emptive PR effort will succeed. But it certainly has a much better chance of succeeding than PR that's delayed till after a strike has started.

* * *

This is not to imply, either, that post-strike PR was always futile. Sometimes a strategy could still be devised that would lead to a good if belated settlement. One such occasion for me came when the "inside" employees of the municipality of North Sydney (the clerical staff in Local 933) walked out after contract talks with the city council collapsed.

This was in the early summer of 1988, but the strike had dragged on past Labour Day by the time I was sent to meet with Local president Kevin MacNeil and servicing rep Gerald Yetman. City officials apparently felt no pressure to resume negotiations. This was the typical stalling tactic of municipal governments when their clerical workers walked out. The more important paper work could be taken over by management personnel, and the less important delayed until the "paper-pushers" were starved into submission.

This belief that clerical workers couldn't maintain a strike and would eventually be forced to return to work on the council's terms was widely held by municipalities across the country. And unfortunately it was usually a safe assumption. They kept their wage and benefit contract offers flagrantly low, relying on the employees to cave in after a few months at most. By that time, the city would have saved enough in unpaid wages to cover the relatively modest costs of the eventual settlement.

Brothers MacNeil and Yetman, however, showed no signs of despair when I met with them, nor did the 36 members — most of them women — on the picket lines around city hall. Their spirits were still high, their resolve unshaken. The financial pinch had not yet started to hurt.

But it would in another few weeks, if the strike lasted that long. CUPE's strike pay of $100 a week at the time, even though supplemented from the

Local's own financial savings, wouldn't cover the members' living expenses much longer.

After giving the situation some thought, a possible way of further supplementing the strike pay occurred to me. It was to persuade some of the other 122 CUPE locals in Nova Scotia that were not on strike at the time to "adopt a Local 933 striker." Gerald and Kevin were all for it, so we phoned the president of CUPE's Nova Scotia Division in Halifax. He, too, was enthused about the "adopt a striker" idea, and agreed to get the project going as soon as possible.

And that's how it worked out. Many of the province's other CUPE locals quickly agreed to "adopt" a Local 933 striker. With this relief from financial shortfall, the clerical workers had no fear of a prolonged strike. They were now getting as much income as they had on the job and didn't care if they had to spend the rest of the fall season on the lawn in front of City Hall.

In fact, it was the city councillors who then caved in. When they realized that the clerical employees could never be starved into submission, they meekly asked that contract talks be resumed. The new collective agreement was one of the best the local had ever managed to gain.

I'm not sure if this strategy for averting strike failures was ever repeated anywhere else in Canada. Maybe not. Voluntary contributions have certainly been made by unions to help workers in other unions during extended strikes, but rarely, to my knowledge, on an "adopt-a-striker" basis.

While I was writing my *Toronto Star* column, one of my more quixotic campaigns was for the creation of a huge national strike fund amassed from the merger of the strike funds of all the major unions. It never materialized, of course, for several reasons having to do with the difficulties of administering such a large fund and amending the constitutions and bylaws of some unions; but I always thought (still do) that such obstacles could have been overcome if union leaders had made a concerted effort. *(My One Big Strike Fund idea is expounded in more detail in Chapter 14.)*

* * *

Not all the assignments of CUPE communicators involved doing PR for strikes. We did the planning and promotion for many general campaigns, at both the national and regional levels. The battles against free trade, wage controls, and excessively high interest rates, for example, taxed the department's time and talents. So did pro-active campaigns for improved health care, child care, and public pensions.

Most days, when we arrived for work at the CUPE national office on Florence Street in Ottawa, we didn't know what calls for our services we'd be getting, or from where in the country they'd be coming.

One morning in the late summer of 1983, Fred intercepted me before I'd reached my desk.

"I just had a call from Tom Mayo in Newfoundland, the rep who services the outside workers at Mount Pearl in Local 2099," he told me. "He needs PR help and he specifically asked for you. I think there's time for you to catch the Air Canada flight to St. John's this afternoon."

I wasn't surprised to get this assignment. As an expatriate Newfoundlander, I was dispatched there quite often.

"What's up, Fred?" I asked. "They haven't gone out on strike, have they?"

"No, believe it or not, they've been locked out for the past few weeks."

I was stunned. CUPE had more than 500 locals across the country, so strikes were not uncommon. But lockouts certainly were. They were so rare that I wasn't aware of any having occurred anywhere since I came to CUPE. Municipal councillors knew how unpopular they would become if they, not the union, were the ones who cut off public services.

So I was puzzled. "Why is the Local asking for me? Why on Earth do they need PR? Surely it's the city, not the union, that's getting all the flak in this dispute."

Fred shook his head. "That's the problem. Most citizens of Mount Pearl, like most people everywhere, don't distinguish between a strike and a lockout. All they can see is that their garbage is not being picked up or their civic parks and pools kept open, so they're blaming the workers more than management. And the local papers aren't helping, either. They do call the dispute a lockout, but just show pictures of the workers picketing City Hall, and the fact that their signs say they're locked out doesn't seem to register."

"Okay, Fred, I'll catch the next plane," I told him, "but I won't be there very long."

"I know you won't," he grinned.

I was actually there and back in four days. When I met Tom Mayo after I got off the plane, I asked him why the outside workers were all walking around with "Locked Out" picket signs.

The question puzzled him. "What else can they do?" he asked, not surprisingly. It was standard practice in any work stoppage to picket the employer's premises, and it was apparently thought to be just as appropriate during a lockout as it would be during a strike. I urged Tom and the locals' officers to reconsider.

"Picketing tends to blur the distinction between a strike and a lockout," I reminded them. "It shows workers walking around with signs instead of providing the essential public services that citizens are being denied, while the city councillors who are actually responsible are nowhere to be seen."

"So what do we do instead of picketing?" Tom wondered.

"The workers simply go back to work," I said. "Or try to. They never wanted to stop working, anyway, so let's have them show up every morning at their usual workplaces and force city council to physically prevent them from entering and going back to work. Then have the newspaper photographers on hand to expose the councillors as the real "strikers" — as the ones who are in fact interrupting the services citizens are paying their taxes for."

It actually took only a few days for this tactic to bring the lockout to an end. After photos of employees being forcibly barred from resuming their work were featured on the front pages of the *Evening Telegram*, the councillors were bombarded with angry phone calls and personal rebukes. Humiliated and embarrassed, they allowed civic operations to be resumed and reopened contract negotiations. The settlement that was reached a few weeks later was one the members of Local 2099 were glad to accept.

The Mount Pearl lockout debacle made headlines all over the country. It was a salutary lesson for Canadian municipalities, very few of whom subsequently made the same strategic blunder.

What they did instead was to devise a much more fiendish and effective strategy that continues to bedevil union leaders, negotiators, and rank-and-file members to this day. Let's call it "takeaway" bargaining. It throws traditional union-management negotiations into reverse. Instead of employers resisting union demands for pay and benefit improvements, the unions find themselves resisting employers' demands for pay and benefit *reductions*.

Labour leaders have had trouble adjusting to such management takeaway tactics — so much so that they have sometimes been provoked into costly, prolonged, and futile strikes.

Fred and I analyzed this devious managerial twist in collective bargaining when it first emerged in the late 1980s. We realized that CUPE and other public sector unions were having trouble coping with it.

"I think it's because union leaders and negotiators have locked themselves into the simple either-or style of bargaining," Fred mused. "It's either reach a settlement or go on strike."

"Exactly," I said. "And, because they can't agree to employers' demands for concessions, the only alternative they see is to strike."

"Even though a strike under those circumstances can accomplish little or nothing," said Fred. "What's the objective? To compel the employer to take away the takeaways? To reduce the extent of the concessions? It certainly won't be to *improve* wages or benefits because the main issue in dispute has become the *employer's* contract proposals for cuts, not the union's proposals for improvements."

Fred and I were convinced that a strike was the worst possible response to a management demand that pay and benefit levels already in a contract be reduced. The best response, we reasoned, was in effect to do nothing except reject such concessions and keep members on the job.

After all, an employer can't unilaterally change any clause in a collective agreement that has already been signed. All such agreed-upon clauses continue in force — *even after the term of a contract has expired* — until a new agreement has been negotiated and ratified by the workers in the bargaining unit.

Granted, working under such a contract means working without any new gains in pay or benefits — but it also means working without any of the *cuts* in pay or benefits the employer is demanding. How long this stalemate lasts, of course, will depend on how impatient the employer becomes with being denied the concessions he's seeking. Will he be provoked into a lockout? Will he finally give up on takeaway demands? Whatever the outcome, the union can be fairly sure it won't lead to *worse* working conditions for the affected members.

The same concessions-free contract can't be expected, however, if the union goes on strike. A strike benefits only employers by lowering their payroll costs, while harming the members with lost wages and the public with lost services. Also lost is the union's opportunity to enlist public sympathy because, once a strike begins, both affected citizens and the media become preoccupied with its impacts and when it will be ended and services resumed.

A strike also effectively terminates the existing agreement and makes the new one vulnerable to management's axe. The likelihood of the eventual settlement leading to gains instead of losses — especially if the strike is a long one — is remote. The best result is probably to maintain the levels of pay and benefits that were in the previous contract — the same outcome that could have been achieved *without* a strike.

After giving this matter a lot of thought, Fred and I collaborated in writing a paper on takeaway bargaining in the public sector that covered every conceivable form this kind of takeaway-driven negotiations could take. Our paper offered detailed suggestions for a union's best response when confronted with any of the possible variations in managerial concession demands. We also outlined the appropriate kind of public relations strategy for each situation, including wage and benefit freezes imposed by federal or provincial government legislation.

Of course, our first and most important piece of advice was: *whatever you do, don't go on strike over takeaways!*

Here are a few pertinent excerpts from our paper:

Some public sector employers feel safe putting the most outrageous takeaway demands on the bargaining table. Why? Because they believe the only response they'll get from the union is a strike threat.

Now, the right to strike is and must remain a cornerstone of free trade unionism; but a strike is not always the best tactic to adopt these days, and certainly not a good response to concession demands. It could mean falling into a trap and being forced to play on the employer's turf.

It's true that employers won't be swayed by logic or reason alone, unless those arguments are backed up by some display of power. But union power in the Information Age doesn't necessarily mean the power to withdraw members' labour. Power can now be exercised through thoughtful strategic planning and controlled tactical moves, especially the development of an effective public education and informational campaign.

Have you made sure your fellow citizens understand and appreciate the value of your services? Have you maintained strong ties with community groups? Do you have good relations with local journalists who can be relied on to fairly report your side of any dispute with employers? The more goodwill, trust, and understanding you can generate in your community, the better your chances of withstanding takeaway demands. Why? Because public employees need to have a good measure of public support and sympathy in any struggle with the politicians who have been elected to "protect the public interest."

Getting the public "on-side" doesn't guarantee victory; but failing to do so almost surely guarantees defeat.

That paper — which we titled "Concession Demands" — was written nearly 25 years ago, and was sent to union leaders for their consideration. It was ignored and never circulated to field staff or negotiators. Perhaps it was thought that such detailed collective bargaining guidelines, coming from a couple of staff scribblers, were not even worth looking at, let alone following. We were probably considered presumptuous for even venturing so far into a realm that was the purview of elected leaders and specialized staff negotiators.

Fred and I recently dug up and reviewed the text of our paper on takeaway bargaining, and found that it has lost none of its relevance and value. If we were writing it today — especially after the disastrous outcomes of strikes over takeaway disputes that have occurred in the past few decades — we would change hardly a word of it.

Union officers and staff who would like to read our "Fighting Concessions" paper may obtain copies from either Fred or me. I can be reached by phone at 613-731-9179 or by email at finn3691@rogers.com; Fred by phone at 613-828-9817 or by email at fredtab@rogers.com.

How many members of ATSU does it take to change a light-bulb?

During my decade in CUPE's Public Relations Department (later properly re-named the Communications Department), I also served for a few years as president of the Administrative and Technical Staff Union (ATSU).

In that capacity, one of my duties was to deliver a speech at ATSU's annual pre-Christmas party. The following excerpt from one of those speeches takes the form of a "light-bulb" joke, which at the time was even more popular that the "knock-knock" joke.

* * *

How many members of ATSU does it take to change a light-bulb? The short answer is "all of us," and the long answer I'm going to provide explains why.

Here's what would happen in the event that a light-bulb burned out on the third floor of the National Office (then at 21 Florence Street).

First, the Accounting Department is asked to check the cash-flow to see if we can afford to replace it. When they say, "No, we can't," the EAs are all appointed as a task force to ascertain if the necessary cash can be taken out of the Defence Fund. Of course, since everything else is considered a legitimate demand on the Defence Fund, they conclude that buying a light-bulb would be, too.

Their decision then gets processed through the bureaucracy and eventually a memo is issued authorizing the purchase, signed by both National Officers with copies to all NEB members and national and regional directors.

The memo is sent to the Technology Office, because a light-bulb is, after all, a piece of technological equipment and therefore must come under this department's purview. At least the purchasing of it.

But before anything else is done, the Research Department is assigned to do a series of studies aimed at testing the relative merits of the various brands of light-bulbs. They're also asked to study the feasibility of switching from a 150-watt bulb to a 100- or even a 60-watter in the interest of fiscal restraint. And this keeps all the staff of this department occupied for several weeks.

Meanwhile, the Job Evaluation Department is asked to evaluate the bulb-changing project with a view to determining its participants' duties and responsibilities. Specifically, the assignment is to decide if the job is too menial to be undertaken by any of the EAs or directors, or whether the list of potential bulb-changers should be confined to the lowly senior officers. And this in fact is the outcome of the JE report.

Now the Department of Organizing and Servicing is asked to actually assemble the bulb-changing team, and of course the Equal Opportunities Department intervenes, as it has every right to do, to make sure there are equal numbers of men and women on the team.

Then the Education Department has to prepare and conduct a week-long course on the intricacies of light-bulb changing, so that all team members become fully trained and qualified.

The actual work is now ready to start, but not until the Health and Safety Department does a thorough check to make sure the light-switch is off, the ladder is sturdy and properly held, and of course to oversee an orderly evacuation if (when) the bulb-changers accidentally set off the fire alarm.

So the bulb eventually does get changed. But no sooner have the ATSU bulb-changers come down off the ladder than the OPEIU files a grievance charging ATSU with infringing on its jurisdiction. We then have to consult the Legal Department to get help and advice on preparing our defence.

Now, you might well ask at this point: what about the Public Relations Department? Well, I think you know, as well as I do, that the P.R. Department gets involved in everything, whether we're asked to or not, even if it's just to kibbitz and second-guess everyone else. So you can be sure we're playing that role at every stage of the light-bulb-changing exercise, offering all kinds of suggestions that as usual are ignored, and of course making up dim light-bulb jokes.

But it's not till the bulb finally gets changed that our work really begins, because then we have to put out a special issue of *The CUPE Facts* on Co-ordinated Light-Bulb Changing, extolling its many benefits for the membership. And of course a feature article has to be written for both *The Public Employee* and *The Leader*. The heading we come up with is: "Third Floor Sees the Light — At Last," but somehow that gets misinterpreted, so we're forced to change it to "National President Illuminates National Office," which is more in keeping with *The Leader's* mandate. And the leader's mandate.

In closing, brothers and sisters, that is why it takes all the members of ATSU to change a light-bulb. Please have a happy and healthy holiday season, and if you need any help changing your Christmas light-bulbs, you know where to come.

Chapter 21

Memorial University tribute

EARLY IN 1994, I had a phone call from Greg Kealey, director of Labour Studies at Memorial University in St. John's.

"Ed," he said, "you haven't been forgotten in Newfoundland for the courage and leadership you displayed here back in the '50s and '60s, both in the early years of the NDP and in the provincial labour movement. And of course the high standards of journalism you maintained as editor of the *Western Star* during the loggers' strike is also still remembered and admired."

"That's very flattering, Greg," I said. "But surely you're not calling just to pay me compliments."

He laughed. "No, I'm calling to tell you that MUN would like to honour you with a degree of Doctor of Laws at the upcoming Spring Convocation. It will be a tangible recognition of your contribution to the province's social and political development. I hope you will accept."

This was such an unexpected honour that I was speechless for a minute or so. I always had trouble accepting praise, and I was afraid that this would be seen as an ego trip. But of course I told Greg that I'd be honoured to come to the convocation, which would be held May 28-29. I knew my wife Dena and son Kevin would take some pride in witnessing the event, as would my daughter Kerri-Anne, but unfortunately she couldn't join us because in late May she would be in the middle of her high school exams.

Many of my relatives and old friends in Newfoundland also attended the ceremony, which began with an introductory oration by the university's Dr. William Pryse-Phillips. He lavished me with so much praise that I was embarrassed. To give you some idea of how excessive it was, here are a few excerpts:

Few dared to carry the torch for liberty against authority when the province's labour movement was attacked and denigrated. But before you stands Ed Finn. He dared to stand by his principles, regardless of consequence.

When the Newfoundland government ruthlessly suppressed the legal strike of the underpaid and mistreated loggers in 1959, he resigned as editor of the *Western Star*, finding intolerable the publishers' instruction to support the government's action.

Later, casting off the yoke of men's opinions and doing what he believed in, he co-founded and led the Newfoundland Democratic Party, forerunner of the national NDP, and ran as that party's candidate in two provincial and two federal elections…

Ed Finn has not been content to see injustice done. His brave, dispassionate voice has been raised fairly in censure and in warning, but also in hope and in commendation for over 30 years, expressing the conscience of its owner, and gaining the trust of all who agree and support the basic liberties of citizens in our society.

So rare are such consistent expressions of conscience and the steadfast defence of liberty that we are bound to mark them with such honour as we can. So I present to you their exemplar, one who always knows the True North, to receive at your hand the degree of doctor of laws *honoris causa*, Edward Horace John Finn.

My cheeks were still burning when I walked to the podium to deliver my acceptance speech. The full text is reproduced here, if only because I think the sentiments it expressed remain relevant today, in Canada as a whole, not just in Newfoundland and Labrador:

As pleased as I am to receive this honour, I wasn't really sure what I'd done to deserve it until I heard Dr. Pryse-Phillips' very flattering introduction.

I thought perhaps that I was here as a representative of Newfoundland's most successful export: Newfoundlanders. We expatriates now outnumber you stay-at-homes by at least three-to-one, so I thought it was fitting that

I shake hands with Memorial University's Dr. William Pryse-Phillips after he introduced me before my address at the university's 1994 convocation at which I was awarded an honourary Doctor of Laws degree.

we get some recognition for the tremendous contribution we've made to the provincial economy by leaving.

Not that Newfoundland's economic problems are anything to joke about. Certainly not for the young men and women graduating this year from Memorial who, even *with* university degrees, may have trouble putting their knowledge and talent to work in the New World Order.

We had a much more serious economic crisis when I was growing up in Corner Brook. It was called the Great Depression. We lived with poverty and deprivation all through the 1930s. But as hard as it was to endure, we never lost hope that living and working conditions could and would eventually be improved.

In part, that was because we knew there were still lots of fish in the sea, lots of trees in the woods, lots of minerals in the ground. But there was something even more important that inspired us and kept us going. And that was our willingness to co-operate, to pull together, to help one another through adversity. We could always depend on our relatives, our friends, on the whole community if necessary, to help the least fortunate among us, and to maintain community standards and values. If any of us had a problem, we all had a problem, and we worked in harmony to find the solution.

I always felt that this spirit of co-operation and social cohesion was deeply ingrained in Newfoundlanders. I know that it was in me, and that I have been its beneficiary. Being the oldest of five children, I had to leave school when I was 16 to go to work in the paper mill to help supplement our meagre family income. If I were at that age today, without even having finished high school — well, I don't have to tell you how limited my prospects would be. But in the 1940s and '50s in Newfoundland, I was not left to fend for myself. I got help, lots of help, as much from strangers as from relatives and friends. Employers were willing to judge me on my potential, not my limited formal education. I never lacked for advice or opportunities. And with that kind of support, I was able to become a journalist and editor, and work for newspapers such as the *Montreal Gazette* and the *Toronto Star*, and even serve as provincial leader of a political party.

Today, without a degree in journalism or even a high school diploma, and certainly without the kind of caring-and-sharing environment I knew in my youth, most doors would be closed to me. The world of the 1990s is bleaker, less hospitable, less tolerant. It's the world of globalization, competitiveness, downsizing, jobless growth, free trade, deficit reduction, deindustrialization, and cutbacks. All the terms that describe a law-of-the jungle society. It's survival of the fittest time again. The cunning, the ruthless, the affluent prosper; the rest fall by the wayside.

It's a time of rampant individualism. Competition is extolled, co-operation scorned. The lesson being drummed into us, over and over, is that we can no longer rely on governments to come to our aid, that unions can no longer protect our jobs or incomes, that we are at the mercy of overwhelming global commercial forces. In such a savagely competitive world, many Canadians regrettably have come to believe they are on our own. Instead of helping or co-operating with others, they feel they must compete with them, fighting and clawing for an elusive share of what is left in the economy after the rich and powerful grab the largest shares.

I don't share this ghastly view of what life is all about. I never have. I still believe that the big corporations that are reshaping the world can be resisted. That we can reverse the downward slide into neo-Victorian squalor, that we can create good-paying jobs for all who are willing and able to work, that our social programs can be preserved. I believe the social and economic troubles that afflict us are not random or unplanned — that, on the contrary, they result from decisions made in boardrooms and legislatures. Different decisions would produce different — and better — outcomes.

That's why I've spent the last 35 years of my life doing what I can to help recreate a compassionate and equitable society — the kind of society I was fortunate to enjoy in Newfoundland when I was a boy and young man. I've worked with the labour movement, with the Action Canada Network, the Council of Canadians, with environmentalists, with women's and church groups, and now with the Canadian Centre for Policy Alternatives. And why? Because, without the efforts of these and other progressive organizations, the kind of society that will ensue for most people from uncontrolled corporate power will indeed resemble the worst conditions of abject poverty and misery that blighted the Robber Baron era in the 1800s.

Finding the countervailing means to prevent such a disastrous decline has been difficult, especially since Big Business has gone global while the rest of us remain confined within national boundaries. With each passing day, it becomes more urgent that new ways be found to curb this corporate power for the common good.

It can be done, but not if we give up on the co-operative approach — not if we keep treating one another as rivals instead of allies. Individually, most of us are powerless. Together, we've at least got a fighting chance.

I thought we Newfoundlanders had learned that lesson back in the Dirty Thirties. But we seem to have forgotten it in the Nasty Nineties. Co-operation has given way to internal bickering. Instead of pooling our resources and working together, we are fighting among ourselves, looking for scapegoats instead of solutions.

You've no doubt heard the old saying, "If you're not part of the solution, you're part of the problem." Well, there's a variation of that dictum that may be more applicable today: "If you're not part of the solution, you'll become part of the *final* solution."

I would compare the situation in Newfoundland today — and indeed all across Canada — with the plight of people in a leaking lifeboat many miles from shore. What do you do in that kind of predicament? Do those of you at the oars pull in different directions? Do you fight among yourselves for the limited food and water or for a seat in the dry end of the boat? Do you throw the weakest among you overboard and hope that will keep the boat afloat longer? Do you try to sell the bailing buckets to the highest bidders? Do you waste your time blaming one another for the leak?

Or do you realize, whether you're in the dry end or wet end of the boat, that you're all in the same foundering vessel and that it's in everyone's interest to co-operate in the bailing and rowing if you are to have a chance of reaching shore?

I'm pretty sure common sense, self-preservation, and co-operation would prevail in a predicament as starkly clear as that. It should be equally clear that Newfoundland as a place to live and work today is also in danger of capsizing, economically and socially, and that the same spirit of co-operation is needed to keep it from going under. Is it too much to expect that, when our home is threatened, we work together to save it?

I wouldn't have had to ask that question 40 or 50 years ago. Not in Newfoundland. Newfoundlanders faced with that kind of challenge would have come together almost instinctively to fight a common foe, whether it was a tidal wave, a forest fire, or an economic depression. Has today's generation of Newfoundlanders lost that co-operative instinct? Are they now incapable of putting aside their internal differences and working together, even for self-preservation?

I truly hope and believe not. I believe that the spark of the community spirit that burned so brightly when I was a boy still flickers in the hearts and minds of my fellow Newfoundlanders. I believe that the young people graduating from Memorial University this year — the leaders of tomorrow — will help to fan that spark into a renewed spirit of co-operation and teamwork.

I leave you with the most important lesson I learned growing up on this island. It is this: there is nothing — no problem, no crisis, no obstacle — that is too difficult for Newfoundlanders to overcome so long as they put their minds and collective purpose to it. As long as they pull together.

* * *

Nearly two decades after I delivered this speech, in the fall of 2011, I was invited to address the centennial anniversary of the Newfoundland and Labrador Federation of Labour at its convention in Gander. If there was one reassurance I gained from the delegates there, it was that the flame of co-operation and solidarity was burning among them more brightly and with more fervour than I have ever seen it displayed before.

I came home from that convention with renewed hope that the same spirit of co-operation would spread across Canada to energize the many activists in NGOs, unions, and other civil society groups who are struggling so valiantly to create a better nation in a better world.

Chapter 22

The CCPA and the **CCPA Monitor**

MY LONG ASSOCIATION with the Canadian Centre for Policy Alternatives started a few years after its founding in 1980. That was when a group of progressive Canadians met in Ottawa to establish a "think-tank" that would produce economic and social studies from a left-of-centre perspective. The need was felt to be all the more urgent because a right-wing research agency — the Fraser Institute — had been churning out papers in support of ultra-conservative policies since the mid-1970s — without sustained rebuttal from the left.

The founders of the CCPA were mainly academic and trade union economists and researchers who were committed to filling the gap in the country's research spectrum. They mustered financial support from the Canadian Labour Congress and some of its affiliated unions. This was enough to maintain a small office and pay for the production of several key studies and the publication of a quarterly newsletter, *Currents*. But the income fell far short of enabling the Centre to maintain even a minimal level of research and publications and still pay the rising costs of operations.

I was working with CUPE during the 1980s and did my best on a volunteer basis to help the CCPA cope with its financial troubles. I wrote articles for *Currents* as well as several booklets the Centre published — on Medicare, free trade, wage controls, and the deficit. In 1985, I was elected to the Centre's board of directors, where the gravity of its revenue shortfall was all too painfully evident. By the time Diane Touchette was hired as office administrator in 1987 — a position she still holds — she found that her main task was juggling the pileup of bills and deciding which ones she could safely defer paying.

The board of directors appointed a sub-committee in 1989 to investigate the financial crisis and determine if the Centre had any chance of staying afloat. I was on that committee, and to us the prospects looked bleak. Our report back to the board was to the effect that only a significant and sustained increase in revenue could keep the CCPA afloat.

Fortunately, a dramatic and ultimately successful rescue effort was then instituted by what then Executive Director Jim Davidson described as "an incredible group of CCPA boosters." They were led by Duncan Cameron, then a political scientist at Ottawa University, who became president of the CCPA in 1988, and Larry Brown, secretary-treasurer of the [then] National Union of Provincial Government Employees, who later succeeded Duncan as president. They spent many weeks appealing to the unions to increase their grants to the Centre, stressing the dire consequences if such a strong research resource for organized labour were to fold.

The unions were persuaded to raise their contributions sufficiently to pay off all the Centre's creditors and start a timely revival process. Additional revenue was secured by enlisting the support of other unions as organizational members. The CCPA's rejuvenation coincided with the great free trade debate of the late 1980s and, with its renewed vitality, the Centre was able to turn out many informative trade-related research and policy papers and play an important role in this major national dialogue.

Apart from providing some writing and editorial support to the CCPA from my position on the board and from my office at CUPE, I wasn't directly involved in its operations prior to 1994.

I had to retire from CUPE upon reaching my 65th birthday in 1991, since like most unions it had a mandatory retirement policy at that age. Duncan Cameron would have liked me to move directly to the CCPA, but its finances were still too shaky to pay for additional staff, so I decided to freelance for a while. Over the next few years, I did contract work for several organizations, including the CLC, which sought my editorial help in drafting a major overhaul of its constitution.

Among other projects I undertook was a year-long public relations stint for the Canadian Owner-Operators' Cooperative, helping this newly-established truckers' group extend cost-cutting benefits to truck owners and drivers across the country.

I was enlisted for another major writing and editing task by Monica Townson when she was appointed to chair the Ontario Fair Tax Commission in 1991. It was a three-year study of the province's tax system launched by the new NDP government headed by Bob Rae. This was a potentially historic project that I thought could lead to significant improvement in the ways Ontarians were taxed, but, regrettably, few of the commission's recommendations were seriously considered when its report was submitted.

This didn't surprise me. Any illusions I may have had about the Rae government's progressive nature were dashed when he backed down from one of his key campaign promises: to establish a public motor vehicle insurance program. Fierce opposition from the private insurance companies soon brought him to heel.

My suspicions had first been raised after I was asked by Rae's office shortly after the election to help implement another of his election promises: to give citizens of the province a role in setting priorities for the government's first budget. The plan was to have Rae and his finance minister tour the province, address public meetings, and solicit opinions and suggestions about how the budget should deal with Ontario's most pressing social and economic issues.

My role was to outline the main aspects of these problems, then draft a set of questions that both individuals and groups would be asked to answer. The results of this public input would then be reflected in the actual budget. After several months of having my draft text altered, rewritten, and parts deleted, I became exasperated and asked for a meeting with Rae's key staffers. I was told there was no need for such a meeting, and that my services on the project were no longer needed.

I was sent a cheque for my work, but nothing was ever said to me (or anyone else) about why the promised budget consultation with the citizenry had been scrapped. No explanation, of course, was required. It was obvious that Rae and his advisors belatedly became aware that seeking public advice about budget priorities might just give citizens the notion that their views would actually help shape the budget's contents. Raising such hopes and then dashing them would be the height of political folly. Ergo, no public input on the budget. Another campaign promise sunk.

The budget of the CCPA, however, had grown enough by early 1994 to sustain a significant staff increase. Bruce Campbell became the new executive director; I joined the staff as senior editor; and political scientist Paul Browne was also hired.

Two major decisions were also made in early 1994, mainly sparked by Bruce, that greatly expanded and solidified the Centre's operation. One was to launch a concerted effort to increase the CCPA's individual membership, which was stalled at less than a paltry 200 or so. This left the organizational membership fees (nearly all from unions) as the source of 95% of the Centre's revenue. But surely, we told ourselves, many individual Canadians, if given the chance, would also contribute to the Centre's growth and influence. Such a large boost to our financial base was essential to enable the CCPA to respond effectively to the rising tide of neoliberalism then engulfing Canada — and most other industrialized countries as well.

The response to our solicitation for more individual memberships was gratifying. Their ranks swelled at the rate of more than 200 a month and continued to grow until, by the middle of the next decade, the total number soared above 10,000. The revenue from individual members eventually came to nearly double that from labour organizations. It was this overwhelming support from the rank and file that enabled the CCPA to expand and become the foremost progressive research agency in Canada that it is today.

The other pivotal decision that was made in 1994 was to start publishing a monthly journal. We called it the *CCPA Monitor*, and its first issue — just 16 pages — came off the press in May of that year. It became a 20-pager the next year, and kept adding pages until it peaked at 40 by 2006. I was the *de facto* editor from the start (and the acknowledged editor by 1997), but quite rightly editorial credit was shared with Bruce, Paul, and Duncan, and with Diane and my daughter Kerri-Anne, who handled the design and layout duties in the early years.

The *Monitor* was mailed free to everyone who became (and remained) a dues-paying CCPA member, and we hoped that it would become popular enough to encourage the renewal of memberships before they expired. And this is what happened. The percentage of renewals has rarely fallen much below 85% — a high rate that can't be attributed entirely to the *Monitor*, although the journal undoubtedly has played a key role in the Centre's growth and effectiveness. The continuing addition of new members more than offset the loss of those who let their memberships lapse. (Many such lapses, of course, were due to deaths, serious illness, or financial setbacks, not to any sudden decision that the CCPA or the *Monitor* no longer merited financial support.)

The *Monitor* was designed as — and has remained under my editorship — a no-frills publication, with an emphasis on conveying important news and views that CCPA members are unlikely to find in the mainstream media. We haven't jazzed it up with photos, cartoons, or a fancy layout because we didn't think it was necessary to induce or entice our members to read it. We believed that what CCPA members wanted was to be enlightened, inspired, and motivated, and that this could be done without graphic or pictorial enhancement. We figured that, as long as we ran articles of varying lengths, maintained a high editorial standard, provided pertinent headings and call-outs, and lightened the pages with occasional humorous fillers, members would not find it difficult to read.

The *Monitor* is also easy to read because, although it is the flagship journal of a research agency, it is not written or published for professional researchers, but for the 95% of its readers who are not academics. What they're looking for are articles and essays that explain major issues in clear, readable prose. Many of the CCPA's other publications — studies, reports, analyses — are written by academics, and thus contain scholarly details and footnotes. But most *Monitor* readers don't need or understand the specialized jargon. They just want to get a general idea of what our studies contain, which is why we summarize and popularize them and remove all the footnotes before they appear in the *Monitor*.

This not to say that approval of *The Monitor's* contents is universal. No monthly journal always appeals to all its readers, and the *Monitor* is no exception. But most of the complaints we receive are related to single articles or to authors with whose views a reader may disagree. Overall, the journal's approval rating has been very high since its inception, especially after we started publishing letters to the editor (Memos from Our Members) which quickly became one of *The Monitor's* most popular features.

I get few complaints about how the journal is filled and edited. On the contrary, some members have told me they now consider the *CCPA Monitor* to be the pre-eminent journal on the left in Canada. I would never make that claim. All I will say is that our writers are doing their best to make readers of the *Monitor* the best informed people in Canada. I leave it to their judgment whether we've succeeded.

During the nearly two decades I've been editor of the *CCPA Monitor*, I've written hundreds of articles, essays, and editorials for the journal. Three collections of these pieces have been published by the CCPA. The first, *Under Corporate Rule*, came out in 1996; the second, *Who Do We Try to Rescue Today?* in 1999; and the third and most recent, *The Right is Wrong and the Left is Right*, in 2007. I doubt there'll be a fourth anthology, given my advanced age (I'm writing this shortly after my 87th birthday), but for readers of these memoirs who haven't read — or have forgotten they've read — my *Monitor* essays, some of the ones I personally regard as among my best are provided in an appendix.

I'm delighted that I've been given the opportunity to end my long tenure in the work force — 70 years and counting — as an editor and writer with the CCPA. It's the most rewarding and fulfilling job I've ever had, privileged to work with an exceptionally gifted and dedicated group of colleagues, the most talented writers and qualified researchers, the most loyal and supportive funders.

Bolstered by such superb assets, the CCPA has become the foremost progressive research agency in Canada. It has spun off branches in British Columbia, Saskatchewan, Manitoba, and Nova Scotia, as well as an Ontario office in Toronto. It has published authoritative and meticulously researched studies on every aspect of national and international affairs. It has attained a credibility and influence that could only be dreamed of a few decades ago.

I'm proud that I have been able to contribute to the Centre's growth and success, and hope to continue doing so as long as my physical and mental faculties permit.

Essays

Back to the "Good" Old Days

"The disparity in income between the rich and the poor is merely the survival of the fittest. It is merely the working out of a law of nature and a law of God."

—*John D. Rockefeller, 1894.*

During the first 70 years that followed this pronouncement by one of the 19th-century's leading robber barons, the worst excesses of unfettered free enterprise were curbed by government regulations, minimum wage increases, and the growth of the labour movement. Strong unions and relatively progressive governments combined to have wealth distributed less inequitably. Social safety nets were woven to help those in need.

Corporate owners, executives, and major shareholders resisted all these moderate reforms. Their operations had to be forcibly humanized. They always resented having even a small part of their profits diverted into wages and taxes, but until the mid-1970s and '80s they couldn't prevent it. Now they can.

Thanks to international trade agreements and the global mobility of capital, they can overcome all political and labour constraints. They are free once more, as they were in the 1800s, to maximize profits and exploit workers, to control or coerce national governments, to re-establish the survival of the fittest as the social norm.

This global resurgence of corporate power threatens to wipe out a century of social progress. We are in danger of reverting to the kind of mass poverty and deprivation that marked the Victorian era. Indeed, this kind of corporate-imposed barbarism and inequality is already rampant in many developing countries.

It could eventually happen in Canada, too, as our manufacturing sector is further dismantled, more good jobs outsourced, more people forced into minimum-wage work, more of the poor denied welfare benefits, more of the elderly denied adequate pensions.

Unfortunately, most Canadians don't seem to know how badly their forebears were mistreated in the workplaces of the 1800s. So the prospect of a reversion to Victorian social conditions doesn't alarm them. A brief history lesson may therefore be in order.

* * *

Working hours in the mines and factories were from sunrise to sunset, about 72 hours a week. Wages, in 2013 currency, averaged less than $3 a day. Workers had to live in shacks or overcrowded tenements. They couldn't afford carpets on the floor or even dishes for their meals.

Most workplaces were dirty, dimly lit, poorly heated. In many factories there were no guards on saw-blades, pulleys, or other dangerous machinery, because owners were not held responsible for industrial accidents. Workers took jobs at their own risk. If they were killed or injured at work, as many thousands were, it was always considered due to their own "carelessness." Uncounted thousands also died of tuberculosis, pneumonia, and other diseases caused by inadequate heat or sanitation.

Conditions in the mines were especially bad, with most miners dying from accidents or "black-lung" disease before they reached the age of 35.

Hundreds of thousands of children, some as young as six, were forced to work 12 hours a day, often being whipped or beaten. A Canadian Royal Commission on Child Labour in the late 1800s reported that "the employment of children is extensive and on the increase. Boys under 12 work all night in the glass-works in Montreal. In the coal mines of Nova Scotia, it is common for 10-year-old boys to work a 60-hour week down in the pits.

"These children work as many hours as adults, sometimes more. They have to be in the mill or mine by 6:30 a.m., necessitating their being up at 5 for their morning meal, some having to walk several miles to their work."

This Royal Commission found that not only were children fined for tardiness and breakages, but also that in many factories they were beaten with birch rods. Many thousands of them lost fingers, hands, even entire limbs, when caught in unguarded gears or pulleys. Many hundreds were killed. Their average life expectancy was 33.

As late as 1910 in Canada, more than 300,000 children under 12 were still being subjected to these brutal working conditions. It wasn't until the 1920s, in fact, that child labour in this country was completely stamped out.

An enterprising union organizer managed to get into a cigar factory in southern Ontario in 1908. He found young girls being whipped if they couldn't keep up their production quota. Many girls wound up at week's end owing the boss money because they had more pay docked for defective cigars than they earned.

A visitor to a twine-making factory in 1907 counted nine girls at one bench alone who had lost either a finger or a thumb.

A surgeon who lived in a mill town related in his memoirs that, over a 15-year period, he had amputated over 1,000 fingers of children who had their hands mangled when forced to oil or clean unprotected mill machines while they were still running.

This callous mistreatment of working people was not only condoned, but even extolled — and not just by the business establishment. The daily newspapers of the time also defended the employers. So did the major religions. In 1888, when labour leader Daniel O'Donaghue proposed a resolution at a public meeting in Toronto calling for the abolition of child labour, all 41 clergymen who attended the meeting voted against it. In Quebec, for many years, the Catholic Church forbade its members to join a union "under pain of grievous sin" — and many bishops and priests went so far as to deny union members a Christian burial when they died.

Blessed by the clergy, the press, and the politicians, employers considered it their God-given right to treat workers as virtual slaves. Said railroad tycoon George F. Baer, "The interests of the labouring man will be cared for, not by the labour agitators, but by the Christian men to whom God has given control of the property rights of the country."

In the United States, another robber baron, Frederick Townsend Martin, was even more candid. In an interview he gave to a visiting British journalist, he boasted: "We are the rich. We own this country. And we intend to keep it by throwing all the tremendous weight of our support, our influence, our money, our purchased politicians, our public-speaking demagogues, into the fight against any legislation, any political party or platform or campaign that threatens our vested interests."

* * *

Today's business executives are not so outspoken, at least not in public, but basically their agenda is not much different from that of their 19th-century forerunners. They envy the robber barons of the Victorian era. They would like nothing more than to recreate the atrocious social and economic conditions that prevailed in those bad old days.

And what's really scary is that they now have regained almost as much of the political and economic power they need to implement this regressive scheme.

A modern descendant of John D. Rockefeller, his great-grandson banker David Rockefeller, put it plainly in a speech he gave back in the 1990s: "We who run the transnational corporations are now in the driver's seat of the global economic engine. We are setting government policies instead of watching from the sidelines."

A long-time proponent of a corporate New World Order, David Rockefeller has also declared that: "The supranational sovereignty of an intellectual élite and world bankers is surely preferable to the national autodetermination practised in past centuries." He also said: "All we need is the right major crisis and the nations will accept the New World Order." (Whether 9/11 or the 2008 financial crash will turn out to be the major crisis he yearned for is yet to be decided.)

In any case, today's CEOs are unquestionably calling the shots. They have harnessed almost all governments to their agenda. The only thing they aren't sure about is how long it will take them to obliterate the last vestiges of the hated "welfare state" and establish the neo-Victorian New World Order David Rockefeller predicted would be the ultimate corporate triumph.

Already, in most of the developing nations, they have brought back child labour. Conditions in most factories operated by or for the transnational corporations in Asia and parts of Latin America are not much better today than they were in North America and Europe in the 1800s. Thousands of boys and girls are being compelled to work 12 hours a day in dirty, unsafe workshops, for 40 or 50 cents an hour.

One 15-year-old girl who started working in a *maquila* sweatshop in Honduras when she was 13, testifying before a U.S. Senate subcommittee on child labour, told how she and 600 other teenaged girls are forced to sew cotton sweaters from 6 a.m. to 6 p.m., seven days a week. They are beaten by their bosses if they make a mistake, forbidden to speak to co-workers, allowed only half an hour a day for lunch, and just two visits a day to the bathroom. She is paid 38 cents an hour to make sweaters that are sold in the U.S. for $90.

This kind of flinthearted exploitation of child labour may never be repeated in Canada, mainly because there are so many children in poorer nations who can more easily be exploited. But don't rule out the possibility that much of our adult work force will be forced back into a modern-day version of serfdom. With our labour laws impaired and laxly enforced, with workers' unions and bargaining rights weakened, with well-paid manufacturing jobs being replaced by low-paid part-time or temporary work, the regression of our labour force into 19th-century-style servitude is far from a dystopian fantasy.

Maybe, if more Canadians take a good hard look back at that era of absolute corporate power, as I've just done, they might be more concerned about reliving that blighted and benighted past — and become active in the struggle to avert it.

Advertising and propaganda

One of the reasons — arguably the main reason — why the big transnational corporations are now running the world is because most people don't believe they are. And, of the minority who do realize they live under corporate rule, some think it's unavoidable and others that it's even desirable.

This unawareness or acceptance of the New World Order is the greatest triumph of the public relations industry. Its propagandists, in the service of business leaders, have perfected the art of media-transmitted mind control. They have honed and refined the mass brainwashing techniques first devised by Edward L. Bernays, a nephew of Sigmund Freud, nearly a century ago.

Not many people today have ever heard of Bernays, but within the glass-and-marble towers of Burson-Marsteller, Hill & Knowlton, Edelman, and other big American PR agencies, he is revered as "the Father of Spin," as the patron saint of mass persuasion.

Bernays got his start in moulding public opinion during the First World War, when he was asked by the U.S. government to popularize its belated decision to enter the war against Germany. He coined the slogan "Let's Make the World Safe for Democracy," and was credited with changing public sentiment in the U.S. from anti-war to pro-war, almost overnight.

In the post-war years, during the Roaring Twenties, Bernays was in great demand by business firms looking for mass marketing techniques to sell their products. One of his biggest clients in the 1920s was the tobacco industry. His first task was to popularize smoking by women, which he did by equating smoking with women's liberation. If you were a woman who believed in equal rights with men, he told them, you should have the same right as men to smoke — even in public. One of his major stunts was to organize what he called a "Torches of Liberty" Easter parade in New York in 1929, in which thousands of marching women all smoked (or at least waved) cigarettes as their symbol of women's liberation — their "torches of liberty." The sale of cigarettes to women increased phenomenally in the years that followed.

Tobacco's harmful effects on human lungs and heart were unknown at the time, of course, so Bernays was able to set up an advertising campaign jointly with the American Medical Association to "prove" that smoking was actually *beneficial* to people's health. This campaign, which featured pro-smoking messages from physicians as well as movie stars and other celebrities, saturated magazine, radio, and TV advertising for nearly 50 years.

Bernays was also the PR genius who popularized bacon as a breakfast food. Nobody had thought of eating these fatty pork strips first thing in the morning until Bernays launched his bacon-for-breakfast blitz.

During the next few decades, Bernays and his growing number of PR colleagues developed the principles and methods by which masses of people could be brainwashed through messages repeated over and over in the media. And it wasn't just products that could be sold in this way — it was also ideas and concepts, no matter how abhorrent. Josef Goebbels, Hitler's minister of propaganda, studied and adopted Bernays's techniques when he was asked to convince the German people that they were members of a superior race that needed to be "purified."

Bernays held the masses in contempt. He once described the public as "a herd that needs to be led," adding that this herd instinct made people "susceptible to leadership." But he always maintained that the best kind of leadership was unobtrusive: that the masses could best be led and manipulated if they weren't aware of the processes used to control them. He didn't believe that democracy was a workable political system, because in his view most people couldn't think rationally and thus needed to be *told* what to think.

Here's a paragraph from Bernays's remarkably candid book, *Propaganda*:

> "Those who manipulate the unseen mechanism of society constitute an invisible government which is the true ruling power. We are governed, our minds moulded, our tastes formed, our ideas suggested largely by men we have never heard of. This is a logical result of the way in which our democratic society is organized. Vast numbers of human beings must co-operate if they are to live together as a smoothly functioning society. In almost every act of our lives, whether in the sphere of politics or business, in our social conduct or our ethical thinking, we are dominated by the relatively small number of persons who understand the mental processes and social patterns of the masses. It is they who pull the wires that control the public mind."

Of course Bernays was himself pre-eminent among the select few entrusted with this task of moulding public opinion on behalf of the world's rich and powerful élites. The big PR firms that now create the desired benevolent image for business leaders and their products are the modern practitioners of Bernays's methods.

The machinations of these thought-control experts, as Bernays cautioned, are carefully concealed from public view. But occasionally the screen is pulled away and the puppeteers revealed, as in the books written by former PR whiz John Stauber and his colleague Sheldon Rampton. In *Toxic Sludge is Good for You*, they exposed the antics of the PR agencies employed to present a favourable image of the industries with the worst pollution records. In *Trust Us, We're Experts*, they explained how the media are used to instill and perpetuate a favourable public perception of the transnational corporations.

According to Stauber and Rampton, as reported by book reviewer Tim O'Shea, "we are the most conditioned, programmed beings the world has ever known. Not only are our thoughts and attitudes constantly being shaped and moulded, but our very awareness [of this process] is subtly erased... It is an exhausting and endless task to keep explaining to people how most issues of conventional wisdom are scientifically implanted in the public consciousness by a thousand media clips per day... If everybody believes something — if it is part of the conventional wisdom — it's probably wrong."

Some current examples of such implanted conventional wisdom, as listed by Stauber and Rampton, may be discerned in the field of health care:

- Pharmaceuticals restore health.
- Chemotherapy and radiation are effective cures for cancer.
- Hospitals are safe and clean.
- All drugs are thoroughly tested before they go on the market.
- You never outgrow your need for milk.
- The cure for cancer is just around the corner.

All are illusions created by the corporate spin doctors through billions of dollars in advertising and public relations.

The mind-control methods devised by Bernays and his successors were evident in the successful efforts to promote free trade, privatization, deregulation, and tax cuts, and to belittle or deny the damage done to the environment by industrial pollution.

The lessons Bernays taught to his PR specialists include the selective use of language, the value of "independent third-party" endorsements, the distribution of canned "news" releases, and the hiring of compliant scientists and experts.

Stauber and Rampton give examples of these lessons.

- **Language spin:** When shaping or reshaping a corporate image, stay away from substance; create images instead. Tell people that complex issues can only be decided by "experts." Focus on emotions, not facts. Put the desired spin on issues, but never state a clearly demonstrable lie. (Which is why we're no longer told that tobacco is good for us.) Speak and write in generalities, using emotionally positive words (like "free" and "trade.") Invent colourful phrases to attack corporate critics, like "tree-huggers," "scaremongers," "conspiracy theorists," "junk scientists," "Luddites," "nanny-staters," "special interest groups."

- **"Independent" third parties:** If an oil company were to deny that burning oil contributes to global warming, its motives might be questioned. But if an "independent" research institute with a credible-sounding name like the Global Climate Coalition says global warming is a myth, people are more inclined to believe it. So the corporations, following Bernays's advice, have funded the establishment of dozens of institutes and foundations [like the Fraser Institute in Canada] that are little more than mouthpieces or front groups for big business. They include the Tobacco Institute Research Council, the American Council on Science and Health, the Alliance for Better Foods, the International Food Information Council, and the Industrial Health Foundation. They all churn out "scientific" studies that "prove" whatever their corporate funders want.

- **Canned news releases:** The corporations and their front groups send the media hundreds of "press releases" every week promoting new "breakthrough" products or defending firms from attacks by NGOs or consumer organizations. Such releases, including radio and TV clips, save lazy journalists the trouble of doing their own investigative work, and often are reported word for word from the release: instant "news" written by corporate PR hacks. On some days, according to Stauber and Rampton, as many as half the articles in the major newspapers and half the items on a TV newscast are based solely on such PR releases.

- **Science for hire:** Prominent scientists can sometimes be induced (even bribed) to endorse or support "research" findings by the corporations' front groups. Their names in a press release can often guarantee publication of something that is pseudo-science at best, or even a blatant PR fabrication. Back in the 1920s, for example, General Motors discovered that adding lead to gasoline gave cars more horsepower. To allay concerns about the damage to public health, GM paid the Bureau of Mines to do some fake "testing" and publish findings that "proved" the inhalation of lead was harmless. This spurious study was then backed up by the world-famous Sloan-Kettering Memorial Institute for Medical Research, founded by Charles Kettering, who also (by a sheer coincidence, of course) happened to be an executive with General Motors. All anti-lead research was then effectively discouraged for the next 60 years, and it wasn't until the 1980s, after the belated revelation that lead was indeed a major carcinogen, that leaded gas was gradually phased out. By that time, many millions of tons of lead vapour had been released into the atmosphere.

* * *

Those of us who are striving every day to "de-brainwash" the victims of corporate propaganda obviously face immensely strong, lavishly financed, exceptionally skilled, and basically unprincipled adversaries. It's a one-sided contest. We lack the resources and the media access enjoyed by the disciples of Edward Bernays.

Nevertheless, it's by no means a hopeless struggle. We have a few advantages. One is that the excesses of our corporate rulers — socially, economically and environmentally — are becoming so glaringly evident that even the most cunning and well-funded spin doctors are having trouble concealing or whitewashing them. A good example is the now discredited corporate effort to deny the reality of man-made global warming. Despite the most intense campaign to dismiss climate change as a myth, most people now realize that it is happening and that the burning of fossil fuels is the main culprit.

Another example is the failure of a concerted PR attempt to justify the genetic engineering of food products. Most people in Canada are still opposed to GM foods, according to an Ekos poll. (Unfortunately, such foods fill our grocery store shelves because — unlike in Europe — food companies are not compelled by law to disclose GM content on the labels.)

Another advantage we now have is the Internet, which (so far) has not fallen under corporate control and is thus providing us with a powerful medium for exposing corporate propaganda and building resistance to it.

Most people, however, still rely on the commercial media for information, so the preponderant "free-market" mantra trumpeted by most of our newspapers, TV and radio networks continues to obstruct us. We lack the access to progressive news outlets enjoyed by people in most continental European countries. The commercial media there have not come entirely under the ownership and control of big business, as they have in the U.S. and Canada. Indeed, some daily newspapers and radio stations in Europe are owned by unions or co-ops, so people there are exposed to news and views from the left as well as the right — which helps explain why most European countries have far surpassed us in social, economic, and environmental policies.

Still, even without a voice in the mainstream media in Canada, we continue to make progress in challenging the corporate propaganda machine. Most Canadians want tax fairness, a more equitable distribution of income, improved public health care, more affordable and accessible higher education, and a cleaner and safer environment.

It is not overly optimistic, in fact, to foresee a time when the "masses," so easily misled and manipulated by Bernays and modern spin doctors, will stop believing everything they're told by the corporate media. It may not even be wishful thinking to expect that a majority of Canadians will soon open their minds to more equitable, more humane, more socially constructive, and more environmentally friendly alternatives to corporate globalization and neoliberalism.

The day may come when most of Bernays's human "herd" realize they are being mentally leashed and driven. The de-brainwashed herd might even turn around, stampede, and trample their corporate herders.

Life and longevity

This essay is being written a few weeks before I celebrate (if that's the right word) my 87th birthday (on June 4, 2013), an event of absolutely no interest to anyone outside my immediate family. I mention it only as a lead-in to the subject I want to discuss here, which is the aging of Canada's population, and to let you know that I'm speaking from experience.

At the last census count, the number of Canadians over the age of 65 (the unofficial dividing line between middle and old age) was just under 5,000,000, or nearly 15% of all the country's inhabitants. The ranks of octogenarians like me, nonagerians, and even centenarians, have been swelling for the past half-century. More people are living longer. The problem is that far too many of them are not enjoying their "golden years."

You've heard the old cliché that "there's only one thing worse than growing old, and that's *not* growing old." But there's another eventuality that's arguably even worse, and that's growing old *and sick*. Very sick. So sick that you become a burden on your family and a financial drain on the health care system.

That's the horrible fate of far too many of our senior citizens. So many that our nursing homes, long-term and palliative care institutions can't accommodate all of them, leaving many thousands bed-ridden or otherwise incapacitated, many in their own homes.

The only reason I'm raising this unpleasant issue is because I'm convinced that a lot of the ills associated with old age are preventable. Well, not indefinitely, of course — we all have to die of something, some time — but for much longer than the age at which many of our elderly now succumb.

This is not a new idea. Many geriatric specialists and health reformers have been saying for years that a switch from curative to preventive health care would improve and prolong human life, and save many billions now spent on remedial surgery, drugs, hospital stays, and home care.

In the absence of an emphasis on prevention in our health care system, we are left to fend for ourselves. Those who don't smoke or overeat, and who keep physically and mentally fit have a good chance of living a long and healthy life. Nothing is guaranteed, of course. Accidents do happen, and we're all predestined to some extent by the genes we inherit. But the lifestyle we adopt can often be the deciding factor in determining our lifespan.

The problem is that many individuals aren't free to choose the kind of lives they'd like to lead. If they're poor, not well-educated, stuck in hard or unrewarding jobs, with arduous family responsibilities, their quality of life is often beyond their control. Without help, particularly from the health care system, they become prone to diseases they would otherwise avoid.

We live in an increasingly hostile world — one filled with uncountable trillions of germs and viruses and toxins that are inimical to our health. To protect us, our bodies have a tremendously powerful defence mechanism — the immune system — that in theory (and for some of us in practice) can repel or destroy even the most dangerous microbial attackers.

A progressive U.S. physician, Dr. Ronald Glasser, wrote a book some years ago called *The Body is the Hero*, in which he argued that, for most forms of sickness, all a doctor can do for a patient is help the immune system do its job.

I couldn't agree more. *Better still would be helping the immune system to prevent the patient from getting sick in the first place.*

Hypothetically, our bodies should be able to keep the immune system strong enough to maintain optimum health and vigor. That would require, among other things, providing the immune system with the "armaments" it needs for an effective defence capability.

There was a time, I think, when it was possible for someone to do that simply by eating the right foods — foods rich in all the vitamins, minerals, and other nutrients that the human body and its immune system require. But that was in a time when such natural organic foods were widely available, when people weren't crowded into cities and workplaces conducive to the spread of disease, and when the air, water, and soil were not contaminated.

Today, much of our food is grown in denatured soil, doused with toxic pesticides and herbicides, and "processed" in ways that leach out much of its natural goodness. And this has happened at a time when our bodies are exposed to many thousands of new harmful chemicals, to smog and polluted water, and to more deadly bugs —and thus more urgently in need of a strong immune system than ever before.

A study conducted a few years ago by Environmental Defence Canada tested the blood of 11 volunteers across the country for the presence of 88 toxic chemicals. It found that every one of these Canadians — including renowned wildlife artist Robert Bateman — had many of these contaminants in their blood. Because only 11 people were tested (such elaborate tests are expensive), Health Canada dismissed the results as "not statistically significant" — but this reaction was typical of an agency with such a dubious record of health protection. The fact that the 11 volunteers varied in age, gender, location, occupation, and lifestyle, and that every one of them had chemically-contaminated blood, is surely very significant.

As Dr. Rick Smith, former executive director of Environmental Defence Canada, said in responding to the test results, "the bottom line is that we are all polluted. It doesn't matter where we live, how old we are, how clean-living we are. We all carry inside of us hundreds of different pollutants, and they are accumulating inside our bodies every day."

The 88 chemicals tested for in the study included heavy metals, PCBs, pesticides, and other carcinogenic and hormone-disrupting substances. They are so pervasive and are carried so widely by air and water and in the food and other products we consume that, short of living in a glass bubble, it has become impossible to avoid them. The strain on our immune systems to keep repelling and suppressing these chemical invaders has also been enormously increased.

Think of the immune system as an engine that, like all engines, operates best when provided with the best fuel and maintenance. But we can no longer obtain the best fuel from our food alone. Our bodies need the extra "ammunition" that can come only from vitamin, mineral, and herbal supplementation.

The traditional medical establishment has been scoffing at this idea for a long time, even ridiculing Nobel Prize winner Dr. Linus Pauling when he promoted megadoses of Vitamin C. But many studies in recent years have confirmed the therapeutic benefits of this and other vitamins and nutrients, particularly those with antioxidants that help the immune system ward off carcinogens.

I started a supplementary vitamin/mineral/herbal regime about 40 years ago. It may be just a coincidence that I've never been seriously ill since then — and I know (I know!) that I'm tempting fate by even alluding to my current wellness, but I'm convinced I would be far less healthy today if I had relied on food alone to nourish and strengthen my immune system.

Of course, it could be an example of the "placebo effect" where a candy pill has the same curative power as a drug because the patient believes in it — but I don't think so. Let's assume, for the sake of argument, that I'm right and that the extra vitamins, minerals, and even the herbal extracts I've been chugging down since I was 40 have helped me to keep fit and fight off the germs. What are the implications?

The first one is that my demands on our public health care system since the 1970s have been minimal. Apart from cataracts and an underactive thyroid (neither of which involves the immune system), I haven't needed medical services other than an occasional check-up — and I have contributed very little to the soaring profits of the pharmaceutical companies.

This is not to imply that a regular multi-vitamin-mineral-herbal intake would be as beneficial for everybody. I don't claim that. We all have different genetic legacies, and many people suffer from tobacco, alcohol, and junk-food addictions that have weakened their immune systems. But I believe that a great many of today's ailing oldsters would be in much better shape if they had known about the need for — and the benefits of — such preventive health care.

A deficiency of Vitamin D, for example, according to recent studies, makes people more susceptible to some cancers and other ailments. Most of us don't get enough of this essential nutrient from the sun, particularly during the winter, so we need to take Vitamin D supplements, at least 1,000 IU daily. But many Canadians don't — because that's a preventive measure and our health care system is almost entirely focused on treatment by drugs or surgery *after* people get sick. Of the $200 billion a year spent on our "illness-treatment" system, less than 2% of it is devoted to prevention efforts — mostly urging us against smoking, overweight, and lack of exercise.

The result is that, when it comes to maintaining our health, we're on our own. We can't access Medicare until our health breaks down, by which time it's often too late.

This is a perverse system. If even one-tenth of the billions now devoted to treating illness were spent instead on averting it, both Canadian seniors and Medicare itself would be far healthier. [Even the relatively few dollars required to ensure that pregnant women get enough folic acid would save millions in treating children with birth defects or lifelong frailties.]

I've been fortunate to be able to shell out the extra amount of cash needed to optimize my immune system. One of the reasons I'm still working is that I probably couldn't afford that monthly expense on just the average retirement income. And, conversely, if I hadn't managed to patronize the health-food stores for so many years, I might be too sick now to keep working.

Many people don't know they need supplementary vitamins and minerals, and wouldn't have the financial means to buy them in any case. So our governments, in their wisdom, won't provide the funds needed to help them stay healthy, but will spend billions to treat them after their health deteriorates.

This approach, of course, is understandable if not defensible in a system in which physicians and pharmaceutical firms can profit only from illness. To them, an outbreak of sustained wellness would be catastrophic. Even the politicians profit from the neglect of preventive measures, since the big drug firms are among the most generous contributors to their election campaigns.

Our entire Medicare apparatus is fixated on the treatment and (if possible) cure of illness rather than its prevention. Doctors, hospital administrators, nursing home operators, medical equipment makers, drug companies — even the scores of charitable cure-seeking organizations — all operate on the assumption that "health care" begins only *after* people get sick. Whether they admit it or not, the fact is that they have a vested interest in sickness, not health. The system is geared almost entirely to treating our ailments. It assumes we'll get sick, is activated only when we get sick, and in fact *depends* on our getting sick to justify all the billions spent on medical staff, technicians, high-tech gadgets, hospitals, clinics, pharmacies, drugs — the whole panoply of a system that is not really about health care. It's about ill-health care, about prescribing the drugs or performing the surgeries that are required when the maintenance of health is ignored.

This is not to denigrate the dedication and integrity of the professionals who staff our health care system. In the toxic-stew environment we're now immersed in, and in the absence of preventive measures, their services are indispensable. They do their best to heal us when we get sick, and sometimes succeed, but surely it would be far better to have a system that helps us stay well. It would also be far less costly, in the long run, to eliminate hunger, poverty, squalor, and the other social causes of illness in this country than to try to cope medically with their debilitating effects.

I've stopped contributing to outfits that are obsessed with finding cures instead of helping people stay well. The Canadian Cancer Association, for example, would be more accurately named the Canadian Cancer *Treatment* Association. When it transforms itself (if it ever does) into the Canadian Cancer *Prevention* Association, I'll gladly resume my financial support.

But it will be difficult to change the prevailing skewed set of health care priorities. Even the champions of Medicare and health care reform are calling mainly for improvements in the existing illness-treatment system: more and better home care, a public prescription drug plan, more doctors and nurses, more hospital beds. All admittedly needed, given the tidal wave of illness that has flowed from the neglect of preventive measures — but it still leaves the social *causes* of illness unaddressed.

We are therefore left, as individuals, to do the best we can to maintain our own health and keep our immune systems as strong as possible. This includes the ingestion of nutritious food supplemented by at least a good daily multivitamin pill plus extra vitamin D and anti-oxidants. The way I see it, in the kind of dangerous environment we are forced to live in these days, our immune system can use all the help we can give it.

The corporate Frankenstein monster

Three decades ago, when I started sounding the alarm about the growth of corporate power, very few other writers or analysts seemed to share my concern. Perhaps it was because the corporations back then exercised their power much less openly and harmfully. They didn't have governments that served them so slavishly, media that eulogized them so profusely, or free trade agreements that extended their influence on a global scale. Their power was also constrained to some extent by government regulations and strong unions.

Today, the economic supremacy of corporations has surged to a level so extreme and intrusive that it can no longer be concealed. A great many writers and speakers are now exposing the dire effects of uncontrolled corporate power on our society, our political system, and on the environment.

I was especially struck by novelist Jane Smiley's essay on the devastating effects of deregulation, which removed most of the legislative constraints on corporate power. In her treatise, she accuses the largest business firms of crimes against humanity. She is as baffled as she is shocked by their indifference to the horrible consequences of their actions.

"Given what these big corporations routinely do," she writes, "we have to ask: are they filled and peopled from top to bottom by ruthless monsters who care nothing about others, and also nothing about the world we live in? Are these CEOs and managers and stockholders so beyond human that the deaths in Iraq and Afghanistan and the destitution of the farmers and the tumors and allergies of children, and the melting of the Greenland ice cap and the shifting of the Gulf Stream are, to them, just the cost of doing business? Or are they just beyond stupid and blind, so that they, alone among humans, have no understanding of the interconnectedness of all natural systems?"

This is a question that most of us have asked ourselves over the years as we witness the corporations ransack the planet's resources, contaminate the environment, mistreat workers, gouge consumers, prop up dictators, widen the gap between rich and poor, and make the planet increasingly less liveable.

It's a question, however, to which there probably is no single answer. More likely, the Big-Business Behemoth now laying waste to the planet is the outcome of several catalyzing events or forces. Here are some that I consider obvious:

- **Deregulation:** An economic system driven primarily by greed is bound to get out of control if it has no checks or limits. The ones that were put in place to curb the 19th-century Robber Barons, then strengthened in the early post-World-War-II period, have now either been dismantled or nullified by lax enforcement. Add to this the collapse of Soviet-style communism, seen (mistakenly) as the only alternative to capitalism, and you have a formula for greed-run-amuck.
- **Globalization:** International trade has freed the corporations from whatever national constraints were left. They now move their operations anywhere in the world where they can find the cheapest labour, the lowest taxes, and the least restrictive environmental laws. Countries have become bidders in a race-to-the-bottom global auction to attract corporate investment at any cost.
- **Technology:** World-wide communications networks that can transfer money anywhere on Earth at the touch of a computer button have immensely empowered the banks and other financial institutions — and weakened any would-be regulators. The ability of these money moguls to blackmail nations with threats of capital strikes, or bribe them with promises of investment, gives them ultimate economic control. (And their abuse of this control, even though it precipitated the latest massive financial crisis, has been maintained by government bailouts.)
- **Rationalization:** The CEOs, stockbrokers, and other business leaders are not monsters in their personal lives. They are, on the whole, model parents, neighbours and citizens. But they have apparently blocked out of their minds all of the negative aspects of the work they do. They have convinced themselves that the benefits of "free enterprise" far outweigh its shortcomings, and that, in any case, it's the only economic game in town, so what choice do they have?
- **Short-term thinking:** Most people (including business leaders) seem genetically incapable of thinking more than a few years ahead, and usually no more than a few months. Unless they, or their pocketbooks, are imminently in danger, they delay protective measures. Global

warming may or may not be catastrophic later in this century. The oil may run out, but only after we're dead. We still have some drinkable water and breathable air. Why worry about an uncertain future?

- **Science will find a way:** Having seen the marvels of electronics and other gadgets that have enhanced our lives in recent decades, there's a tendency to believe that scientists and inventors will come up with ingenious solutions to all the terrible problems we face. Alternative fuels, purifying anti-pollutants, cures for cancer and other deadly diseases — surely these scientific breakthroughs will come to our rescue. (Well, maybe, but more likely not. Wishful thinking is no substitute for strong corrective measures.)

- **The juggernaut effect:** Out-of-control capitalism has gained so much momentum that it's futile for any individual to yell, "Stop the world, I want to get off!" This applies to most business executives, too. Any CEO who suddenly developed a conscience and wanted to turn his company into an ethical, responsible, "good corporate citizen" would instead turn it into a vulnerable swimmer in a sea full of corporate sharks. He would be castigated by shareholders unwilling to forgo lower dividends, and his firm would become the target of a hostile takeover by a less scrupulous rival.

- **The death of democracy:** The governments of most countries (some in Europe are exceptions) have become the political arms of big corporations. Elections and other trappings of democracy remain, but most politicians today see their role as facilitating business activities and removing barriers to their profit-making imperative. Deregulation, free trade, tax cuts, and lax environmental laws take precedence over the broader public welfare. Democracy has given way to plutocracy.

- **Religious fundamentalism:** Hard as it is to credit, millions of people see all the economic, social, political, and environmental upheaval as part of God's preparations for Armageddon. I heard one of the 150 or so Christian-right preachers with a radio talk show in the U.S. tell his listeners not to be worried about these societal breakdowns, that they are all integral to the Creator's grand Second Coming, which is to coincide with the end of the world, coming soon. Hey, brothers and sisters, calm down. Jesus will lift you and all other true believers directly into Heaven. The Rapture will save you from the grisly fate set to befall the godless non-believers.

- **The eat-drink-and-be-merry syndrome.** Given the transience and uncertainty of life, a sizeable segment of the population (no doubt including many corporate freebooters) decide to live as enjoyably as they can as long as they can. If this means grabbing and consuming the largest possible share of the world's resources, so be it: "All that matters is that I and my family live our lives in comfort. So I'm depriving others of their means of livelihood, including future generations. Tough, but it's a jungle out there, and if I'm not among the winners, my life will be miserable among the losers."

* * *

If you have other explanations for our lemming-like march to the abyss of social collapse, economic chaos, ecological disaster, and perhaps even extinction, let's hear them. But I think I've covered the main ones. The death of true democracy is no doubt the key factor, because only governments have the potential to restrain the corporate rampage, as they did in the late-Victorian and post-Depression years. But these were governments that could legitimately be called democratic. Most governments today have been either subverted or intimidated by the corporations. They take their orders from Wall Street (or, in Canada, Bay Street), not Main Street.

Many NGOs and individual citizens are doing their best to restore democracy and compel their governments to govern once again in the public interest. It's a worthy effort that deserves support, and we mustn't lose hope that it will eventually succeed. But it's a race against time, and time is running out.

The reign of the corporations, of course, will not last indefinitely, in any case. Maybe not even more than another couple of decades. Their throne stands on a very shaky platform: a foundation largely consisting of oil — and the oil, too, is running out. This depletion of our main energy source is inevitable. It will bring the whole structure of global corporate rule crashing down — regardless of whether prior efforts to curb corporate pillage and pollution succeed or not.

A much preferable outcome, of course, would be for the corporations to be dethroned as global rulers by an uprising of citizens and voters, and for this to happen in time for the development of renewable energy sources to replace fossil fuels. For such a timely rebellion against corporate rule to be launched, however, many more people will first have to be jarred out of their present ignorance, complacency, or despair. The CCPA and other progressive NGOs — with the support of their members — are doing their best to provide the crucial facts, figures, and analyses that are needed for such an ambitious educational project.

Trying to topple the Big Business Empire is a formidable endeavour, granted. But the alternative is dooming future generations to a societal collapse that is much more likely to be bring planetary rupture than rapture.

The "Big Business Bang" Theory

After nearly two decades of editing and writing articles for *The CCPA Monitor*, I've come to divide our contributors into two broad categories. Finding suitable one-word labels for them, however, is difficult without being guilty of generalizing. They all concern themselves in some way with social, economic, political, and environmental issues and the struggle for global justice, but some — let's call them the "specialists" — focus on one particular problem. There's poverty, pollution, inequality, war, the erosion of democracy, the myriad problems with health care, child care, education, trade, labour, politics, the tax system, civil liberties, mega-farming, and the media. On all of these and many other ills besetting our troubled world, *Monitor* writers have provided thoughtful, well-documented, often brilliant diagnoses and suggested remedies.

Then there are the writers and thinkers who try to connect these problems and see them all as symptoms of one overall global malaise. Privately, I think of these analysts as "world-viewers." That's not a satisfactory term, by any means, but it does reflect the holistic approach they take. (If there were a personal noun — holist? holisticist? — I'd use it, but the lexicographers haven't yet provided one. So "world-viewer" will have to do.)

Again, a caution against generalizing. Most of our "specialists" are not so fixated on their particular problem that they see it in isolation from everything else. They do see the connections, especially the economic and political ones. Nor do all our "world-viewers" ignore the localized symptoms. They often focus on individual problem areas before taking the global perspective.

The point I want to emphasize is that, in our struggle for a better world, we need both specialists and world-viewers. They complement one another. Without the specialists, the world-viewers would lack the specific information they need to map an effective counter-strategy. Without the world-viewers, the specialists would lack a broader framework into which their specific findings could be interlocked and acted upon.

In each issue of *The Monitor*, we try to offer space to both kinds of commentators. We need contributors who care deeply about a particular social or economic injustice. We need the writers and activists who are passionate about protecting Medicare, about eradicating poverty, about cleaning up the environment, about preventing wars, about developing renewable forms of energy, about saving the rainforests, about replacing free trade with fair trade, about serious political reform. At the same time, we need writers who look at the bigger picture, who see the accumulation of all these separate problems worsening to the point where the very survival of planetary life is at stake.

As someone who has read and edited thousands of articles and essays of both kinds — and who, as an editor, has occasionally been chided by readers for "filling *The Monitor* with doom and gloom" — I think we have done a reasonably good job of exposing and describing the problems, but perhaps not such a good job on the solution front. Not, mind you, that we've neglected the need for alternative policies — that's what the CCPA is all about, after all — but that perhaps we haven't made "the one big connection" as effectively as we should.

Is there one big connection between all the social, economic, environmental, and political problems we are concerned about? If we were to take a cause-and-effect approach, could we identify one overriding cause of all the troubles that beset us? If we could, it would certainly simplify, solidify, and intensify our reform efforts. Instead of dissipating our resources trying to tackle each of the many problems separately, we could come together in a concerted campaign to tackle their common cause. That, in turn, would give us a much better chance of averting global collapse.

At the risk of being branded a monomaniac or a simpleton or a crazy conspiracy theorist — or all three — let me give you this common cause: **excessive and destructive corporate power.** Call it corporatism, neoliberalism, ultraconservatism, *laissez-faire* capitalism, corporate globalization, the corporate agenda, private enterprise, right-wing fundamentalism, the Washington Consensus, or any of the other descriptive tags applied to a world overwhelmingly dominated by Big Business. Whatever you call it, you'll find it to be the root cause of virtually every social, economic, political, and environmental problem we are now grappling with. And, by extension, it's also the primary cause of the rapidly worsening global crisis.

I've been nattering on about the damaging effects of corporate power for quite some time, but, on flipping back over the pages of *The Monitor* for the past 19 years, I was struck anew by the number of articles on a wide range of issues that did indeed — directly or implicitly — expose corporate blame. Let's recap some of them:

- **Health care:** Many writers on this subject have traced the deterioration of Medicare to its deliberate sabotage through underfunding and understaffing by politicians eager to justify opening this vital service to private for-profit operators. But, as one headline put it, "Privatization is a health problem, not a solution." Experts on prescription drugs also question the benefits of the $30 billion a year that Canadians are spending on the products of the big pharmaceutical drug companies, which, as one writer noted, "are hooked on ever-rising profits."

- **Poverty:** Countless articles have cited the many broken promises by Canadian governments to eradicate poverty, notably the all-party pledge in Parliament in 1989 to eliminate child poverty by 2000. Instead, the rates of poverty and homelessness have soared. Why? Because these social blights stem from the ever-widening gap between rich and poor, which in turn is an inevitable result of an economic system that glorifies profiteering and blocks a more equitable distribution of income. No wonder, as one of our writers put it, "we now live in an era of inequality that is historically unprecedented."

- **Pollution:** Hardly an issue of *The Monitor* goes out that doesn't contain an article deploring the contamination of our air, water, soil, and food by industrial toxins. The release of these pollutants — few of which are tested or regulated — cause most of the cancers that afflict us, but are treated by their corporate makers and dispensers as "just another cost of doing business." On a larger scale, of course, pollution of this magnitude threatens the viability of the biosphere itself.

- **War and peace:** A *Monitor* index revealed that the arms sales of the top 100 manufacturers of weapons now total more than $236 billion a year. As our writers have explained, wars have become very profitable, so we should expect more of them. At least one-third of the multi-billion-dollar cost of the Iraq war, for example, swelled the coffers of the big arms corporations. One headline declared that "War is driving the economic agenda we're fighting."

- **Trade:** Many experts in this field have described NAFTA and WTO trade deals as essentially "charters of rights and freedoms" for transnational corporations, extending their power and influence to encompass the globe. Far from helping to boost employment and economic prosperity for everyone, these one-sided treaties have worsened poverty and inequality while creating obscene riches for a privileged minority. We now have a global economic system in which the pursuit of profits is unconstrained by any concern for the public good — "a world in which 20% of the people consume 80% of the resources."

- **Labour:** Corporate leaders have always been anti-labour, accepting unions only grudgingly and always looking for ways to attack and undermine them. As corporate power has increased — especially the ability to move jobs to regions with the lowest wages, taxes, and environmental laws — so has the corporate assault on organized labour. It's an attack that has been avidly supported by most governments in Canada, which have not only failed to protect and promote collective bargaining rights, but — as our labour relations writers emphasize — have repeatedly violated these rights themselves.

- **Taxes:** Reductions in taxes on business and the rich, along with lavish tax breaks for these élites, have highlighted the budgets of the federal and most provincial governments over the past 20 years. The non-collection of these billions in corporate tax revenue has unfairly shifted the cost of public services and programs to lower-income taxpayers, while providing governments with a handy excuse for cutting these programs. Globally, we have a tax system that, as a *Monitor* report revealed, allows transnational corporations to hide over $600 billion in tax [evasion] havens.

- **Politics:** Corporations have always wielded a great deal of political clout, being the major funders of most Conservative and Liberal politicians' election campaigns and being free to propagandize their views during elections and finance strong lobbying pressure between elections. With the even greater power bestowed on them by free trade and deregulation, they now effectively dictate government policies — to the point where some observers fear the conversion of our governance to a form of fascism. As one headline reads, "Governments now see themselves as the political arms of business." And another heading concludes that "the business of government has become the government of business."

- **The media:** Numerous *Monitor* articles have remarked on the transformation of the commercial media into propaganda organs for corporations and their free-market dogma. This is hardly surprising, since the privately-owned newspapers, TV and radio networks are owned by and operated as profit-making corporations themselves. In addition, of course, they depend for most of their profits on the corporate ads that fill their pages and air-time. Little wonder that our media articles carried headlines such as "Commercial press lacks balance and fairness," and "Democracy can't work if corporate propaganda prevails."

* * *

I could go on to cite the damaging effects of corporate influence on our education system, monetary policy, natural resources, civil liberties, science, and a host of other sectors. But I think I've made the point that, no matter which social, economic, political, or environmental problem you happen to be mostly concerned about, its origin (and aggravation) can be traced to some aspect of corporate rule.

Isn't it time, then, to at least *think* about developing a unified effort to address the common corporate cause of all our problems, including the biggest problem of all, which is the threat to humankind's very survival?

This assumes, of course, that our species *deserves* to survive, which is not at all a given, and it also assumes my "Big Business Bang Theory" has some credibility. You decide.

If uncontrolled capitalism is the problem, what's the solution?

If you agree with the case I made that all our most pressing social, economic, and environmental problems are caused and perpetuated by unbridled corporate power, the obvious question that arises is: how can that horribly misused power be tamed? How can the barbaric economic system spawned by that power be replaced by a truly fair and democratic system?

Before any effective reform can even be considered, two prerequisites must be met. First, there will have to be a fairly widespread public awareness of the urgent need to curb corporate influence — an awakening that would-be reformers can build upon. And secondly, the movement to challenge the predominant business élite will need to be soundly led and coordinated.

I'm beginning to think the first requirement has come close to being achieved. The scores of thinkers and activists whose critiques of corporate rule have graced the pages of the *Monitor* for more than a decade are now more mainstream critics than mavericks. Anti-corporate articles and op-eds by such critics as Maude Barlow, John McMurtry, Naomi Klein, and Vandana Shiva are popping up in magazines, journals, and some newspapers all over the world — and of course even more frequently in online news-sites. The upsurge of Occupy Wall Street, Idle No More, and other public protest movements on a global scale have all specifically targeted the abuse of corporate power.

Corporations and their CEOs are now commonly portrayed as villains in movies, TV shows, and books. The proliferation of insider-trading and other "white-collar" crimes make front-page news. Few people have escaped some personal bad experience with a business project or investment — and most are now aware that by far the biggest polluters of the environment are the industrial corporations and the products they make.

I recently read *Forty Signs of Rain*, a science-fiction novel by Kim Stanley Robinson about the imminence of catastrophic climate change. In it, his protagonist, an environmental activist named Charlie Quibler, writes an angry memo to the executive director of the National Science Foundation, which merits quoting:

> "Humanity is exceeding the planet's carrying capacity for our
> species, badly damaging the biosphere. Neoclassical economics

cannot cope with this situation, and indeed, with its falsely exter-
iorized costs, was designed in part to disguise it. If Earth were to
suffer a catastrophic anthropogenic extinction event over the next
ten years, which it will, American business would continue to focus
on its quarterly profit and loss. There is no economic mechanism
for dealing with catastrophe. And yet government and the scientific community are not tackling this situation either; indeed both
have consented to be run by neoclassical economics, an obvious
pseudo-science. We might as well agree to be governed by astrolo-
gers... Free market fundamentalists are dragging us back to some
dismal feudal eternity and destroying everything in the process,
and yet we have the technological means to feed everyone, house
everyone, clothe everyone, educate everyone, doctor everyone. The
ability to end suffering and want, as well as ecological collapse, is
right at hand, and yet the NSF continues to dole out its little grants,
fiddling while Rome burns!"

Granted, this outburst came from a fictional character, but I'm convinced
now that the frustration it reflects is shared by most real-life scientists and
activists. They know the gravity of the economic, social, and ecological crises
we're facing; they know what needs to be done to avert the calamity Charlie
Quibler is ranting about; but they are just as much at a loss as he is about
how to jolt corporate and political decision-makers out of their complacent
reliance on a fatally flawed and ultimately destructive economic system.

This complacency, of course, stems from their belief that, with the
demise of communism, capitalism has become the only viable economic
system. (Future historians may trace the inevitable collapse of capitalism
— whether through economic folly or ecological cataclysm — to the earlier collapse of communism, since that historic event led to the uncontrolled cancerous growth of a globalized free-market system.)

One of our members in Saskatchewan called to speculate that many
CEOs might secretly *want* governments to re-impose regulatory restraints
on their business operations. None of them individually can opt out of the
current cutthroat system, he pointed out, since that would trigger a share-
holder revolt or a hostile takeover, but they might welcome a government
"restraining order" that applied to all of them.

There may indeed be some rational business leaders of this kind out there — CEOs who can see past the next quarterly report to the yawning abyss they are careening toward. There may even be some rational politicians who can see past the next election to the disastrous consequences of continuing to serve solely corporate interests. But, regrettably, if such corporate and business paragons are to be found, they have yet to make their appearance. All the indicators cast doubt on their existence, and thus on the likelihood of voluntary economic reform.

The desperately needed changes in policies and priorities apparently will only come from the application of strong political pressure — pressure that is strategically focused, concentrated, and unrelenting. Sporadic lobbying will not suffice, nor will the extraction of glib election promises, nor the currying of favour with MPs and senior mandarins. All of these activities have been carried on by thousands of progressive individuals and organizations for many years, to little or no effect. Only a powerful and concerted campaign involving and supported by *all* the members and groups in civil society will have a chance of succeeding.

And that's the rub. About 10 years ago, Tony Clarke of the Polaris Institute and Maude Barlow of the Council of Canadians —winners of an "Alternative Nobel Prize" — convened a meeting of the leaders of Canada's major NGOs and unions. Their aim was to do exactly what I've been talking about: persuade these social, economic, labour, and environmental leaders to pool their resources — to join together in one big overall campaign to supplant corporate rule with true democracy and an equitable economic system.

The civil society delegates were verbally supportive. They acknowledged the need for a joint effort. They talked vaguely about bringing it about. But in the decade that has since elapsed, they are all still acting independently and are no closer to forging a common front.

This tendency for each NGO or union to follow its own agenda, and to unite with others only occasionally for demonstrations and meetings, has long been a deterrent to more effective collaboration. I've bemoaned this dissipation of effort many times. A column I wrote on the subject nearly twenty years ago still applies, and I quote from it in the next several paragraphs.

* * *

The present situation can be likened to a river in which many people — old, young, men, women, white, black, Aboriginal, etc. — are being swept downstream. Strung out along each bank are various rescue teams, one for each category of victims. The anti-poverty group tries to save the poor, the seniors' group tries to pull out the seniors, the women's group concentrates on the drowning women, and so on. It's an evocative metaphor.

Each organization has strong swimmers, and is equipped with ropes, lifebuoys, nets, poles, and other rescue equipment. It prides itself on how many people it saves. Not all of them, of course. Many are carried away out of sight and drown. But to rescue even some is considered a great achievement.

These organizations exist to pull people out of the river, or at least make the attempt. That is their *raison d'être*. Their activities are reactive, not proactive. This is not to say that their leaders are unaware that somewhere upstream there are other groups — the chuckers or flingers or heavers — whose purpose is to throw people *into* the river. They know that, and sometimes they will even go and try to persuade the chuckers to stop chucking. (They call it "lobbying.") But that is as far as they will go. They know why the chucking and heaving is going on, and who is responsible. They know that there is a privileged powerful minority whose members are never in any danger of getting wet themselves — so rich that they can easily afford to pay the heavers and chuckers (sometimes called "politicians") to do their dirty work for them. The more people who get thrown in the river, you see, the fewer left to share the nation's wealth.

It's a pathetic sight when the rescue group leaders hike up the river to remonstrate with the political heavers. "Please stop throwing so many of our members in the river," they beg. Usually on bended knee. The politicians promise to stop eventually. Maybe next year. Or the year after that. But they never do. Or they say they have no choice but to keep filling the river with throwaway people because, after the rich and powerful finish gorging themselves, there's not enough food or shelter or work for everyone in a system based on the survival of the fittest. Some have to be discarded, and it's only fitting that they be the weakest and the most vulnerable.

The rich and ruthless élite will sometimes fool the would-be rescuers by replacing one bunch of chuckers with another. The flingers take over from the heavers, or the slingers take over from the hurlers. "Surely," the rescue groups reassure themselves after voting in the latest election, "surely this new gang of people-drowners won't throw in as many as the last crowd." And they don't. They throw in more.

It never seems to occur to the rescue organizations to blame the economic system itself and those who run it for all the drowning victims, or to wonder why the people with the most money and power are never among those sacrificed.

Maybe it's because the rescuers are so busy saving as many victims as they can, so busy collecting donations to buy their nets and ropes and life-buoys, that they don't have time to think about changing a system that is so harmful to so many. Or maybe it's because they are now so accustomed to their role of rescuers, and so organizationally structured, that they can't even conceive of a river into which nobody is thrown. How, then, could they justify their existence? On what basis could they continue to appeal for donations?

Now, admittedly, saving people from drowning (or from poverty and hunger) is a noble pursuit. But surely preventing them from being tossed into the river in the first place would be even nobler.

Could it be done? We'll never know as long as groups concerned about the victimization of the weak and poor confine their activities to pulling them out, instead of joining together to confront and foil their corporate and political assailants.

To desist from such a preventive approach is in effect to tolerate a system in which civility and compassion have been displaced by the law of the jungle. It is to concede that there is nothing to be done to change this brutal system except try to rescue and comfort its victims.

* * *

Not much has changed in the nearly 20 years since I first penned those words. If anything, the number of "drowning" victims has doubled or even tripled, as have the number and size of the rescue groups. And the rescuers have come no closer to forging a broad and more reform-minded alliance.

It's not that they are resigned to a system so unfair that the need for charity becomes permanent. In one of its recent annual reports, for example, the Canadian Association of Food Banks clearly would prefer that hunger be eliminated by political reform so all the food banks could be closed.

Not all the charitable organizations, however, seem so anxious to make themselves redundant. There is some legitimate concern about their approach to making the world a better place. Critics take them to task for not being as politically active as they could and should be. "Avoidable starvation, preventable illness, and predictable disaster are supremely political events," says one critic, David Ransom. "They result in good measure from people being forced to consume the poisonous brew of free-market economics and fake democracy that is concocted by corporate globalization and neoliberal politics." What are the NGOs doing, he asks, to find and apply an antidote to this venomous concoction?

Not nearly enough, it seems. Yes, each in its own way, they are doing a great deal to mitigate the hardships inflicted by free-market economics and corporate greed — but that's still an exercise in trying to save and comfort the victims. It's still pulling people out of the neoliberal river instead of preventing them from being thrown in.

The rescuers will remain indispensable as long as the current economic and political barbarism prevails. Much more urgently needed today, however, are NGOs committed to pooling their resources in a determined, coordinated, all-out effort to achieve economic reforms — reforms that, if successful, will make their rescue operations (and their very organizational existence) unnecessary.

Might I suggest that Tony and Maude call another meeting of civil society and labour leaders? Maybe the NGOs and unions are finally ready to launch a collective effort to prevent economic victimization rather than trying separately to cope with it.

Maybe they'll agree it's time to give solidarity — *real* solidarity—a chance.

The Decline of Collectivity

Shortly before he died, former Alberta Premier Peter Lougheed astonished us by denouncing what he called "the decline of collectivity" in Canada. "We are becoming increasingly Americanized," he warned, "and this imposes an un-Canadian individualism on our ethic."

Coming from Lougheed, whose province had spearheaded the country's Americanization, this concern was completely unexpected. Never considered a Red Tory — or, in the current far-right parlance, a "squishy" one — he nevertheless was alarmed by the extent to which his party's current leaders were pushing the corporate agenda. He was particularly disturbed by their promotion of the American-style cult of individualism, which puts personal rights ahead of community values.

Like many others on the left, I was surprised that Lougheed used the term "collectivity" so approvingly, as something to be preferred over individualism. Usually conservatives — even "squishy" ones — equate collectivism with socialism or even communism, and the word leaves their lips dripping with scorn and venom.

They have the advantage of being able to point to both fascist and communist states (Hitler's Germany and Stalin's Soviet Union being the prime examples) where collectivism was taken to the extreme of almost completely suppressing individual freedom. In the insect world, they can also point to the regimented conformity of the anthill and the beehive.

The consequences of unrestrained individualism, on the other hand, are not so easily demonstrated. Even the social breakdown in the United States is not seen by most people as the result of the glorification of individual liberty, to the detriment of community (i.e., collective) needs. This is largely because, in a capitalist economic system, any constraint on the freedom of individuals — or, for that matter, of individual business firms — is considered abhorrent, even if such limits are imposed in the broader public interest. To contend, in today's born-again *laissez-faire* system, that the common good should be society's primary goal is to be guilty of the worst kind of heresy.

But weren't governments originally established to protect and advance *collective* interests? And wasn't such an overriding purpose inherently hostile to the cult of individualism? Indeed it was, and so the corporate, political, media, and academic champions of "individual rights and freedoms" had to reverse this prime government mandate. They had to convert government into a mechanism for promoting private and individual interests instead.

So regulations that had curbed the socially harmful activities of individual persons and companies were weakened or eliminated. Social programs that helped the poor and unemployed — and thus interfered with the free operation of the markets — were gutted. Public services and institutions that allegedly could be provided more efficiently by the private sector were privatized. Taxes that "stifled or discouraged" private initiative were slashed.

"The best government," we were told by its wreckers, "is the least government."

Governments have thus been transformed from guardians of the public good to boosters of private profit, from seekers of social justice to destroyers of the welfare state. It matters not at all, apparently, that the main beneficiaries of this anti-government rampage have been the big corporations and the wealthy élite. The other 90% of us should be content that we are now as free as the plutocrats to live in mansions, dine and shop at the ritziest restaurants and boutiques, and spent our winters on the Riviera. And they, for their part, are as free as we are (if we still have jobs) to shop at Giant Tiger, eat at McDonald's, and spend their winters shovelling snow.

Many Canadians, however, even if they haven't embraced the cult of individualism willingly, have come to believe they have no choice. They have lost trust in our economic, social, and political institutions — or, rather, have had that trust betrayed.

The glue that holds any society together is faith in its governments, corporations, courts, churches, unions — faith that these institutions, no matter how flawed, will always be committed to serving and protecting people from poverty, unemployment, sickness, and other afflictions. That glue is coming unstuck in a country where governments put private interests ahead of the public interest, when corporations put the pursuit of profits ahead of the well-being of workers and their communities, when unions have been stripped of much of their capacity to protect their members.

No wonder that so many Canadians have come to the conclusion that they're now on their own — that each of them is in a struggle for survival, with no help from any quarter.

Self-preservation is always a powerful motivator, but especially so in a society that seems to be reverting to a survival-of-the-fittest mentality. The reaction of people plunged into that kind of jungle-law environment is predictable. If their employers are downsizing and outsourcing work, if their governments keep destroying jobs through free trade and social service cutbacks, if their unions' rights and ability to help them have been reduced —in that kind of ruthless system, people will feel they are on their own.

Their tendency will be to start looking at their co-workers, their neighbours, immigrants — indeed, anyone outside their immediate family circle — as rivals for the slim pickings of a shrinking economy. Individualism will run rampant. Co-operation and solidarity will be overwhelmed by a single-minded devotion to self-interest.

The erosion of our health care system, unemployment insurance, and other social programs spurs this flight to individualism. These programs are the tangible expressions of our willingness to look after one another's needs, to pool our contributions for the common good. As underfunding dismantles them, we are being thrown back, each of us, on our own resources.

Whether Canadians voluntarily embrace individualism or feel compelled to adopt it, the consequences are equally horrendous. Why? Because it rests on a philosophy that is fundamentally flawed and dangerous.

This is the spurious notion that, if each person and corporation is left free to pursue individual advantage, the "market" (or its "invisible hand") will somehow make sure that the overall result will benefit everyone. In fact, as we have seen, the outcome is the precise opposite. Only the strongest, the smartest, the luckiest, and the fiercest prosper — at the expense of those less strong, less smart, less lucky, and less unscrupulous.

It is one of the worst flaws of human nature that the actions we take as individuals may benefit us separately, at least in the short term, but harm us collectively. These individual actions may be reasonable, even brilliant, if assessed solely on the basis of their immediate personal gains; but collectively they can prove disastrous.

The invention of the combustion engine was a giant step forward in human mobility, but in millions of automobiles its emissions pollute the air we breathe.

One person carrying a handgun for protection may be acting intelligently as an individual, but millions doing the same thing create a violent and perilous society.

A company that outsources thousands of jobs to cheap-labour countries may increase its profits and please its shareholders; but when most other firms do the same thing, the ensuing collapse of consumer spending cuts their domestic sales and triggers a recession.

A corporate tycoon, free to amass unlimited wealth, enjoys an opulent lifestyle, but the billions of dollars he and other business leaders hoard or hide in overseas tax havens are unavailable to help the 12 million children globally who die every year from the hunger and disease that adequately funded programs could prevent.

The basic point is that unrestrained individualism can be much worse for a society than unrestrained collectivism.

Curtailing and humanizing individual enterprise doesn't mean we have to become like the ants or the bees; but it does mean that some limits, some regulations, some minimum community standards have to be in place to protect collective rights and meet collective needs.

Otherwise we fall back into the worst kind of medieval society, brutalized by huge income disparities, masses of poor and jobless, urban slums, and high levels of crime and social unrest.

This process of social decay is well under way in the United States, and is increasingly discernible in many Canadian communities, too. It will continue and get worse as long as the cult of individualism holds sway in our boardrooms and legislatures.

Surely, if a committed conservative like Peter Lougheed could have had that insight, it is not beyond the comprehension of most Canadians.

Thinking the apocalyptic unthinkable

Whether our "civilization" will survive this century is now — or should be — the main concern of everyone. It's no longer a far-fetched Chicken Little "the-sky-is-falling" bugaboo. Enough evidence has been found to show us beyond doubt that the next several decades will be the most perilous to confront humankind since the dawn of recorded history.

So many global threats loom ahead that the chance we can avoid their combined devastation is minimal. They are rapidly converging. Destructive climate change — mostly man-made — is accelerating. The easily accessible deposits of oil and natural gas that support our way of life are dwindling. The proliferation of hair-trigger nuclear weapons could unleash a global holocaust. The spread of deadly viruses could trigger a global pandemic. A severe water shortage is developing that threatens the lives of billions.

If we are smart enough, diligent enough, co-operative enough, and lucky enough, we may escape most of these catastrophes. We could drastically cut our greenhouse gas emissions and pollution, and so avert the worst consequences of global warming. We could get serious about disarmament, develop vaccines against our microbic foes, and even learn to decontaminate and share our water.

The one threat we absolutely can't avoid, however, is the exhaustion of a gift of Nature that our modern "civilization" was founded and is wholly dependent upon: fossil fuels. They are a non-renewable resource, built up over many millennia, that we have been squandering for the past century. More deposits are being discovered, but almost all are very difficult to extract and costly to consume. The supply of easily acquired fossil fuel will start to run out over the next few decades and may be entirely depleted before mid-century. And, long before the last drop goes into the last tank, the ever-worsening shortage will cause social, economic, and political upheaval on a colossal scale. Civilization as we know it will almost inevitably collapse.

This apocalyptic forecast will be rejected by most people. As the famous psychologist Carl Jung once observed, "people cannot stand too much reality." And that's especially the case when the reality they face challenges most of their assumptions about the world they live in.

It's comforting to look for and cling to tempting escape hatches. Surely the oil and gas will be replaced by alternative forms of energy: solar, wind, tidal, geothermal, hydrogen, methane. And nuclear — especially nuclear.

The problem with relying on any of these alternatives, however, is that none of them — or even all combined — will ever provide the cheap, effective, and widely available power now derived from fossil fuels.

To fully explain the decline of fossil-fuel energy and the limitations of all the renewables would take a book-length exposition. That's what Jeff Rubin does in *The End of Growth*, and what James Howard Kunstler did earlier in his stark and scary book *The Long Emergency*. One by one, Kunstler analyzed all the alternative fuels and explained why they won't rescue us. Cheap natural gas supplies, like oil, are also running out. Hydrogen-powered cars and industries are a pipe-dream. A return to coal may keep some of the economy going, but at intolerable costs to the environment. Hydroelectric capacity could be increased somewhat, and so could nuclear power, but they both depend on plants and machinery that could only be manufactured en masse in a fossil-fuel-driven economy. (And nuclear power has a deadly and still unsolved radioactive waste storage problem.)

Solar and wind energy are attractive alternatives, but they require solar panels, wind turbines, and other equipment that could only be made in large quantities by oil-and-gas-powered factories. As Kunstler points out, "the batteries, the panels, the electronics, the wires, and the plastics all require mining operations and factories using fossil fuels." And the components would have to be transported to the sites of the solar and wind-farms by trucks, planes, or ships that now are also fuelled by oil. "Could these systems exist," Kunstler asks, "without the platform of an oil economy to produce them?"

If our governments and corporations decided to face the future energy crisis instead of ignoring it, we'd have some hope of making a less chaotic transition. If, say, 20% of our present use of fossil fuels were devoted to making the hardware and component parts that renewable energy sources will need (instead of the current 2%), some of the social and economic convulsion could be abated. There's no sign, however, of such a sudden outbreak of political or corporate enlightenment, so we have to lower our expectations.

* * *

We live in a world created by and based on cheap energy. Fossil fuels power fast air, sea, and land transportation. They fuel the massive increase in agricultural output that in turn has permitted the explosive five-fold growth of human population in little more than a century. All the manufacturing and technological marvels of the past 100 years — from telephones to high-definition TV and I-pads, from prop-planes to jet airliners, from ball-point pens to plastic electronic gadgets — all have their origin or creation in cheap fossil fuels.

The days of this "advanced" civilization are numbered — and so is the comfortable lifestyle it has sustained for the élite minorities in both the rich and poor nations. Most of the gadgets and services to which we've become accustomed will be lost long before the oil is gone. No more comfortable suburban homes dependent on fossil fuels for heating and car-commuting. No more big-box stores and malls because the "free trade" that generates cheap-labour-made goods from China will have stopped.

Our species doesn't exactly have an admirable record of dealing with scarcities. Instead of sharing shrinking resources equitably, we tend to fight over them. With drinkable water, arable land, and even food becoming increasingly less available along with the oil, what are the prospects of avoiding horrendous conflicts over diminishing supplies? Not that bright.

Kunstler and other pessimistic analysts foresee a future by mid-century in which 80% or more of the planet's present population will have perished — victims of famine, disease, wars, and ecological blight. The survivors will be those who have set up sustainable communities with the capacity to grow sufficient food for their inhabitants. But they will have few of the amenities now so common in the early years of the century. In effect, they will have regressed to a way of life not much different from the pre-industrial-revolution era.

* * *

Such a doom-and-gloom outlook is not of course inevitable (yet). Facing reality, however, also means assessing the danger of ignoring reality. One of the problems facing those now raising the alarm — even reputable ecologists, energy experts, and other scientists — is the reluctance of most of their readers and listeners to make that mental leap from the prosperous and productive present to the stark, bleak, shortage-ridden future that lies only a few decades ahead. It's a difficult intellectual exercise, and one that most people will resist as long as they can cling to any excuse for denying or delaying the need for it. The snail's-pace increase in global warming and decrease of cheap oil also makes it easier for short-term-wired humans to ignore a crisis that looms so far into their future.

For those of us in civil society groups, the challenge is even more formidable. If we recognize the gravity of the slow depletion of cheap fossil-fuel energy (and not all of us do), what's our reaction? Most of us are involved in some way in what we call "the struggle for a better world." That struggle has many aspects. It includes efforts to reduce poverty, help the hungry and homeless, work for a more equitable society, clean up the environment, pursue peace and disarmament, oppose corporate globalization, and strive for real political democracy. All very commendable projects. But if we really foresee a breakdown of the whole socioeconomic system that spawns all these inequities, do we continue to try to ameliorate each of them separately for the time left before the entire system begins to fall apart? Or do we turn our collective efforts toward trying to avert world-wide societal and economic collapse?

The two approaches, of course, are not mutually exclusive, except perhaps for the religious fundamentalist "end-timers" who have pretty much abandoned any effort to deal with current social, economic, or environmental concerns that are not related to what they believe is the imminent Second Coming apocalypse. Why worry about the depletion of oil, about global warming, about poverty or disease or anything else when the world as we know it is to come to an end soon, anyway? We may dismiss these people as fanatical imbeciles, but their numbers are now in the millions in the United States, and even in the hundreds of thousands in Canada. With their growing political influence, they constitute one of the biggest barriers to effective disaster-averting political action.

We on the left have to resist a similar tendency to slack off the pursuit of immediate reforms that, even if achieved, wouldn't last more than another few decades. Why keep opposing globalization, free trade, and other manifestations of corporate power if the end of oil is going to bring the whole unfair system crashing down well before mid-century, anyway? Well, if for nothing else, because *it is this same excessive corporate power that is forestalling the political action required to prepare for and cope with a post-fossil-fuel future.* Fighting poverty and inequality in the short-term and striving to preserve a habitable planet in the long term are not mutually exclusive endeavours. They can be pursued in tandem.

* * *

A pertinent question that some may wish to ask in this twilight of our oil-driven civilization is whether the human race *deserves* to survive.

Considering our irresponsible abuse and misuse of the planet and its resources, not to speak of the callous mistreatment of billions of our fellow humans, what do we have to offer in our defence? What human accomplishment or virtue can we cite that comes close to offsetting all our crimes and failings as a species? Do we deserve to become extinct (to *make* ourselves extinct) as yet another of Nature's biological failures? She made the mistake of endowing us with what we in our hubris call intelligence, and we've misused it to vandalize the planet and brutalize most of the creatures on it, including most members of our own species.

Mark Twain, before he died, became bitterly cynical about the human race. Farley Mowat, a renowned contemporary Canadian author, has become almost as despairing as Twain about humankind's future, or even our right to *have* a future. Based on their keen observations of human history and behaviour, their scathing appraisals of their species are hard to rebut.

The best I can do is to repeat something I wrote to Farley a few years ago. I told him that any species capable of producing someone of his intellectual stature and compassionate nature should not be universally condemned and relegated to the evolutionary scrapheap. The same could be said about Mark Twain and hundreds of other humanitarian writers and artists, about the many thousands of good and caring social activists, scientists — and even a few politicians — who have striven tirelessly over the centuries, no matter how unsuccessfully, to lessen human barbarism and make our society truly civilized.

Whether the valiant efforts of the "do-gooders" are enough to redeem all the terrible violence and villainies perpetrated by the leaders of our species — and tolerated if not approved by the majority — is a dubious premise. However, even if the scales are still badly overbalanced by the mountains of human evil, perhaps the goodness of a Mahatma Gandhi or a Florence Nightingale or a Leonardo da Vinci or an Elizabeth Fry or a Tommy Douglas might be enough to earn us a stay of execution.

On condition, of course, that we spend the next 20 or 30 years — starting now — doing all we can to save ourselves and future generations.

The Right to Strike

"Workers' complaints multiplied, and strikes grew more frequent — strikes among the miners, the tradesmen, even among the police." Thus did historian W.W. Tarn describe labour relations conflict in Egypt in 230 B.C. According to Tarn, the first recorded strikes in history were conducted by workers building the great pyramids of Egypt many thousands of years earlier.

References to strikes have been found on the tablets and papayri of ancient Persia, Sumeria, and other long-vanished civilizations.

The Roman Empire sustained numerous strikes by goldsmiths, coppersmiths, potters, shoemakers, dyers and carpenters.

In the industrial towns of France and Italy in the 13th and 14th centuries, the craft guilds went on strike repeatedly against the ruling merchant class. Textile workers at Rouen staged a lengthy strike in 1281. Woolworkers in France went on strike in 1371.

Strikes occurred in England as early as the 1300s, with a contemporary writer complaining that even priests had struck for higher compensation.

In their monumental *Story of Civilization*, Will and Ariel Durant tell us that in 1579 textile workers went on strike in Germany, and that throughout the 16th century in Europe "strikes were numerous, but were crushed by a coalition of employers and governments." (Who says history doesn't repeat itself?)

Major strikes also took place in the factories of Amsterdam in 1672, and in the silk-making plants of Lyons in 1774.

This brief history lesson is for the benefit of those present-day Canadians who seem to believe that the strike is a diabolical invention of modern unions.

These are the people who keep urging, on radio hot-line shows and in letters to the editor, that unions be stripped of their right to strike — especially unions in the public sector. They apparently think that simply outlawing strikes would ensure "labour peace" — that all forms of labour-management conflict would then suddenly disappear.

What would more likely happen is an increase in conflict and chaos. Strikes would proliferate, not diminish, even if they were made illegal.

We should learn from the events of the past. There has never been a period in human history that was entirely free of strikes, ever since some people were obliged to work for others. The relationship between workers and their bosses almost inevitably breeds resentment and dissension. And when their discontent rises to an intolerable level, workers will walk off the job — whether they have unions or not, and also regardless of the kind of political and economic system in which they live.

Most of the strikes of bygone eras occurred under totalitarian regimes that banned strikes and ruthlessly suppressed them. Strikers were severely punished, their leaders hanged, beheaded, or exiled.

Not even such brutal deterrents, however, could prevent strikes. They have continued to erupt down through the ages.

It is important, when looking at the incidence of strikes in Canada today — most of them provoked by corporate aggression or government cut-backs — to keep them in historical perspective, and to realize that strikes preceded modern unions by more than 8,000 years.

The first recorded strike in what was to become Canada, for example, occurred when the voyageurs at Rainy Lake (a territory now located in northern Ontario) went on strike for higher pay in August of 1794, more than half a century before the first union made its appearance here.

The evidence is clear, for those open-minded enough to see it, that unions do not instigate labour strife — that instead they do their utmost to avert it.

The late renowned economist Kenneth Galbraith called unions "managers of discontent," in the sense that they serve as an agency for resolving workers' grievances — and thus in most cases preventing their escalation into work stoppages.

"The clauses in unions' collective agreements that regulate pay, benefits, seniority, and conditions of promotion are voluminous," Galbraith pointed out. "Any unilateral application of such rules by management, however meticulous, would seem arbitrary and unjust. By helping to frame the rules and by participating in the grievance machinery, the union serves invaluably to mitigate the feeling (among workers) that such systems are unfair."

No union ever calls a strike from whim or malice, or with the idea that a strike would somehow be preferable to a mutually satisfactory agreement. The reverse is true. Union leaders regard strikes as costly and troublesome, and make every effort to avoid them. When they do stage a strike, it is as a last resort, after all reasonable attempts to negotiate a peaceful settlement have failed, or when they are backed into a corner by an intransigent employer or an anti-union government.

So effective are unions in averting strikes that they have been accused by some left-wing critics of acting as enforcers of labour peace on behalf of employers.

In his book *Strike*, Jeremy Brecher went so far as to claim that the function of unions today "is to set the terms on which workers will submit to the managers' authority. . . Once employers accept a contract, the jobs of union officials depend on their enforcement of the contract — that is, preventing strikes."

A more fair and balanced view, by economist J. Raymond Walsh, is that "union leaders, far from fomenting trouble, spend most of their time settling disputes before the strike stage is reached."

The underlying reality is that conflict is built into our private enterprise system. It is a system in which workers can only get more if their employers take less, a system in which both sides are continually at odds over how the revenue from products or services is to be shared between them.

In such an inherently adversarial system, the wonder is not that there are so many strikes, but that there are so few.

Without unions to represent workers and channel their anger and frustration constructively through collective bargaining, the nation's workplaces would be far more turbulent and unproductive. Strikes would still break out, and workers could resort to more damaging forms of protest, such as slowdowns, sit-ins, and mass absenteeism.

Instead of hobbling unions, curbing their bargaining rights, and even trying to get rid of them, those who yearn for a labour relations paradise should be thankful that unions exist. They should acclaim the unions' success — despite the growing hostility to them by employers and governments — in still managing to settle 95% of contract negotiations *without* a strike.